Published under license from the Harlequin Football Club by
Vision Sports Publishing in 2016

Harlequin Football Club
The Twickenham Stoop Stadium
Langhorn Drive
Twickenham
Middlesex
TW2 7SX
www.quins.co.uk

Harlequins

Vision Sports Publishing
19-23 High Street
Kingston upon Thames
Surrey
KT1 1LL
www.visionp.co.uk

VSP

ISBN: 978-1909534-62-9

© Harlequin Football Club
Text © Brendan Gallagher

Author: Brendan Gallagher
Editor: Jim Drewett
Designer: Neal Cobourne
Production Editor: Ed Davis
Editorial: Paul Baillie-Lane
Sales and Marketing: Toby Trotman
Print Purchasing: Ulrika Drewett

150th Anniversary Co-ordinator for Harlequins: Paddy Lennon

Back cover pictures: Getty Images (top left and bottom right),
Colorsport (bottom left) and Harlequin FC (top right)

A CIP record for this book is available from the British library
Printed and bound in China by Hung Hing

MIX
Paper from
responsible sources
FSC® C017606

Nunquam Dormio

150 Years of Harlequins

Brendan Gallagher

VSP

Contents

PLAYER'S CIGARETTES

W. W. WAKEFIELD.

1158

HARLEQUIN F.C.

ADMIT TO GROUND
(STANDING ONLY)

Price **£3.00** (incl. V.A.T.)

Foreword

By Bob Hiller, President, Harlequin FC

The 2016–2017 season is the 150th (sesquicentennial) anniversary of our great club, the Harlequin Football Club. In true Harlequin fashion, this gives us the opportunity to celebrate, in style, our wonderful history and heritage. This book forms just one part of those celebrations, alongside many other planned activities and events.

I find it somewhat surreal that I should be writing this foreword as President of Harlequin FC. Never in my wildest dreams did I imagine that I would attain such an honour. Often, when we look back on our lives, we can identify events that, at the time, appear to be relatively insignificant but, in retrospect, they turn out to have been life-changing. One such event occurred in my life regarding Harlequins.

While still at Bec School, I was playing for a Surrey Under-18 XV against a Middlesex Under-18 XV at Old Deer Park in Richmond. At the end of the game, I was walking off towards the pavilion when a tall, distinguished-looking gentleman approached me and asked if I would like to join Harlequins. To my everlasting shame, I replied, "Well sir, I think that I would but, at the moment, I am rather committed to Bec Old Boys." On my return to school the next day my headmaster, on hearing what I had said, made an immediate telephone call and I could hear him saying, "Of course he wants to be a Harlequin". Thus began my close association with Harlequins which has already lasted 55 years.

I discovered later that the gentleman in question was David Brooks, who was the driving force behind Harlequins at that time. He subsequently became President of Surrey and the Rugby Football Union and he was also the manager of my first British and Irish Lions tour to South Africa in 1968. The final twist in this story is that, when I was appointed as President of Harlequins, I was replacing the previous incumbent who had sadly passed away – David Brooks.

The history of our club is a wonderful and fascinating story of our journey from being a purely amateur club 'of no fixed abode' to being one of the premier professional clubs in the country with a truly magnificent stadium. Of course, as with any club, there have been highs and lows but the true Harlequin spirit still prevails and we aspire to continue playing the attractive, adventurous rugby that spectators want to see and players want to play.

I hope that, in dipping into this book and reading about the major events and characters in the club's history, you will also get a flavour of the warmth and sense of fun that is prevalent within Harlequins. Our author, Brendan Gallagher, has been diligent and enthusiastic in his efforts to do justice to the people and stories that make our history interesting and enjoyable and I thank him for his efforts.

Running and developing a successful rugby club such as Harlequins over many years demands a massive effort by a large number of people. I would like to take this opportunity to thank everyone who has contributed to our success, of which there are far too many to mention individually.

People often ask me about my favourite memories from my time at Quins. Of course there are many matches and results from my playing career that spring to mind but most of all I remember the fun, friendship and comradeship that I have experienced in my 55 years at the club and I thank you all for that!

Enjoy the book.

Bob Hiller

The Harlequins Way
By Brendan Gallagher

Every so often in the hurly burly of sport comes an opportunity to pause for a second and examine where you have come from and in which direction you are travelling – to put your foot on the ball to borrow from our footballing cousins. This season Harlequin FC will be celebrating its 150th anniversary and such a milestone offers the perfect opportunity for players and supporters alike to catch their breath just a little and take it all in.

Like all the oldest clubs in the land who have somehow 'survived' through to the modern professional era, there have been some ups and downs along the way throughout Harlequins' existence and these will be chronicled faithfully in this book. What is undeniable about Quins, however, is that a very particular ethos and ambience has surrounded the club since its earliest days and continues to permeate into everything it does. There is a very distinctive 'Harlequins Way' which entails a singular approach to rugby and possibly even life itself.

Throughout the decades, perhaps encouraged by its bold, extrovert colours, Harlequins has always looked to make a splash. To play rugby with a certain panache and style, to boldly experiment at the cutting edge of the game on and off the field, to 'tour' like there is no tomorrow and appreciate, at all times, that there is a life outside of rugby.

At the very start of this project I thought it might be helpful to ask a clutch of illustrious Quins what they believed constituted the essence of the club. Fun and a certain *joie de vivre* seemed to be the constant theme…

One of my first matches for the Wanderers as a youth was against the Cardiff Second XV at the Cardiff Arms Park club ground. I say Cardiff Second XV but the programme indicated they had five or six full Wales caps playing. Anyway, early in the game I collected the ball just inside our 25 and hit a torpedo kick touch-finder right out of the middle. It was the best kick out of hand in my entire career and bounced into touch 80 yards away for a line out right on the Cardiff line. I was rather pleased with myself and trotted around a little, perhaps looking for a word of encouragement from the old hands. Eventually the skipper, Roger Whyte, came up to me and didn't look best pleased: "A word in your ear, young Hiller. We don't like to kick in the Wanderers. Ever."

Bob Hiller

One of the things I loved about Quins was that just about everybody involved with the club – not just the first team squad but the club generally – was really good at something. Legal, money, finance, city trading, computers and IT, police inspectors, chippies, school teaching, academics, you name it. There were so many talented people around the place and a culture of excellence almost without you noticing it. And loads of big characters. We took our rugby seriously but after the games I don't remember talking rugby that much, there was always something else to discuss.

Peter Winterbottom

Somehow in my time, as the game headed towards professionalism, Quins still managed to get the balance right and that was a difficult trick to pull off. My favourite memory is turning up at the car park at The Stoop early one morning to get the bus down to Bristol. I had never in my career won a match at Bristol but had high hopes this time around. However, as I looked around the bus it suddenly dawned on me that four or five of the big names who had been announced in the team on Thursday night weren't present. This wasn't entirely unknown at the time, what with England players wanting to rest that hamstring niggle, an emergency meeting in some City boardroom or a pressing social engagement. I resigned myself to yet another sound thrashing at Bristol, but I was entirely wrong. Those who stepped up from the Seconds were magnificent and we stole off with a famous win, which I thought was quintessential Harlequins.

Paul Ackford

For me Quins is summed up with an unlikely mental image I carry in my head, and that is back in the day when Roger Looker – retired prop, whizz-kid lawyer, high flying businessman, and then chairman of the club – would always end a long Saturday evening in the corner of the bar with his old front row partner in crime Terry Claxton – a lorry driver and proud of it – surrounded by empty beer glasses. They had the utmost respect for each other's very different skills and abilities. It was the most unlikely of friendships, yet at Quins it somehow seemed completely normal.

Colin Herridge

Now, at the end of researching this book, those words ring truer than ever. Fun, a zest for life, ambition and the pursuit of excellence – alongside an ability to see the bigger picture – have been constants at Harlequins and remain as valid today as they ever have been. *Nunquam Dormio* proclaims the club motto and alas we have never been able to identify which club member came up with that little gem. My Latin O-Level tells me the literal translation is *I Never Sleep* – but for me the modern day meaning is clear. Always on the case. 24/7. On and off the field.

Happy reading...

1895

1912

1936

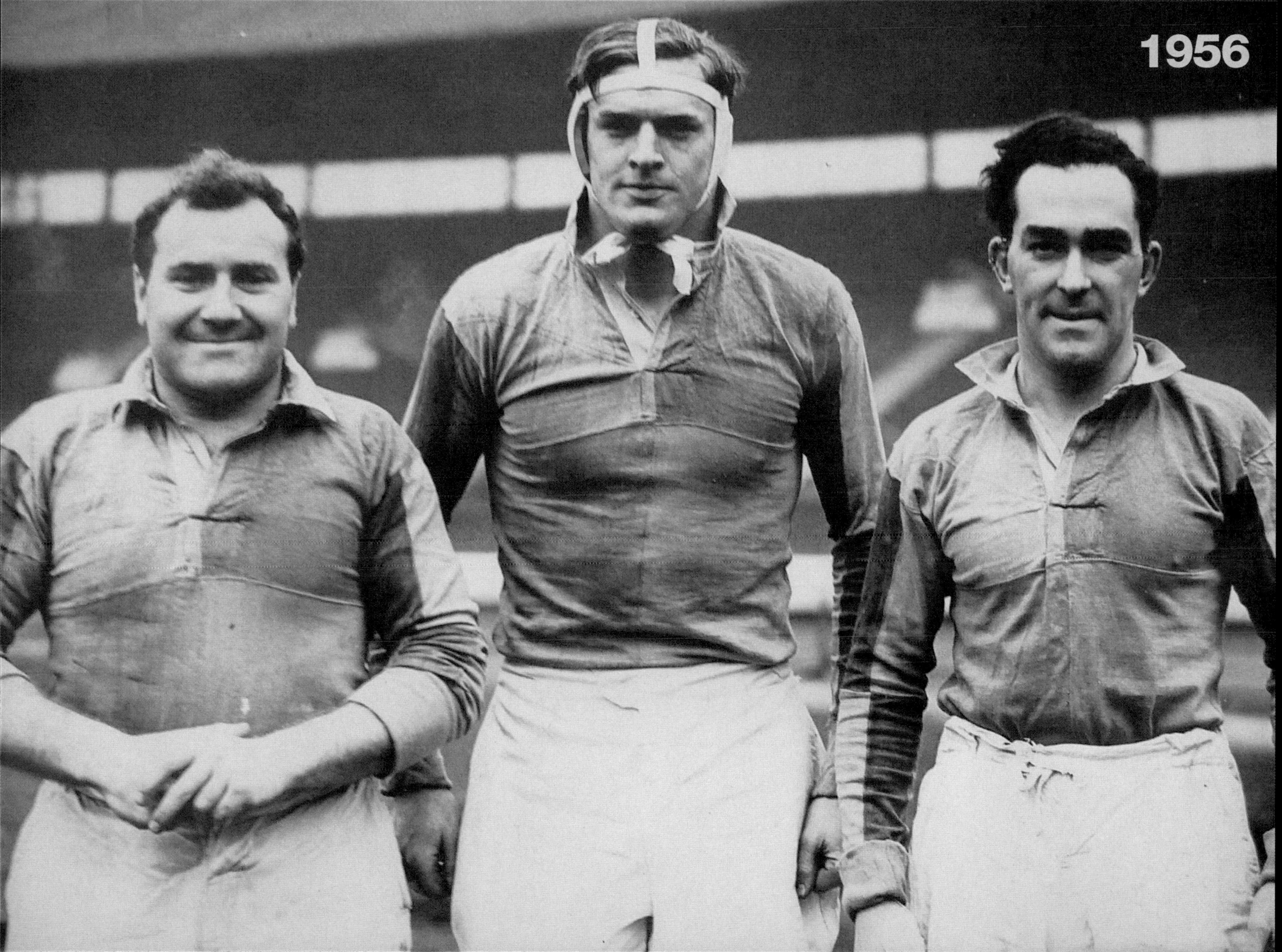

1956

1986

1991

2000

2008

2015

1

The Birth of a Club

1866–1905

1

Harlequins' considerable playing achievements and contribution to English rugby alone would guarantee a chapter in any of the game's history books. But in parallel to the main narrative runs an inspirational sub-plot that centres on a particular brand of rugby – a consistent approach to Kipling's twin imposters of success and failure – which has given the club a unique and compelling identity over the decades.

Title page: The Harlequin FC team of 1885–86 in a typical Victorian portrait. The players are all wearing knickerbockers and some of their jerseys appear to be homemade. Standing (*from left to right*): H K Gow, C Job, T A M Forde, H J Hill, W F Compton, P Smith, J H P Murray, F Johnstone, W R M Leake, H Jones; Seated: P C Cooke, A B Cipriani, F W Burnand (captain), H S Johnstone, H Gurney, G B James; In front: R Walker, W Williams, W Walker

Right: Hampstead Heath as it would have looked in 1866

Opposite: When Hampstead Football Club needed to find a new name beginning with 'H' they settled upon 'Harlequin' – a colourful and quick-witted character from traditional theatre

The rugby at Harlequins, even in defeat, is played with panache and the determination to entertain as well as to win, while outstanding and sometimes maverick individuals, their talent uncompromised, have always been encouraged to express themselves within the team. Incredibly, this approach has largely survived the professional era and has produced both successful and pleasing rugby, while in the club's bars you can always sense an awareness of the bigger picture. For 80 minutes the game and result matter massively and no quarter is asked or given, but underpinning this is always the understanding that sport should never be confused with real life. This is the 'Harlequins Way'.

As the club celebrates its 150th anniversary it is fascinating to discover the historical reasons why it has developed its distinctive ethos and style – what the French prefer to call *ambience*. It has not been an entirely random or mystical process: distinct traits, themes and characteristics can be seen throughout the Harlequins story.

So let us go back to the dawn of rugby time and the nascent Hampstead Rugby Club from which Harlequins emerged. Officially, Hampstead Football Club (HFC) – who played at what is still the cricket ground in Lymington Road – was founded in August 1866, and there are a number of references to the club playing fixtures in the 1866–67 season so it is entirely

appropriate to celebrate Harlequins' 150th anniversary during the 2016–17 campaign. Only four clubs still in existence today in England preceded them – Blackheath (1862), Richmond (1861), Bath (1865) and Manchester (1865). Harlequins has undeniably been one of the great constants in English rugby, even if on occasion it has clung on by its very fingertips.

One of the young dynamos at this early stage was undoubtedly William (W E) Titchener, who was both the first Club

Secretary, at the age of 17, and then captained the side a couple of years later. Titchener lived in Hampstead and arranged for the team to change at the Freemasons Arms at Downshire Hill, which effectively became the club's first headquarters.

These early years were a revolutionary period in rugby history, every bit as tumultuous as the switch to professionalism in 1996 following the International Rugby Board's (IRB) decision to make the game 'open' the previous year. Rugby union in the Victorian era was a new sport fighting hard to establish its niche separate from the fast emerging football code. New rugby clubs were starting up, establishing player bases, passing the hat round to raise money to rent grounds, and trying to attract crowds. Financially it was a constant struggle for the clubs to balance the books and keep their heads above water. The list of clubs that flared briefly for a decade or less, never to be heard of again, is long and at various times Harlequins could easily have faded away, their name found only in rare copies of *The Sportsman* in the British Library.

These were the pioneering days of rugby. Although some matches, including early internationals, were contested with 20 players or more, finding enough players to make up a team was frequently a considerable challenge. Matches were of indeterminate duration and there were often local laws applying. On one noted occasion in 1868, Hampstead contested the issue with the City of London School for three hours and changed ends twice before agreeing to call the match a draw. Goals of course then determined the result, with tries being of no value other than to earn a kick at goal. This did not sit well with some clubs and occasionally you see mention of a 'winning draw' when a side crossed the line more than their opponents but finished with the same number of goals.

With playing numbers in flux, and with virtually none of those who did attend actually coming from the local area anymore, the watershed moment for Hampstead came in 1870 when it was decided to reconstitute and re-name the club so as to appeal to all aspiring rugby players in London.

Right: The report, published on 31st August 1870 in *The Sportsman*, that announced the club's new name and colours to the world

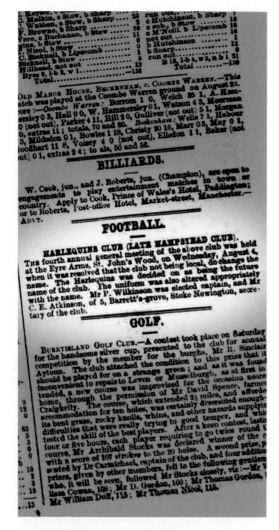

With its tenancy at Hampstead in doubt, the embryonic Harlequins club could not afford to be stuffy or elitist. Far from it. Any port in a storm, frankly.

The decision to re-name the club was made at the annual meeting of Hampstead Football Club in 1870, warranting a brief mention in *The Sportsman* periodical which reported that the summit was held at the Eyre Arms in St John's Wood and that it was the club's fourth annual meeting. To preserve the 'HFC' monogram, which had already been established, it was suggested that the newly constituted club also begin with the letter 'H'. Equally it was decided that Hampstead's motto – *Nunquam Dormio* (I Never Sleep) – should also be preserved, both as a maxim in life and to maintain that link with the very recent past. There were no objections to either proposal.

So what to call the new club? Legend has it that some unidentified committee member was deputed to scroll through the dictionary reading out any words beginning with 'H' that might possibly work as a new club name. Mainly he was greeted with dissenting shakes of the head, but there was a distinct murmur of approval when he read out 'Harlequin'. It certainly had possibilities. Various definitions of harlequin were then cross-checked: a devil in medieval legend; a person who makes funny moves; a fantastic player of tricks; a waggish trickster; a court jester. Yes, that seemed to strike a chord in the room and hinted at the jovial and distinctive chaps around town that the players rather fancied themselves to be. The Harlequin Football Club it was.

Then came another huge decision, although it probably did not seem so at the time, and that was to change the club colours from black and gold to the wildly eccentric, but now iconic, chocolate brown, French grey, magenta and light blue quarters, which is how various harlequins and court jesters have historically been depicted. Having settled on such distinctive colours, the jersey immediately helped define the club. Harlequins was never going to be run-of-the-mill, drab, average or routine.

The radical decision to reconstitute and re-name the club, and to opt for such an unusual jersey, seems rather seminal, the style and tone of the club almost being defined by its rebirth and the image it wanted to portray. This was a young, ambitious club that, rather than accept the fate of others and close down, rebooted itself on more cosmopolitan grounds: a group of young athletes who deliberately chose an extrovert name and dazzling club colours. This was a club that was already a little out of the ordinary and evidently keen to make a splash one way or another, even if its long-term future at this juncture was uncertain.

The re-launch of Hampstead as Harlequins had a momentum of its own, which was immediately reinforced with a number of players coming over from the disbanded Belsize Park RFC, and a glance at the fixture list for that first season under the new name and colours (1870–71) speaks eloquently of a very different era. Among Harlequins' opponents were St Mary's Hospital, Godolphin, Flamingoes, St Bartholomew's Hospital, Wimbledon Hornets, Clapham Rovers and Mars.

Old Cheltonians were also interesting early opponents in the 1870s because they played by their own rules and scoring systems. Radical chaps that they were, the Old Cheltonians attributed a numerical value to tries, penalties, conversions and drop-goals, and preferred to finish their matches with a numerical score. Eventually this system was to be universally adopted throughout the game.

Rugby union at this point was still in the early stages of its evolution. There was no thought of league or cup competitions – indeed that level of competition was the very antithesis to what the game was then about – but the rivalries were keen with local honour and bragging rights at stake.

to have played the majority of his rugby for Harlequins and had been with the club since the Hampstead days, but his connection with the Law XV was considered more prestigious at the time.

Harlequins, however, was definitely growing in stature, as evidenced by the fact that on 26th January 1871 it was one of the 21 clubs represented at the historic meeting at the old Pall Mall restaurant in Charing Cross which saw the Rugby Football Union (RFU) founded. Of those 21 clubs only Harlequins, Richmond, Blackheath and Guy's Hospital still exist today in any format that we would recognise. Wasps should have made it 22 but their representative got his wires crossed, went to the wrong public house and eventually retired in high dudgeon.

Often referred to as the 'father of the club', William (W H A) Smith (known to one and all as simply 'W A'), an internationally renowned cyclist who specialised at racing the penny-farthing and was the fiercest looking of sportsmen, was a prominent member of the Harlequins pack around this time and was just embarking on a marathon spell with the club, including serving as the Club Secretary and then a 16-year stint as President. On the field he was known for the robust physicality

of his play and he brooked no argument off the pitch when he concentrated on administrative chores.

Running the club was almost a full-time job for harassed secretaries, with a constant fight to find a suitable ground where the rent was reasonable and a pitch could be marked out. Harlequins, as we will see elsewhere, lived a nomadic existence and played at numerous venues before the club became the long-time tenants at the newly built Twickenham Stadium in 1909. It was also an era when organised training and team nights were virtually unheard of, and informing players of their selection – either by post or, more haphazardly, the printing of teams in co-operative newspapers – was another mountain to climb, especially when Harlequins started fielding two or three sides. Despite the communication difficulties, however, it was an early club rule that a 2s 6d fine – the infamous Rule 14 – be levied for players who failed to appear when selected. That way the onus was very much on the individual to find out and not vice versa.

By March 1874, with the formation of a Second XV, Smith was reporting a membership of 109, but the club's fortunes were yo-yoing dramatically and by 1878 it had fallen to 69 despite an influx from the recently disbanded Flamingoes. Club members were required to pay an annual subscription of 7s 6d, which was not an inconsiderable sum in those days, but being an amateur really did mean paying for the privilege of playing. This was undoubtedly a difficult time for the club, as its future lay in the balance, and much credit goes to the outstanding forward Frederick Burnand whose five-year captaincy (1878–83) did much to keep Harlequins alive.

The newly constituted Harlequin Football Club started with a bang in these nascent days, winning 12 matches in its first season and improving the following year when it suffered just two defeats. Percival Wilkinson was an early star at half-back and arguably the club's first international, although he was listed as coming from the Law FC when he appeared in the second international of all time, England playing Scotland at The Oval in front of 4,000 fans in 1872. Wilkinson appears

Harlequins 1880–81: The oldest known photograph of a Harlequins team in existence. Standing (*from left to right*): F G C Burnand, C Job, A Claremont, C E Grasermann, A T Waley, J C Howe, A E Stoddart; Seated: H Watts, E H Coles, A Tillyer (captain), C E Macrae, H L Stoddart, L Waver; In front: E Kell, F S Watts, F W Burnand

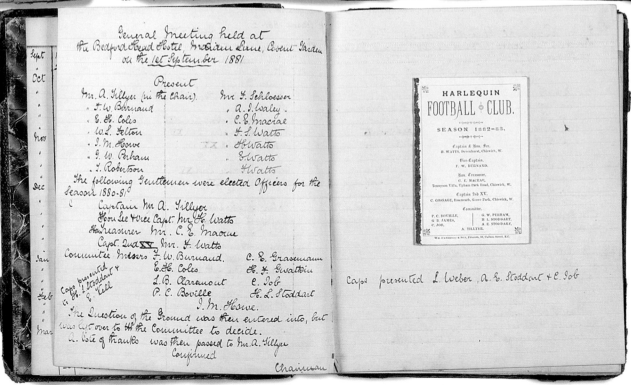

Right and above: A handwritten minute book covering the period 1880–86, which includes early fixtures, minutes of meetings and club rules

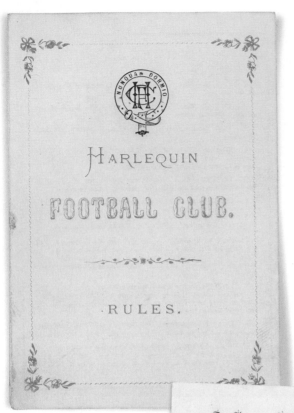

Above: The Harlequin Football Club 'Rules' from the 1883–84 season

Right: A notice informing an unnamed player of his selection to play for Harlequin FC against Wimbledon School on 30th October 1883, with the match to start at 3pm 'wet or fine'

Right: The earliest known surviving Harlequins cap

Above: Cyril Wells, a Harlequins great who effectively invented the position we know today as fly-half

Important players of real character also emerged in the decade that followed. Fly-half William Leake, a Cambridge Blue and then a cleric and schoolmaster at Dulwich College, was the first player officially recognised in the RFU records as a Harlequin to play for England when he appeared against Wales in 1891. Likewise, Arthur (A B) Cipriani was also a great clubman who served at various times as captain, often alongside the formidable Smith, and he played 15 consecutive seasons of first-team rugby for the club, logging 195 appearances.

Another extraordinarily talented and sometimes elusive character was Andrew (A E) Stoddart, who captained England at cricket and rugby and was also a key member of the first Lions rugby tour to Australia and New Zealand, which he embarked on very soon after playing cricket for England during their first tour Down Under in 1888. A former Wisden Cricketer of the Year (1893), he was an attacking back, alternating between Harlequins and Blackheath (as was normal in those days), and seems to be present in many of the club's early team pictures.

Towards the end of the decade, Cyril Wells – another product of Dulwich College and later a teacher at Eton – joined the club and made an instant impact. At Cambridge, Wells was a cricket and rugby Blue who specialised at fullback, but at Harlequins he converted to half-back and played an important part in the development of Harlequins' attacking and handling game. Adrian Stoop – much more of whom anon – rightly gets most of the plaudits as the high priest of Harlequins' distinctive style, but by all accounts Wells did a considerable job preparing the ground. Prior to Wells arriving on the scene and assuming his new role, both half-backs had traditionally positioned themselves directly behind the scrum. It was his initiative to insist that one of them – namely him – stood back and received the ball in the position we would now recognise as fly-half.

The fine condition of the Chiswick ground, where Harlequins were playing by the 1890s, may also have had an influence. "The Harlequins ground was always in good condition," Wells recalled. "The grass was short and thick, the ground level, almost like a cricket ground. The accommodation, however, in the pavilion was rather primitive – only four or five basins of cold water for the whole XV. Afterwards a hip bath with hot water was introduced but the changing room arrangements were never good. I don't think players were so particular in those days."

It is Wells we have to thank for the description of a remarkable game that Quins – if we can now call them that – played at Leicester on their Christmas tour of 1895, which they won 6–0. Always looking to be at the cutting edge, Leicester had decided to protect their enviable Welford Road ground from snow and frost with sand rather than straw, but a thaw and heavy rain had dramatic consequences.

"When the match was played the turf looked like a seashore with large pools of water dotted here and there," Wells explained. "On that same occasion some of us left behind our jerseys and knickerbockers as they were far too wet and full of sand to take away."

Left: Cyril Wells' 1894–95 cap

Above: An early photo of Harlequins in action, date and opposition unknown but possibly from the 1890s. Note the shape of the ball and the fact that the players are wearing buckle belts

Wells then added a rather censorious caveat that hinted that some clubs possibly overindulged on the social side when on tour. Not Quins, of course.

"Harlequins did well on tour because they were a very steady set of fellows compared with some of the other clubs who were apt to do very poorly on tours."

Throughout the mid-1890s Quins were regularly running three teams, but, as many small businesses will testify, with expansion comes much risk and by 1897 the club was finding the £20 a year rent required at Chiswick excessive and so moved first to

Catford and then to Wimbledon Park. The situation remained precarious and the club could have folded at any time as the 19th century drew to a close. An AGM convened for 30th January 1900 amounted to a crisis meeting and members were unashamedly asked to put their hands in their pockets and donate. A hastily organised whip-round raised £66 9s 6d right there on the spot – an outstanding effort – and Harlequins lived to fight another day. The club was a long way from being secure but it was still in the game.

Meanwhile, rugby life continued away from financial and committee worries with a

Quins 'A' XV playing Rugby School during the Easter of 1900, where a precocious youngster named Adrian Stoop caught the eye. Blackheath, considered a bigger and more prestigious club at the time, were understood to have already been in touch with the rising star. However, a recent Rugby XV captain and future England forward, Vincent 'Lump' Cartwright, who alternated between playing for Quins and Nottingham, knew Stoop and his family and was instructed to persuade him that the emerging Quins club was much the better bet. Among other considerations, he would be virtually guaranteed first-team rugby.

Everything eventually worked out as if by design. Stoop went up to Oxford but failed to make the Blues team in his first year – in those days it was almost as difficult to win a Blue as win a full cap – so he was free to play for Quins for much of that time and the connection was cemented before he concentrated on Varsity rugby for the next three seasons. Indeed, Stoop's very first game for the club was against Oxford in 1901 when he scored Quins' only try in a 27–3 defeat.

In 1901 Harlequins hosted the Racing Club of Paris, and so began a strong if intermittent French connection, while the following year the club was on its travels yet again in search of a home ground, this time settling at the Heathfield Club on Wandsworth Common where the rent was now £35. Costs continued to escalate and in 1905 another whip-round was required, and this time £23 13s 9d was raised to keep the wolf from the door.

The tide was turning, however. At that 1905 AGM the youthful Stoop was elected as Secretary, as well as vice-captain, and other capable individuals were emerging. 'Holly' (H E) Ward joined the club as a player that year, but his greatest contribution was to be as a Harlequins institution, not least as the club's frugal treasurer from 1912–50, during which all thoughts of disbanding and being forced to close down were banished for evermore.

It was not readily apparent at the time but the club was, in retrospect, on the cusp of a golden era. Even before the heady Stoop years it is worth noting just how far the Harlequins name had already spread. Early in 1903 came a request from Pretoria in South Africa asking permission to name their club Harlequins and to wear the same distinctive quarters. The request came from the struggling Civil Service Club where they simply could not attract the number of playing members needed to be competitive in the rapidly expanding and strengthening South African scene. They needed to become an open club, looked around for a template, and a number of players originally from England, notably 'Bird' (J E C) Partridge, the club captain who was an officer in the Welsh Guards stationed in Pretoria, mentioned the example of Harlequins. Pretoria Harlequins continue to thrive today, with the late Kitch Christie, South Africa's 1995 World Cup-winning coach, probably its most noted old boy.

If imitation is the sincerest form of flattery then Harlequins had well and truly arrived. Starting from humble but distinctive beginnings, it had fought its way to pre-eminence as a club, overcome the disadvantage of frequently having to up sticks and move, and established a tradition for attacking rugby on the pitch and camaraderie at all times. It was a good start, but even better times were just around the corner.

THE DAILY GRAPHIC, MONDAY, OCTOBER 5, 1903.

STOUT PLACING THE BALL FOR A GOAL KICK

PULLED OVER.

HARLEQUINS BREAK AWAY.

FRANK STOUT THE RICHMOND CAPTAIN

FRANK GILLETT

RUGBY FOOTBALL: THE MATCH BETWEEN THE HARLEQUINS AND RICHMOND AT WANDSWORTH COMMON.

CLOSE QUARTERS

HARLEQUIN WANDERERS

In the course of its 150-year history, Harlequins (previously Hampstead Football Club) has played 'home' fixtures at no fewer than 19 recorded locations – 15 of them between 1866 and 1909, the year when the club took up residence at the newly built Twickenham Stadium.

1. 1866–69 Hampstead Cricket Club
Hampstead Football Club – following its formation in 1866 – played its first three seasons on this site before relocating to the Highbury area.

2. 1869–71 The Old Sluice House, Highbury
The Old Sluice House was situated not far from where the famous football ground of Arsenal FC was to spring up. Here, Hampstead changed its name to Harlequin Football Club.

3. 1871–72 Pages Cricket Ground, Tufnell Park
The club spent one season at the Pages Cricket Ground, which is believed to have been situated near modern-day Carleton Road.

4. 1872–73 Swiss Cottage
The exact location of this ground is unknown, although the Britannia pub in Belsize Park apparently provided training and catering facilities.

5. 1873–74 Putney Heath
After one season in Swiss Cottage, the club relocated to Putney Heath, making use of the Green Man pub on top of Putney Hill.

6. 1874–75/76 Fairfield, Kensal Green
Next season saw Harlequins relocate back north of the Thames as the club moved to Kensal Green and the King William IV tavern. Some sources suggest that Quins made use of this site for two seasons, although Teddy Wakelam, in his book *Harlequin Story*, asserts that the club was once again on the move prior to the 1875–76 campaign.

7. 1875/76–79 Stamford Brook
After the spell at Kensal Green, the club made Hammersmith its next temporary HQ, with players and members refreshing themselves at the Queen of England pub.

8. 1875/76–77 Beaufort House, Fulham
During its spell at Stamford Brook, there is strong evidence to suggest that the club occasionally made use of Beaufort House as an alternative ground.

9. 1879–81 Turnham Green
In 1979 Quins made the short move to Turnham Green, the changing facilities and refreshments being provided by the Packhorse & Talbot, a still thriving pub situated on Chiswick High Road.

10. 1881–85 Devonshire Park, Chiswick
The start of the 1881–82 campaign saw the club make another small move as it relocated to Devonshire Park for four seasons.

11. 1885–97 Chiswick Park Cricket Ground
After a spell at Devonshire Park the club decamped to the nearby cricket ground. This appears to have offered an excellent playing surface that drained well and the origins of Quins' attacking game became established while at this venue. However, the rent gradually became too high and players wearied of the poor changing facilities.

12. 1897–99 Catford Sports Ground
Situated close to Catford Bridge station, with changing facilities available in a pavilion at the ground.

13. 1899–1901 The Polo Grounds, Wimbledon Park
The precise location of this ground is unknown, although fixture cards from the period state that it was within a three-minute walk of Southfields station. It is suggested it may have been located at the end of Gartmore Gardens.

14. 1901–09 Heathfield Cricket Club, Wandsworth Common
Described as being only seven minutes' walk away from Wandsworth Common station, potentially placing it at the site of the modern-day Sinjun Grammarians Cricket Club.

15. 1909–Present Twickenham Stadium
In 1909, after some hard negotiating, Harlequins became the tenant club at the newly built RFU stadium at Twickenham. Between 1909 and 1914, in addition to First XV matches, the club's other XVs also occasionally played here.

16. 1919–25 Home Park, Hampton Wick
While retaining the use of Twickenham, Quins sought out a second venue where the club itself and its junior sides could be based and where the First XV could play when the larger stadium was unavailable. Home Park was eventually found, with Kingston Public Baths providing the changing rooms.

17. 1925–63 Fairfax Road, Teddington
Having purchased the site two years earlier, Quins moved into a ground which was to serve as the club base for decades – although the First XV played the vast majority of its fixtures at Twickenham Stadium.

18. 1954–59 White City
In the second half of the 1950s, the First XV played certain floodlit matches at the White City stadium. It is unclear whether this was either because Twickenham was not available or it was an attempt to increase revenue by attracting larger crowds. Initially crowds were increased but, after two or three seasons, they decreased and the venue was eventually dropped.

19. 1963–Present The Twickenham Stoop Stadium
In 1963 Quins moved to a 14-acre site – which already housed an athletics track – opposite Twickenham Stadium on the other side of the A316. Initially it was used as a training ground but quickly it became Harlequins' ground of choice. For a period the club retained the right to stage a certain number of regular games at Twickenham Stadium, although these were increasingly limited to early season outings, often against Welsh opposition. In recent years, the club has hired Twickenham for the regular Yuletide 'Big Game', which is promoted as a massive festive day out for the whole family and has consistently attracted crowds in excess of 75,000.

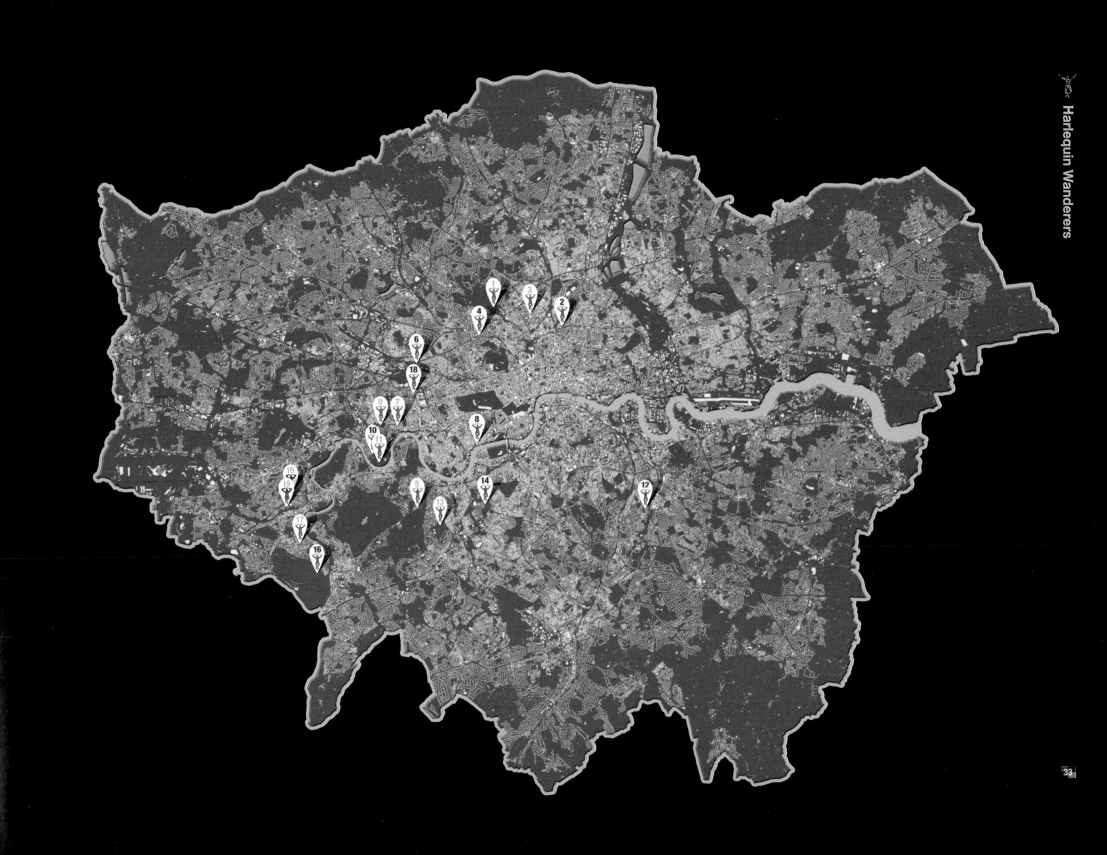

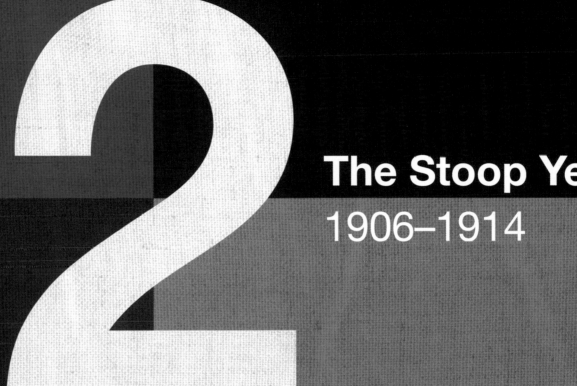

The Stoop Years

1906–1914

2

What has been dubbed by rugby historians as 'The Stoop Era' ran from 1906 to the start of the First World War in 1914, and during this period the force of nature that was Adrian Stoop was both captain and Secretary of Harlequins. With Stoop at the helm, on and off the field, the club reached new heights and developed a playing style that started to truly set it apart from its rivals.

The son of a fabulously wealthy Dutch oil magnate and emigre, Stoop was a man of independent financial means – he was gifted a marble quarry on his 21st birthday – who became fanatical about the game while at Rugby School and proceeded to devote virtually his entire life, save for a distinguished military career during the Great War, to the club.

As a rugby player and de facto coach, Stoop chased perfection and, under his guidance, Quins became the leading club side in the land while the national team's fortunes flourished in parallel. Although the notion of ever being 'paid' to play rugby would have been anathema, his total dedication to training and playing hinted at modern-day professional attitudes, while there was more than a whiff of the very up-to-date notion of 'marginal gains'. Off the field he also helped to engineer the move to Twickenham in 1909 when the RFU started looking for tenants after they had expensively completed the construction of their ambitious new 17,000 capacity stadium.

Stoop could do it all. Many would claim that he is the inventor of modern back play and, certainly, his theories on the core skills of rugby were adopted for decades before the game itself changed. Reading between the lines, he was something of a maverick and martinet, and you suspect that he might not have suffered fools gladly. Famously, after his beloved Rugby School had once been heavily

beaten by Cheltenham, he sent a Quins 'A' team of near First XV strength down to Cheltenham a few weeks later to administer severe retribution for their impertinence.

It is also clear, however, that he was a generous and devoted friend to those who came under his spell and were dedicated to the cause. A life-long fitness fanatic who trained first as a gymnast before catching the rugby bug, he played his last game for Quins at the age of 55 when he took a team down to Eastbourne College. It was he, in the mid-1930s, who meticulously supervised Douglas Bader's physical rehabilitation after the legendary fighter pilot's double amputation following a serious plane crash.

Looking back a century or more later, Stoop's supreme quality appears to have been as a recruiter and trainer of raw talent, especially among the backs, so perhaps we should add 'coach' and 'director of rugby' to his many titles, although 'supremo' is probably the only term that does his influence justice. It was he who cast his eyes around and used his acute sense of raw athletic talent to pull together a squad and then train them assiduously. He also introduced the previously unthinkable – given the prevailing amateur ethos – midweek evening practice sessions at Preece's military indoor riding school, where the perfect, dry conditions enabled his team to develop their passing skills.

Who were these players, this eclectic bunch of individuals that Stoop transformed

into the team that would play rugby from the Gods, often attacking in thrilling fashion from behind their own line? Stoop's long-time half-back partner was Herbert Sibree MC (Military Cross) – born in Antananarivo, Madagascar and the only member of his God-fearing family not to become a missionary – who arrived from the defunct Kensington Club as a fullback. However, Stoop was having none of that and quickly converted Sibree to scrum-half.

John Birkett – the son of Reginald Birkett, who scored England's first ever international try – was always a great rugby talent, but pitched up at Harlequins from Haileybury College and the Brighton FC club as a half-back. Stoop,

Title page: When Adrian Stoop (*seated, centre*) was photographed in this team picture during the 1902–03 season, no-one could have envisaged the huge impact he would make not just on Harlequins but on the game of rugby as a whole

Right: A break in play as Quins' big guns consider the next move against Oxford University. Taking part in the discussion are (*from left to right*) John Birkett, Herbert Sibree, 'Roc' Ward, Adrian Stoop and Gordon Elmslie, with an Oxford University player stood between Stoop and Elmslie

however, had no need of new half-backs – Sibree was his man at scrum-half and that was the end of the matter – so he converted Birkett into possibly the best centre of his era.

Douglas 'Danny' Lambert was mainly a footballer at Eastbourne College and a jovial member of the Quins 'A' XV pack until a trial match early one September when he sprinted after Stoop and caught him from behind to prevent a certain try. A famous quickfire exchange ensued:

"Who the hell was that?" enquired Stoop as he picked himself up.

"That was Lambert, the 'A' team forward, sir," came the response.

"Well, he's the first team wing now," replied Stoop instantaneously.

Lambert was also a prodigious goal-kicker and went on to win seven England caps, although you sense he never quite convinced the England selectors. Certainly, he must be the only ever player to be dropped after scoring five tries in a Test, as he did against France in 1907.

Kenneth Powell, meanwhile, was no sort of rugby player at all when Stoop spotted him at the Rugby School athletics day. Powell was essentially a superb high hurdler – he came fifth at the 120-yard hurdles at the 1912 Olympics in Stockholm after winning his semi-final – and a very considerable tennis player. The agile Powell could run like the wind and Stoop, the great planner and plotter, could visualise him finishing off the many try-scoring chances he knew his multi-talented Quins back division would conjure up.

Later during his tenure as captain, Stoop pulled another rabbit out of the hat. Henry Brougham, from Wellington College, was a brilliant cricketer and racquets player – he won a bronze medal at the 1908 Olympics at the latter and scored a fine 84 in the 1911 Varsity cricket match in the former – and played rugby just for fun.

Stoop, however, caught sight of him playing for a Brasenose College XV at Wellington College on an afternoon when he had attended to check the form of promising youngsters Frank Perkins and Wilfred Schloss. Stoop was immediately impressed with Brougham's untutored skills and, on

talking to the young man afterwards, was amazed to hear that Brougham was already a social, largely non-playing member at Harlequins. Before very long he was starting on the wing, both for Quins and for England.

Ronnie Poulton – to become Poulton-Palmer just before his death – was a once-in-a-generation rugby talent and Stoop's task in his particular case was to beat off the opposition and ensure he joined Harlequins, with Blackheath again among the many clubs also seeking his services. Just as Old Rugbeian Vincent 'Lump' Cartwright had been delegated to ensure the young Stoop joined Harlequins, Stoop kept in touch with the Poulton family and eventually landed his man. Again fate intervened with Poulton who, as was the case with Stoop, missed out on his Blue at Oxford in the first year, which enabled him to play more often for Harlequins and establish a strong relationship with the club.

There were also other notable players. Fullback George Maxwell-Dove used to catch the overnight sleeper from Cumbria down to

Above: An illustrated tribute to the great Harlequins team assembled and marshalled by Stoop that appeared in *The Sketch* in November 1910

Harlequins 2nd October 1909: The first match at Twickenham. Standing (*from left to right*): G R Maxwell-Dove, J H Denison, B H Bonham-Carter, G V Carey, W G Beauchamp, T Potter, R E Hancock, R O C Ward; Seated: H J H Sibree, D Lambert, A D Stoop (captain), W A Smith (President), J G G Birkett, J G Bussell, R W Poulton (later Poulton-Palmer); In front: F M Stoop, G M Chapman

London every Friday night because this was a team he considered it well worth the effort to be part of. Over 80 years later another young back would commute from Durham University to play for Harlequins most weeks, a certain Will Carling. Meanwhile Stoop's younger brother, Tim 'Freek' Stoop, was a very strong centre indeed and might have won more than his four England caps had he not been dogged by injury.

Although they rarely received the plaudits, Quins also possessed a number of very considerable forwards contending for a place in the First XV. Cartwright had retired to become a top referee, but Curly Hammond was still a stalwart on and off the field. This is a man who, in a famous incident related in the *Harlequin Story* by Teddy (H B T) Wakelam, was dubbed the 'Beer King of Germany' when he accepted a challenge from a local dignitary on one of Quins' tour games in Frankfurt against the German national team. In response to the challenge, Hammond polished off ten glasses of beer one after another, the last four while standing on a chair – thus setting a high benchmark for future Quins on tour. 'Roc' (R O C) Ward was another always seen in the thick of the action, again on and off the field. Alas like many of this era he was lost in the Great War, commanding a tank on the Western Front. William (W B) Grandage was an outstanding pack leader and forward and another who would be killed on the Western Front.

The 1906–07 season was when Harlequins first started to make waves, with a campaign including 17 wins and seven defeats, and the press started mentioning the 'Stoop system'. And it was much the same the following season, although Stoop himself was inactive for the majority of that winter after breaking a collarbone against United Services in October. The injury put him out of action for much of the season and then the following campaign he broke the same bone again, this time against London Scottish in a game in which Birkett also dislocated his shoulder, although 13-man Quins clung on to record a deserved 13–9 victory.

Unable to play for the best part of two seasons, Stoop switched his energies to coaching – not a term anybody would have recognised at the time – and getting the paperwork together to apply for the lease at Twickenham. By the end of 1908 the RFU had spent nearly £10,000 developing the ground, built where a Quins member, Billy Williams, had run a market garden. That considerable outlay was all for three or four games a year – a couple of Home internationals each year and perhaps an incoming touring side once every four or five years. That made little sense the ground would become a white elephant, with the pitch and stands suffering from underuse and neglect. Stoop bided his time and then pounced on 27th November 1908 through a formal letter to the RFU suggesting, in effect, a ground share with Quins leasing the use of Twickenham. Such an arrangement ticked a lot of boxes and, in an outstanding piece of business, Stoop secured an arrangement whereby Quins could play a minimum of 13 First XV games there for the next two years for the annual payment of £100 rent. This was very quickly increased to a five-year arrangement and thereafter it was renewed regularly by the club.

Harlequins' first match at Twickenham, and in fact the very first match at the ground, was on 2nd October 1909 against old rivals Richmond. A crowd of 2,000 attended as Gordon Carey had the honour of kicking the game off, and in no time Birkett had raced in for the first of four Quins tries, although a strong performance from Richmond pegged Quins back and in the end they were grateful enough to claim a 14–10 win.

THE FIRST MATCH ON THE NEW RUGBY UNION GROUND.

HARLEQUINS BEAT RICHMOND BY FOURTEEN POINTS TO TEN AT TWICKENHAM.

Above: An artist's impression of the very first match at Twickenham Stadium between Harlequins and Richmond

Right: The match programme for a fixture between Harlequins and Blackheath in 1910

Below: A shirt belonging to Eric (E S) Unwin, dating from 1912, which was presented to the club by his family

Immediately Stoop and the club set about building what we would now call its 'fanbase'. Over 100 years ago Twickenham would be considered an out of town venue and not the easiest ground to visit, meaning strenuous efforts were required in order to attract sizeable crowds and turn the 'gate' into a valuable source of revenue – one of the strategies employed allowed each member to bring two ladies into the ground for free. Ultimately, however, it was the quality of rugby that counted most and that season Quins remained unbeaten all the way through to February when the First XV lost 12–5 to an Oxford University side inspired by a certain Poulton-Palmer.

These were heady days – the 1909–10 international season also saw Quins players come to the fore, with Stoop and Birkett taking starring roles in England's memorable win over Wales at Twickenham, the first over the Welsh for 12 years. Quins ended the season with just four defeats, one of those coming on the final day with a 17–15 reverse at Newport – the Welsh clinching the issue with a try in the seventh minute of injury time after what most observers considered to be the club game of the season. Stoop's influence was clear – in 23 games that season Harlequins amassed 129 tries. The following season was another riot of action, with just seven defeats in 29 games, the high point being a 32–0 drubbing of Northampton.

Another barometer of success came in the form of the club's balance sheet. At the end of the 1905–06 season Harlequins showed a profit for the season of £61 6s 8d, but as gate receipts rose massively so did the club's profit. At the end of the 1910–11 season Quins, burdened initially by the cost of renting Twickenham, albeit at an exceptionally good rate, reported a surplus of £23, but two years later the figure was £1,163. You do not have to be much of an accountant to appreciate such a healthy trend, sparked mainly by the club's ability to now attract a decent paying gate for games at Twickenham.

In June 1913 the club decided to invest £1,000 in India stock, having dipped its toes cautiously in financial waters in 1908 with an initial investment of £50. At that stage nobody was anticipating the war ahead, even the politicians did not really see that one coming, but such prudence was to prove invaluable in

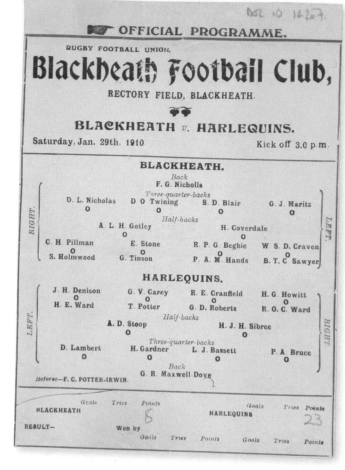

OFFICIAL PROGRAMME.

RUGBY FOOTBALL UNION.

Blackheath Football Club,
RECTORY FIELD, BLACKHEATH.

BLACKHEATH *v.* HARLEQUINS.

Saturday, Jan. 29th, 1910.   Kick off 3.0 p.m.

BLACKHEATH.
Back
F. G. Nicholls

Three-quarter-backs
D. L. Nicholas   D O Twining   S. D. Blair   G. J. Maritz

Half-backs
A. L. H. Gotley   H. Coverdale

C. H. Pillman   E. Stone   R. P. G. Begbie   W. S. D. Craven
S. Holmwood   G. Tinson   P. A. M. Hands   B. T. C. Sawyer

HARLEQUINS.

J. H. Denison   G. V. Carey   R. E. Cranfield   H. G. Howitt
H. E. Ward   T. Potter   G. D. Roberts   R. O. C. Ward

Half-backs
A. D. Stoop   H. J. H. Sibree

Three-quarter-backs
D. Lambert   H. Gardner   L. J. Bassett   P. A. Bruce

Back
G. R. Maxwell-Dove

Referee—F. C. POTTER-IRWIN.

	Goals	Tries	Points		Goals	Tries	Points
BLACKHEATH			8	HARLEQUINS			23
RESULT—		Won by					
	Goals	Tries	Points		Goals	Tries	Points

1920 when the club was able to re-launch from a relatively secure financial footing after the First World War and five years of enforced inactivity.

What was the secret of Harlequins' string of outstanding performances and growing reputation? What was the so-called 'Stoop system'? Fitness and attention to detail was certainly one aspect – Stoop was an advocate of no smoking, drinking alcohol in moderation, four pints of water a day, breathing through your nose, clean lightweight boots and midweek training – but it was his determination to play what we would

Left: A collection of caps earned by the great Adrian Stoop, courtesy of the World Rugby Museum, Twickenham, including (top left and right) his Rugby School cap, featuring embroidered inscriptions on the inside; his Harlequins cap for the 1909–10 season (bottom left); and his England cap (bottom right)

LIEUT. A.D. STOOP,
5TH BATTY THE QUEEN'S, ROYAL
WEST SURREY REGIMENT,
the famous ENGLISH RUGBY
INTERNATIONAL, & Captain of
the HARLEQUINS for many seasons.
"The Field," Oct. 30, 1915.

Above: A hero both on and off the pitch – an illustration of Lieutenant Adrian Stoop that appeared in *The Field* in 1915

was considered deeply radical and daring at the time.

Playing the game in this way came naturally to Stoop and, indeed, we have already seen that Cyril Wells was an early proponent of attacking half-back play at Harlequins. But the 'Road to Damascus' moment for Stoop probably came at Stamford Bridge on 4th October 1905 when he was reduced to a hapless bystander as Dave Gallaher's All Blacks team ran a strong Middlesex side – which included his Quins captain Curly Hammond – ragged, scoring eight tries in a 34–0 victory. New Zealand, and indeed the triumphant, outstanding Wales team of the era, were setting new standards which Stoop was determined to match and better.

Stoop was a man way ahead of his time, as witnessed by the passing technique he trained Harlequins to adopt, outlined here in an extract from a famous essay he penned for the *Rugby Football Annual 1913–14*. Many consider it the definitive word on the subject:

"As the receiver is seldom able to give his whole attention to the ball but usually is largely occupied with watching his opponent, it is essential that a pass should be made so that it is easy to take. And to ensure this, three points should be borne in mind. 1: the passer and runner must be running on a parallel, if not diverging line. 2: the ball must travel in a horizontal direction. 3: it must fly without spin with one end pointing towards the receiver.

"It is quite a simple matter to prevent the ball from spinning. It should be held in both hands at one end, with the other pointing away from the body. But to obtain the force necessary to make the ball travel horizontally and at the same time to keep control over its

direction is by no means easy and it is an art which in most cases requires considerable practice.

"The force is obtained by the muscles of the back while the arms are used merely to control the direction. As an illustration let us suppose the pass is to be given to the left. The action of the body is the same as we are throwing some object which is held between the teeth over the left shoulder with the greatest possible force.

"It takes the form of a swing from the right hip using the muscles down the right hand side of the back, finishing up with a hollow back and the chin pointing towards the left while the shoulders have swung through an angle of about 45 degrees. The arms should be held straight, though not necessarily rigid and the only conscious movement of them should be raised towards the end of the swing. At the commencement they are merely used to connect the ball with the shoulders. At the end of the swing we are looking in the direction in which the ball is to travel, and the direction of the ball will be that in which the arms are pointing when the ball is released.

"The same considerations apply to a pass given by a scrum-half but as in his particular case every fraction of a second is of the greatest importance… there should be no picking up or swinging back with the ball. It should be swept straight off the ground to the stand-off in one movement. It is by practice and practice alone that such a pass off the ground is obtained, for in no other way are muscles of the back and sides strengthened in the manner in which the pass demands."

Perhaps the final word on Stoop should lie with Wavell Wakefield, the dominant playing figure at Harlequins during the 1920s when

probably recognise today as 'total rugby' that set Quins apart: supremely quick and accurate passing, with the ball given and taken without breaking stride, scissor movements, devastating cross-field kicks and a willingness to turn defence into attack whenever possible. The rugby that Quins played around 1910 would be readily identified by the modern-day spectator, but it

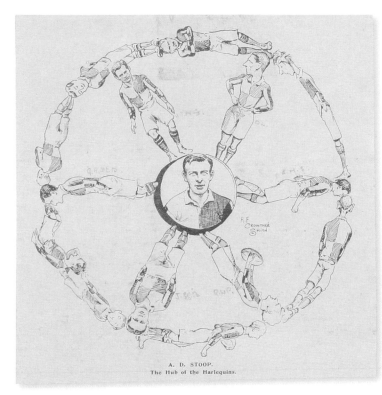

A. D. STOOP.
The Hub of the Harlequins.

Stoop and the Harlequins arc synonymous; certainly it's hard to think of one without the other, and of his profound influence on the club and his mass service to it there can be no doubt whatsoever. I know I speak for every Harlequin when I express our deepest gratitude for all he did for us through the years as captain, Honorary Secretary and President."

Harlequins ended the 1913–14 season with a 26–6 win over United Services, but the world was about to fall off a cliff and that was the last game Quins contested in he worked closely with Stoop. Here is a telling extract from his address at Stoop's memorial service in 1957.

"Adrian Stoop was a dedicated man. He concentrated the whole force of his strong personality into creative thinking about rugby football and this integration of purpose gave him, in this sphere, more than a touch of genius. He sought quality. By deep thought, by continual practice and by physical fitness he achieved quality. He demanded quality in others and not infrequently got it.

"His name will rank always with the legendary names of those who have made outstanding contributions to the game of rugby football and we in the Harlequins are particularly proud to think that it was through our club that his remarkable qualities came to full fruition. Indeed we might say that Adrian

five years. By the start of what was meant to be the 1914–15 season the First World War was underway, with able-bodied men from the nation's rugby clubs among the first to volunteer. Harlequins held a final committee meeting at Carr's Restaurant on 17th September 1914 and it showed just one entry: a resolution was proposed and passed that, on account of the war, all fixtures be cancelled and that, forthwith, a £500 donation be paid towards the refurbishment of the Star and Garter Hotel, which was being established as a home for badly disabled servicemen on top of Richmond Hill. As Wakelam eloquently wrote in *Harlequin Story* you could, on a clear day, see the top of the Twickenham stands from Richmond Hill, a poignant link with the many Quins who didn't come back.

Ode to Adrian Stoop
Athletic News, 15th November 1909

A 'half should be the perfect blend
of weasel and of fox:
Like a stag to dart,
With a lion's heart
To face the rugged shocks

Which would affright a timid youth
considering his skin
These virtue group
themselves in Stoop
The agile Harlequin

Just see him hov'ring near the pack
and darting around the scrums
swiftly to nip
with eager grip
The ball when out it comes.

Note too with what elusiveness
away he will gaily spin
Both in an out
And around about
The tricky Harlequin

He cogs not with black selfishness
That most unpleasant vice
But hands the sphere
with words of cheer
to someone in a thrice

Well passed, well run, well passed again
that wing three quarter's in
A rattling cry
spectators cry
Stoop-endous Harlequin.

Left: An unusual illustration (source unknown) showing Stoop as the 'hub' of Harlequins – discovered in the Stoop family scrapbook (see overleaf)

Right: The remarkable scrapbooks covering the life and career of Adrian Stoop that appear on the following pages were donated to the World Rugby Museum at Twickenham by the Stoop family. It is not known exactly which of the great man's relatives compiled them, although Adrian's nephew, Peter Stoop, is considered a likely candidate

ADRIAN DURA STOOP. MC.

BORN 27 May 1883   DIED 27 Nov 1957

EDUCATED @ DOVER COLLEGE / RUGBY SCHOOL / UNIVERSITY COLLEGE OXFORD.

RUGBY HISTORY —

PLAYED FOR RUGBY SCHOOL 1900/01

" OXFORD UNIV 1902/03/04

" ENGLAND 1905/06/07/10/11/12

" HARLEQUINS 1905 — 1914

ENGLAND SELECTOR 1927 — 1931

PRESIDENT R.F.U 1932/33

MARRIED AUDREY NEEDHAM. 1917

HAD 4 SONS   BUNNY   Killed in Italy 1944
DICKY   Killed Motor Racing 1970
MICHAEL   Born 1922
BILLY   Killed in Motor Acc.t 1937

ALSO PLAYED FOR BARBARIANS & MIDDLESEX AND SURREY & THEIR PRESIDENT

PRESIDENT OF HARLEQUINS 1920 — 1949.

HE WAS OF DUTCH PARENTAGE

AUDREY HIS WIFE

THE KINDEST AND MOST GENEROUS PERSON

DIED @ HARTLEY WINTNEY   OCT 1981
AGED 84.

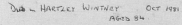

ON HONEYMOON 1917.

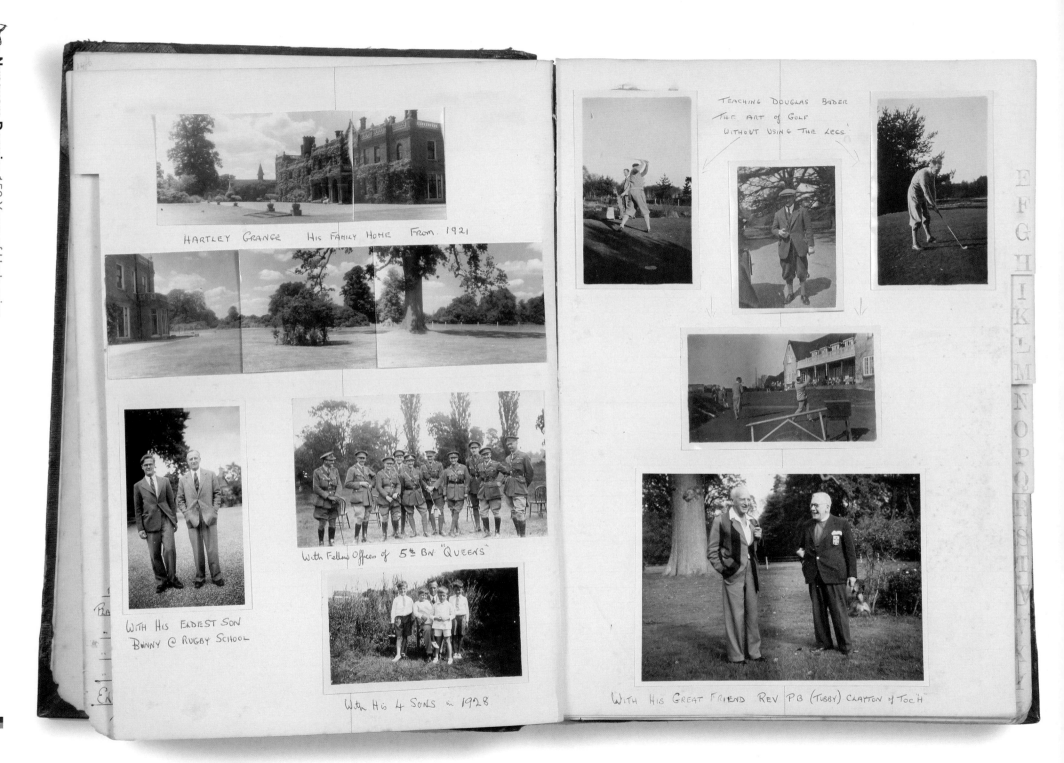

HARTLEY GRANGE   HIS FAMILY HOME   FROM. 1921

TEACHING DOUGLAS BADER
THE ART OF GOLF
WITHOUT USING THE LEGS

WITH FELLOW OFFICERS OF 5TH BN "QUEENS"

WITH HIS ELDEST SON
BUNNY @ RUGBY SCHOOL

WITH HIS 4 SONS in 1928

WITH HIS GREAT FRIEND REV P.B (TUBBY) CLAYTON of TOC H

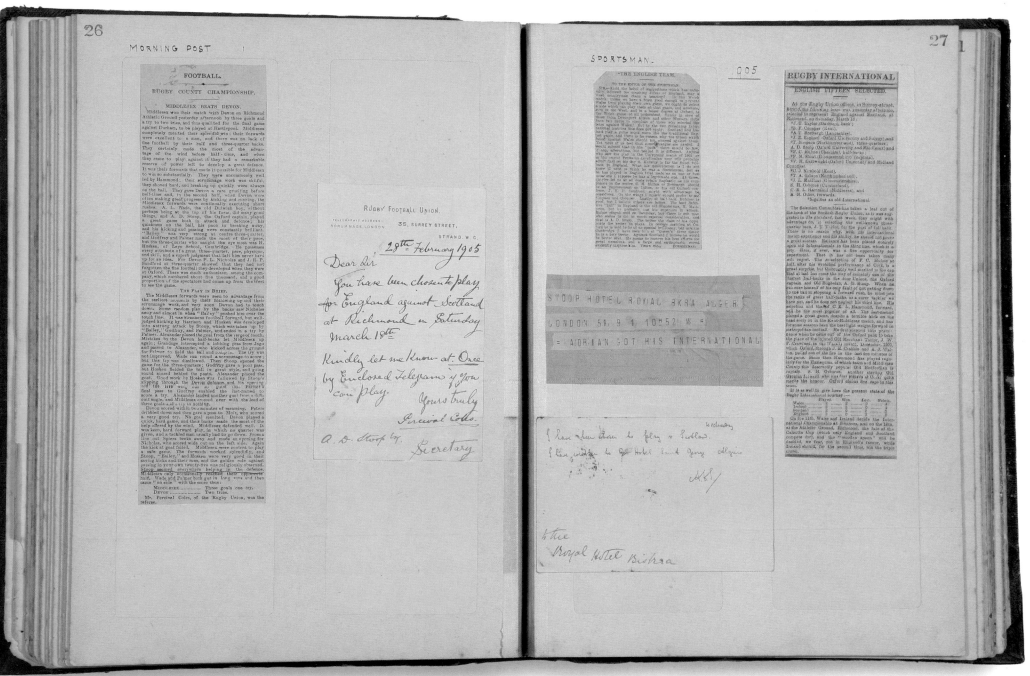

3 36

37

Jan 15th 1910

Jan 24 1910

ENGLAND BEATS WALES FOR THE FIRST TIME IN TWELVE YEARS.

ENGLAND, 11 POINTS; WALES, 6 POINTS, IN 2ND RUGBY INTERNATIONAL, PLAYED AT TWICKENHAM ON SATURDAY.

ENGLAND'S GREAT RUGBY VICTORY.

Long Run of Welsh Successes Broken by a Brilliant Win at Twickenham.

FIRST MINUTE REVELATION.

ENGLAND'S FORWARD RUSHES.

FOOTBALL.

THE HARLEQUINS AS SCORERS.

LONDON SCOTTISH BEATEN AT RICHMOND.

THE IMPORTANCE OF TACKLING.

The Harlequins seem possessed of some uncanny spell that they cast over opponents to destroy their power of tackling. It was marked at Twickenham when three Scottish sides played there; it was quite pronounced when Oxford let off the Harlequins on the Iffley-road field in Michaelmas term; it recurred on Saturday at Richmond Athletic Ground. The Harlequins now crossed the Scottish line eight times and won by three goals and five tries to nothing.

THE CANTER IN THE SECOND HALF.

GENERALSHIP OF A GREAT HALF-BACK.

The match was a great triumph for A. D. Stoop.

"LONDON SCOTTISH v. HARLEQUINS.

THE SCOTS OUTPACED.

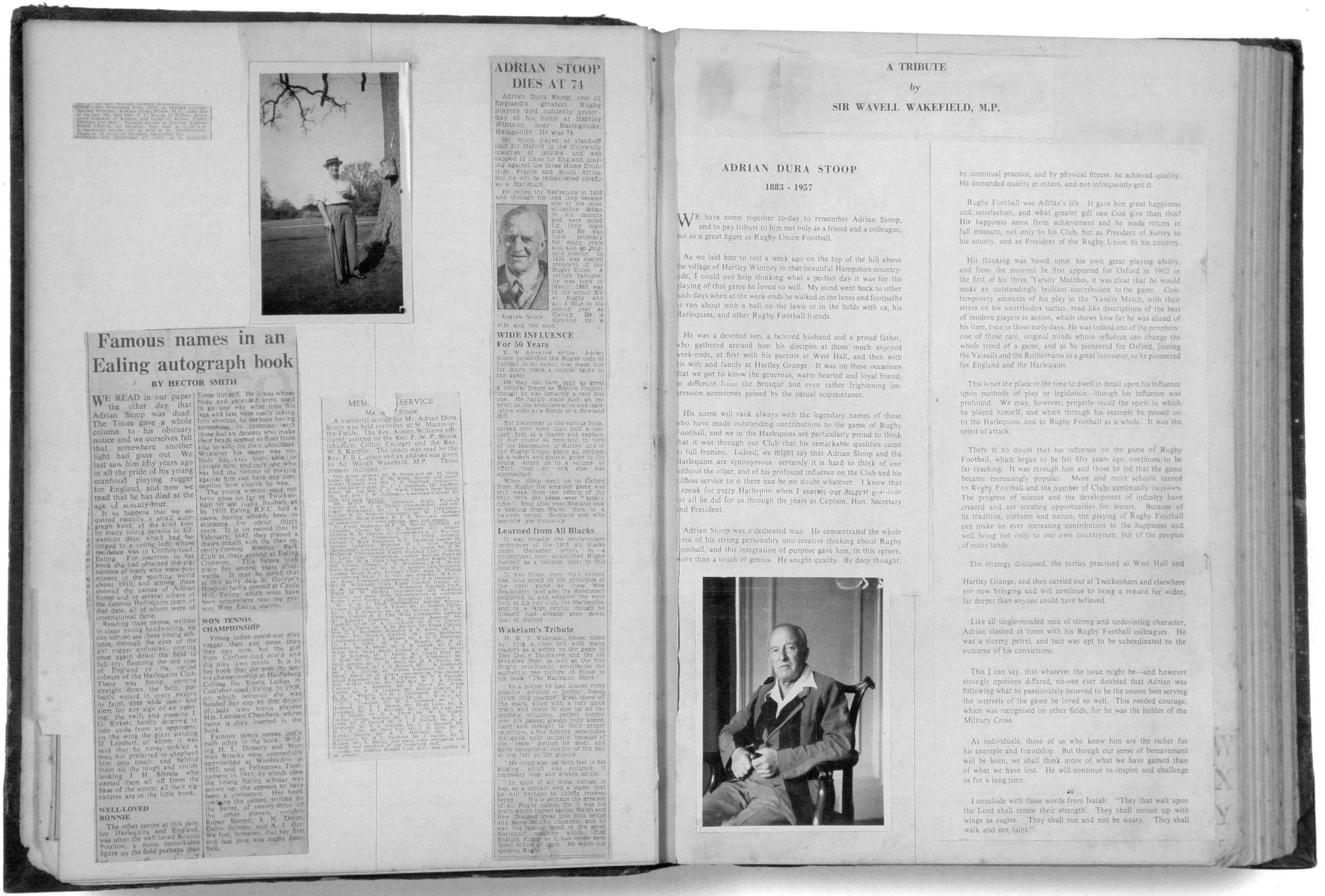

Famous names in an Ealing autograph book

BY HECTOR SMITH

WE READ in our paper the other day that Adrian Stoop was dead. The Times gave a whole column to his obituary notice and we ourselves felt that somewhere another light had gone out. We last saw him fifty years ago in all the pride of his young manhood playing rugger for England, and now we read that he has died at the age of seventy-four.

It so happens that we acquired recently a small autograph book, of the kind kept by many young persons in Edwardian days, which had belonged to a young lady whose residence was in Corfton-road, Ealing. For insertion in her book she had obtained the signatures of many who were prominent in the sporting world about 1910, and among these showed the names of Adrian Stoop and of several others of the famous Harlequins team of that date, all of whom were of international fame.

Reading these names, written in clear young handwriting, we can almost see these young athletes, through the eyes of the girl rugger enthusiast, coming once again down the field in full cry, flaunting the red rose of England or the varied colours of the Harlequins Club. There was Stoop, coming straight down the field, perfectly poised in every swerve or feint, eyes wide open and alert for any sign of an opening; the swift and massive J. G. Birkett, hardly deigning to turn aside from an opponent; on the wing the giant striding D. Lambert, of whom it was said that he never tackled a man but preferred to shepherd him into touch; and behind them all the tough and untidy looking J. H. Sibrete who started them all off from the base of the scrum; all their signatures are in the little book.

WELL-LOVED RONNIE

The other centre at this date, for Harlequins and England, was often the well-loved Ronnie Poulton, a more remarkable figure on the field perhaps than Stoop himself. He it was whose body and extended arms used to go one way what time his legs and feet were really taking him another, he perhaps having something in common with those Indian dancers who make their heads appear to float from side to side on their shoulders. Whatever his secret was nobody has ever been able to imitate him, and only one who has had the honour of playing against him can have any conception how elusive he was.

The young woman need not have gone so far as Twickenham to see rugby football as by 1910 Ealing R.F.C. had a name, having already been in existence for about thirty years. It is on record that in February, 1882, they played a drawn match with the then recently-formed Rosslyn Park Club at their ground at Ealing Common. This fixture took place for several years afterwards. It may be noted that at this early date St George's Hospital had a ground at Castle Hill, Ealing, which must have been somewhere near the present West Ealing station.

WON TENNIS CHAMPIONSHIP

Young ladies could not play rugger then any more than they can now, but the girl from Corfton-road could and did play lawn tennis. It is in her book that she won the tennis championship at Heidleberg College for Young Ladies in Castlebar-road, Ealing, in 1908, on which occasion she was handed her cup by that doyen of lady lawn tennis players Mrs. Lambert Chambers, whose name is duly inserted in the book.

Famous tennis names jostle each other in the book: Wilding H. L. Doherty and Norman Brooks were successfully approached at Wimbledon in 1907, and at Felixstowe Tournament in 1910, by which time the young Ealing scholar was grown up, she appears to have been a contestant. Her book contains the names, written on the pages, of twenty-three of the other players, notably Roper Barrett, S. N. Doust, Daisy Sunden, and A. J. Orr. We feel, however, that her first and last love was rugby football.

MEM… SERVICE

Mr. A… Stoop

A memorial service for Mr. Adrian Dura Stoop was held yesterday at St. Martin-in-the-Fields. The Rev. Austen Williams officiated, assisted by the Rev. P. W. P. Brook (chaplain, Clifton College) and the Rev. W. S. Kemble. The lesson was read by the Rev. P. B. Clayton and an address was given by Sir Wavell Wakefield, M.P. Those present included:—

ADRIAN STOOP DIES AT 74

Adrian Dura Stoop, one of England's greatest Rugby players died suddenly yesterday at his home at Hartley Wintney, near Basingstoke, Hampshire. He was 74.

Mr. Stoop played at stand-off half for Oxford in the University matches of 1902-3-4, and was capped 15 times for England, playing against the three Home Countries, France and South Africa, but he will be remembered chiefly as a Harlequin.

He joined the Harlequins in 1905 and through his lead they became one of the most attractive teams in the country and were noted for their open play. He was their secretary for many years and also an England selector. In 1932 was elected president of the Rugby Union. A retired barrister, he was born in March, 1883, was in the school XV at Rugby and got a Blue in his second year at Oxford. He is survived by a wife and two sons.

ADRIAN STOOP

WIDE INFLUENCE For 50 Years

E. W. SWANTON writes: Adrian Stoop personified the Rugby code of football to an extent that made him for many years a unique figure in the game.

He may not have been so great a natural player as Ronnie Poulton, though he was certainly a very fine one. He hardly made such an imprint on the administrative and legislative sides as a Royds or a Rowland Hill.

Yet his energy in the various fields, spread over more than half a century, first as a player and captain, in due course as president in turn of the Harlequins, of Surrey, and of the Rugby Union, above all perhaps as a coach and general guide to the young, added up to a volume of effort that no one else has approached.

When Stoop went up to Oxford from Rugby the amateur game was still weak from the effects of the split with the north over "broken time." Year after year England took a beating from Wales, then in a halcyon period. Scotland won with scarcely less frequency.

Learned from All Blacks

It was, broadly, the revolutionary techniques of the 1905 All Blacks under Gallagher which, in a triumphant tour, established Rugby football as a national sport in this country.

It was Stoop, more than anyone else, who seized on the principles of the open game as these New Zealanders (and also the Welshmen) exploited it, and adapted the style both of his own club, the Harlequins, and to a large extent, though he himself had already gone down, that of Oxford.

Wakelam's Tribute

H. B. T. Wakelam, whose name will ring a clear bell with many readers as a writer on the game in THE DAILY TELEGRAPH and the old MORNING POST, as well as the first Rugby broadcaster, contributes the authentic pen picture of Stoop in his book "The Harlequin Story."

"As a player he had almost every possible attribute — perfect hands (from long practice), great speed off the mark, allied with a very quick brain and power to sum up an immediate situation, perfect control over his passes, always truly aimed, hard and straight to their proper objectives, a fine defence (sometimes maligned, quite unjustly, because of the 'team' method he used), and quite exceptional control of the ball at his feet on the ground.

"He could also use both feet in his kicking, which was accurate, if necessary long, and always astute.

"In spite of all these virtues, it was as a captain and a leader that he will perhaps be chiefly remembered... His is perhaps the greatest of all Rugby names, for it was his brain which turned earlier Welsh and New Zealand ideas into still better and more fruitful channels, and he was the master mind in the great Harlequin machine which lifted English Rugby as it has never been lifted before or since. He made our modern Rugby."

A TRIBUTE

by

SIR WAVELL WAKEFIELD, M.P.

ADRIAN DURA STOOP

1883 - 1957

WE have come together to-day to remember Adrian Stoop, and to pay tribute to him not only as a friend and a colleague, but as a great figure in Rugby Union Football.

As we laid him to rest a week ago on the top of the hill above the village of Hartley Wintney in that beautiful Hampshire countryside, I could not help thinking what a perfect day it was for the playing of that game he loved so well. My mind went back to other such days when at the week-ends he walked in the lanes and footpaths or ran about with a ball on the lawn or in the fields with us, his Harlequins, and other Rugby Football friends.

He was a devoted son, a beloved husband and a proud father, who gathered around him his disciples at those much enjoyed week-ends, at first with his parents at West Hall, and then with his wife and family at Hartley Grange. It was on these occasions that we got to know the generous, warm hearted and loyal friend, so different from the brusque and even rather frightening impression sometimes gained by the casual acquaintance.

His name will rank always with the legendary names of those who have made outstanding contributions to the game of Rugby Football, and we in the Harlequins are particularly proud to think that it was through our Club that his remarkable qualities came to full fruition. Indeed, we might say that Adrian Stoop and the Harlequins are synonymous: certainly it is hard to think of one without the other, and of his profound influence on the Club and his selfless service to it there can be no doubt whatever. I know that I speak for every Harlequin when I express our deepest gratitude for all he did for us through the years as Captain, Hon. Secretary and President.

Adrian Stoop was a dedicated man. He concentrated the whole force of his strong personality into creative thinking about Rugby Football, and this integration of purpose gave him, in this sphere, more than a touch of genius. He sought quality. By deep thought, by continual practice, and by physical fitness, he achieved quality. He demanded quality in others, and not infrequently got it.

Rugby Football was Adrian's life. It gave him great happiness and satisfaction, and what greater gift can God give than this? His happiness came from achievement and he made return in full measure, not only to his Club, but as President of Surrey to his county, and as President of the Rugby Union to his country.

His thinking was based upon his own great playing ability, and from the moment he first appeared for Oxford in 1902 in the first of his three 'Varsity Matches, it was clear that he would make an outstandingly brilliant contribution to the game. Contemporary accounts of his play in the 'Varsity Match, with their stress on his unorthodox tactics, read like descriptions of the best of modern players in action, which shows how far he was ahead of his time, even in those early days. He was indeed one of the prophets: one of those rare, original minds whose influence can change the whole trend of a game, and as he pioneered for Oxford, joining the Vassalls and the Rotherhams as a great innovator, so he pioneered for England and the Harlequins.

This is not the place or the time to dwell in detail upon his influence upon methods of play or legislation—though his influence was profound. We may, however, properly recall the spirit in which he played himself, and which through his example he passed on to the Harlequins, and to Rugby Football as a whole. It was the spirit of attack.

There is no doubt that his influence on the game of Rugby Football, which began to be felt fifty years ago, continues to be far reaching. It was through him and those he led that the game became increasingly popular. More and more schools turned to Rugby Football and the number of Clubs continually increases. The progress of science and the development of industry have created and are creating opportunities for leisure. Because of its tradition, customs and nature, the playing of Rugby Football can make an ever increasing contribution to the happiness and well being not only to our own countrymen, but of the peoples of many lands.

The strategy discussed, the tactics practised at West Hall and Hartley Grange, and then carried out at Twickenham and elsewhere are now bringing and will continue to bring a reward far wider, far deeper than anyone could have believed.

Like all single-minded men of strong and undeviating character, Adrian clashed at times with his Rugby Football colleagues. He was a stormy petrel, and tact was apt to be subordinated to the outcome of his convictions.

This I can say, that whatever the issue might be—and however strongly opinions differed, no-one ever doubted that Adrian was following what he passionately believed to be the course best serving the interests of the game he loved so well. This needed courage, which was recognised on other fields, for he was the holder of the Military Cross.

As individuals, those of us who knew him are the richer for his example and friendship. But though our sense of bereavement will be keen, we shall think more of what we have gained than of what we have lost. He will continue to inspire and challenge us for a long time.

I conclude with these words from Isaiah: "They that wait upon the Lord shall renew their strength. They shall mount up with wings as eagles. They shall run and not be weary. They shall walk and not faint."

THE ARCHETYPAL HARLEQUIN

Although Adrian Stoop was a massive influence at Harlequins during the early years of the 20th century, it was Ronald Poulton – later Poulton-Palmer – who became recognised as the archetypal Quin.

Poulton was ridiculously talented. A member of two Grand Slam-winning England teams, he looked like a young Greek god, was modest to boot, and judging by contemporary reports played like a cross between Richard Sharp and David Duckham. Born into a relatively wealthy academic background, he was nonetheless socially conscious and worked hard on behalf of those less privileged before dying a poignant soldier's death on the Western Front in May 1915.

It was of course Stoop, recuperating from his first broken collarbone injury in the 1906–07 season and thus with time on his hands, who 'discovered' Poulton at his old school, Rugby, although in truth his talent was there for all to see. Indeed the *Rugby Football Annual* 1907, edited by Charles Alcock (who potentially took the text from the school's termly magazine *The Meteor*), gave him quite a write-up for the previous season when he was playing – against opponents two years his senior – in the Rugby First XV: "R.W Poulton (10st 3lb): A centre three-quarter of great promise, very fast and has a useful swerve; plays a most unselfish game. His defence is not as strong as it might be." Alcock also made note of Poulton's fellow centre that season, who was to achieve fame elsewhere: "R.C Brooke (11st 2lb): A reliable centre three-quarter who although not brilliant is usually in his place and makes good openings. He tackles too high." Ultimately, it would be a close-run thing as to who was the most lyrical in their later lives.

Stoop, who was well aware that perennial rivals Blackheath were also on the case, wrote formally to Poulton in December 1907, asking him to join Harlequins and to play for the club over the

Right: Ronald Poulton-Palmer: an England and Harlequins legend

An artist's impression of
Poulton-Palmer scoring for
Oxford in the Varsity match

holidays. The bashful schoolboy wrote to his parents, seeking permission: "Of course, it is quite an exception and I certainly should not suggest doing it again. It only means being away half a day. I should be back by dinner... it would be awfully good fun playing."

In the event the game did not materialise, but Poulton joined the club and made his debut at the start of the following season, scoring a try in a 39–12 win over Richmond. That autumn he took up his place reading science at Balliol, but could not force his way into an Oxford University side of near international quality, so he played regularly for Harlequins while at university. It was on the strength of those performances for Quins, guided by Stoop, that Poulton was picked by England to play against France in January 1909, despite being omitted from the Varsity match. Poulton remained a regular for Harlequins until the 1913–14 season when his work commitments took him north and he played for Liverpool, although he remained a Quins member.

Poulton's father, Professor Edward Bagnell Poulton, a noted evolutionary biologist, wrote an extraordinary book – *The Life of Ronald Poulton* – in homage to his son after the First World War, in which he stated: "Adrian Stoop's influence had much to do with the selection, a bold act to recommend, or pick, a man whose physical strength had not yet fully matured and who had been left out of the inter-Varsity match shortly before. But Stoop is a remarkable judge and an equally remarkable trainer of footballers and Ronnie completely justified his selection."

Poulton learned from Stoop that pace was not everything. As he commented himself: "Fast running is not as important as people believed. Adrian Stoop is not a fast runner but extremely successful in getting through, often achieved by a deceptive pace that was slower than it seemed to be, so that an opponent running

to intercept overshot the mark and crossed Stoop's tracks at a point he had not yet reached." Tricky stuff.

Throughout his club and international career he was plain Ronnie Poulton, but then his wealthy uncle, George – head of the Palmer biscuit empire – died suddenly in October 1913 and his will stated that Poulton would inherit the entire estate after 21 years if he changed his surname. In the meantime, he could draw an annual stipend of £4,000, approximately £200,000 in today's values. The name change came into effect after he played his final game in 1914 but before he travelled to France to serve with the Royal Berkshire Regiment on the Western Front. He was killed by a sniper on 5th May 1915 at Ploegsteert, Belgium.

Poulton was a captain so modest that he refused to be photographed with the ball, the traditional mark of seniority, when the time came for team photographs. He devoted most of his precious leisure time to running working men's clubs as well as what we would now recognise as youth clubs. He did not have to work for a living but put in 50–60-hour weeks, including Saturday mornings, learning the trade on the shop floor at Palmer's factories in Reading and Manchester, all the while attending evening classes in the latter.

Poulton-Palmer had a social conscience, knew his own mind and did not hesitate to make himself unpopular, doing so with the RFU when he supported a handful of players down in Devon – farmers and fishermen – who were being slipped a few bob to compensate them for the day's work they lost when competing for their teams each Saturday. The captain of England happily put his head above the parapet when he wrote to *The Sportsman* newspaper following their life bans:

"Was this not the opportunity to put the game on an immovable basis among all classes of

Above: Poulton-Palmer served, and died, on the Western Front with the Royal Berkshire Regiment

the community by making an alteration in the laws of the game relating to professionalism so as to legislate for a carefully arranged payment for 'broken time' for men who are paid weekly and monthly? It is difficult to see how such an offence can be construed as professionalism. A man does not, or under careful regulations, would not receive any addition to his normal weekly

Above: His Royal Berkshire badge is housed at the World Rugby Museum

wage but would be paid merely for the hours of work missed through football. He would then be exactly in the same position of many businessmen who, in the enjoyment of a settled income, leave their work early to catch the necessary train to the match. Such an action that the RU [Rugby Union] committee have taken will do much to prevent the expansion of the rugby game and so reduce the value to England of the most democratic of sports."

Written just before he departed for the Western Front, his words, alas, fell on deaf ears.

On hearing of Poulton's death, Dicky Lloyd, the Ireland captain during the 1914 Five Nations, commented:

"During my experience of Rugby Football Ronald Poulton was the greatest player I ever came in contact with. It was the glorious uncertainty of his play that appealed to friend and foe. I studied his play very carefully and I don't ever remember him doing the same thing twice... It will be a long time before a Rugger crowd will have the pleasure of seeing another Poulton as he was a born genius once he got the ball into his hands. It was as much a pleasure to play against him as with him for he was always the same fascinating figure apparently doing nothing but always doing a great deal."

The heroic Quin's grave is in Hyde Park Corner (Royal Berks) Cemetery, near Ploegsteert, Belgium

53

3 Rebuilding in Style

1918–1929

3 **Harlequins had reached new heights under Stoop** before the First World War, radically developing the notion of back play and contributing significantly to a resurgent England team. Like all of England's major clubs, Quins suffered grievously in the Great War – some 63 known club members were killed during the conflict – and it required a huge concerted effort to get the club up and running again when peace was finally declared on 11th November 1918. The club had been dormant for over four years, and even when the fighting ceased many of the players who had survived were scattered amongst military units throughout Europe and the Middle East and would remain so for a year or two.

For the duration of hostilities Harlequins, along with all its regular opponents, ceased to operate as a rugby club. There is no record of any club matches during the First World War, so complete was the dispersal of available manpower to the Western Front and other theatres around the globe. Occasionally rugby-playing soldiers on leave or temporarily garrisoned in England – including one or two Quins – would congregate to play charity games, but no more. For Harlequins it was an abrupt end to

a golden era and, for a while at least, the party was over.

The first tentative steps were taken to effectively re-launch the club at a committee meeting on 18th December 1918 when the sensible decision was taken not to start playing again until the start of the 1919–20 season, which allowed time for the surviving older players to return to Britain and something like normality and a recruitment drive aimed at the top rugby-playing schools to begin.

Holly Ward, only recently returned from a prisoner of war camp in Germany, and Teddy Wakelam, back in London for a few months before being required by his regiment again in Poland, were the main touch line scouts and showed a good nose for a player by immediately recruiting wing Richard Hamilton-Wickes from Wellington, scrum-half John Worton from Haileybury and Sandhurst, and Howard Marshall, a second row at Oriel College, Oxford.

Ward struck gold when he enticed a young RAF officer and wing forward, Wavell Wakefield, to the club. Wakefield, a product of that well-known rugby nursery Sedbergh School, was an outstanding player – in the back row or second row – by any criteria and a big personality who made things happen

with Quins, the RAF and England. He might have been a comparatively junior officer with the RAF but he was far and away their best player and set about devising plans for the 'junior' service to win their first ever Inter-Services Championship.

His theory was that their thin layer of good-quality players should all join top clubs rather than play a vastly inferior standard of rugby with their squadrons and then join forces against the Navy and Army. Just about all his senior officers disagreed strongly, but he then boldly took his plans directly to the Chief of Air Staff, Lord Trenchard, who immediately understood his reasoning and gave Wakefield the green light. Wakefield thus became a Harlequin early in his career and a mutually beneficial tradition of co-operation with the RAF was established (Wakefield was, incidentally, justified when the RAF took their first ever title in 1923).

The Harlequins captaincy for the 1919–20 season was given to the redoubtable Noel (N B) Hudson, who initially only had two players of any experience to call on in Birkett and Wakelam, but there were a couple of encouraging wins, not least a surprise victory over a strong Guy's Hospital side. For the match against the medics, Wakelam records that a young Afrikaans-speaking gunner

Harlequins 1919–20: Standing (*from left to right*): H R Paterson, W G Hewett, S P Simpson, W P Ward (Honorary Secretary), C K Brown, R G Howell, B L Jacot, H J H Sibree (Honorary Treasurer); Seated: J Hughes, W W Wakefield, J G G Birkett, A D Stoop (President), N B Hudson (captain), H B T Wakelam, R H King; In front: J R B Worton, V G Davies, A L Gracie

subaltern was drafted into the pack from the Royal Artillery mess in Woolwich to decipher the line out calls of the South African-dominated opponents.

By the start of the 1920–21 season, Wakefield was in charge on the field as captain and Stoop was back on the committee, and the club really started to crank back into action with the recruitment campaign in full swing. The 'A' XV went on a virtually season-long tour of the country in search of emerging talent, with fixtures against Cranleigh, Wellington, Rugby, Marlborough, Eastbourne, Haileybury, Eton, Bedford, Brighton, Radley, Emmanuel, Wandsworth, Felsted and Dulwich to name just a few.

The club also recruited well from elsewhere. Vivian (V G) Davies, an old boy of Marlborough, began a long and illustrious career at the club – which led to England honours – when he answered an SOS call from Stoop who was a man short when taking a team down to Eastbourne College.

Davies was a neat fly-half whose two caps saw the worst and best of England during this era. He made his debut at fly-half in a calamitous 28–6 defeat against Wales in Cardiff in 1922, but signed off, on the wing, two years later as part of a very fine team performance in a 17–11 defeat against the All Blacks. Davies was one of a

number of Quins who served in both world wars. He survived the Great War while serving in the Duke of Cornwall's Light Infantry, but was killed in action in December 1941 while serving as a captain in the Royal Artillery.

The second great 'find' was down to that great clubman and very fine fullback George Maxwell-Dove, who spotted the Anglo-Scot Bill (A L) Gracie running rings around the opposition playing for the 50th Rifles in the British Army of the Rhine. Gracie was quickly invited to join Quins on his return to 'Blighty' and within a year he was playing for Scotland.

Gracie was the son of missionaries working in Ceylon (modern-day Sri Lanka) and was a contemporary of his future Scotland colleague Eric Liddell at Eltham College in south-east London, which traditionally educated the sons of missionaries who were serving abroad. He had started to study law at Jesus College, Cambridge but joined the Inns of Court Regiment in 1915 and by the following year was serving on the Western Front in the King's Royal Rifle Corps.

By all accounts Gracie was a clever Stoop-like player, albeit blessed with rather more pace, and at Test level he will forever be known for scoring the

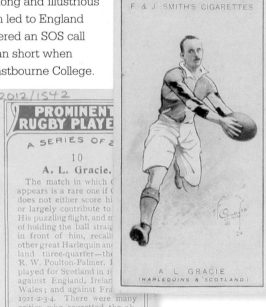

winning try against Wales in 1923, after which he was chaired off the ground by the Welsh supporters! He later recalled the try:

"Running, slightly diagonally to the left to go between Arthur Cornish (Wales) and 'Codger' Johnson (Wales) whom I saw in a flash was in two minds – whether to go for me or run between me and Liddell and prevent me passing to the latter … As I went on, the way opened up for me and the tactics to be adopted were as plain as a pikestaff. Whether I dummied or not I do not remember but I was just able to swerve round my opposite number and in doing so saw I had Male (Welsh fullback) on the wrong foot and all I had to do was to carry on over the line. But here I nearly spoilt everything. The dead-ball line at Cardiff was desperately close to the goal line and in trying to touch down near the posts I recklessly ran along the dead ball line, only inches off it, till the close proximity of Cornish and Albert Jenkins made me decide to drop on the ball."

Gracie stepped down from international rugby rather abruptly in 1924, despite the pleading of the Scottish selectors, which meant Quins saw more of him. He was another to serve in the Second World War, again with the King's Royal Rifle Corps, and ended up as the Camp Commandant, Allied Forces Headquarters (British Section), North Africa and Italy.

For the 1921–22 season, with Wakefield unavailable before Christmas due to his relocation to Cambridge on a two-year RAF scholarship, Wakelam took over as captain and the season was notable for a high-profile 'Harlequins Past and Present' game at Twickenham, which served mainly as a gathering of the clans and celebration of the club being back together and in rude health.

Right: A cigarette card depicting Harlequins great Bill Gracie

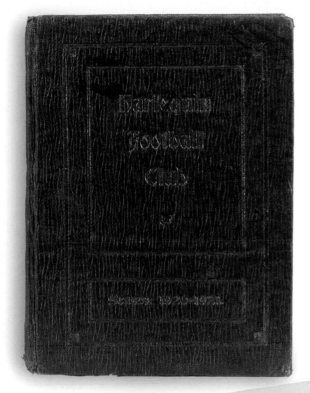

206

R.U. 1705 Rich.

Walker 462 Rich
38 Heath Rd.

Keith
22 Pudding Lt ... Bristol

AVAILABLE ONLY FOR
HARLEQUIN F.C. MATCHES

Admit

A. D. Stoop.

Byfleet

Surrey.

Fixtures—1st XV.				Season 1920-21					
Date.	Opponents.	Ground.	For G	T	P	Against G	T	P	
1920									
Sep. 18	Harlequin Trial	Home							
25	Bedford	Home	1	2	6	26	—	—	W
Oct. 2	Gloucester	Home		2	—	8	2	—	10	W
9	Richmond	Home		3	3	8	4	1	W
16	United Services	Home		2	6	4	1	15	W
23	Guy's Hospital	Honor Oak		3	7	36	L
30	Cambridge University	Home	3	1	18	1	3	14	W
Nov. 6	Newport	Newport	1	1	8	5	3	24	L
13	London Scottish	Richmond	2	2	3	19	L
20	Oxford University	Oxford		2	6	2	3	8	L
27	Blackheath			3	3	22	L
Dec. 4	Rosslyn Park	Home T. match	5	4	37	L
11	Old Merchant Taylors	Richmond O.D.P.	4	2	26	1	3	W
18	Richmond	Richmond T.	2	6	13	1	3	14	W
25	Christmas Day	Leicester							
27	Royal Air Force	Home	4	1	23	2	6	W
1921									
Jan. 1	London Hospital	Hale End T. Trials	Scratched					
5	Royal Navy	Twickenham	2	—	15	2	—	10	W
8	Blackheath	Blackheath	2	10	4	12	L
15	**England v. Wales**								
22	Army	Home	2	2	21	1	6	W
29	St. Bartholomew's Hos.	Home	4	3	19	1	3	W
Feb. 5	Northampton	Northampton	2	2	14	1	2	11	W
12	**England v. Ireland**				15				
19	United Services	Portsmouth		1	9		3	L
26	Oxford University	Oxford	4	1	26	W
26	**Army v. Navy**								
Mar. 5	Leicester	Home	1	2	11	1	3	W
12	Old Merchant Taylors	Home	4	1	25	W
19	Old Leysians	Home	3	1	2	5	L
26	Swansea	Swansea		6	2	3	17	L
28	Cardiff	Cardiff		1	5	1	4	8	L
Apr. 2	London Scottish	Home	2	30	1	9	W
9	Bristol	Home	3	15	1	3	W
					491			286	

Above and left: A season ticket for the 1920–21 campaign belonging to Adrian Stoop, serving as the club's President at the time, with the scores for each match meticulously filled in

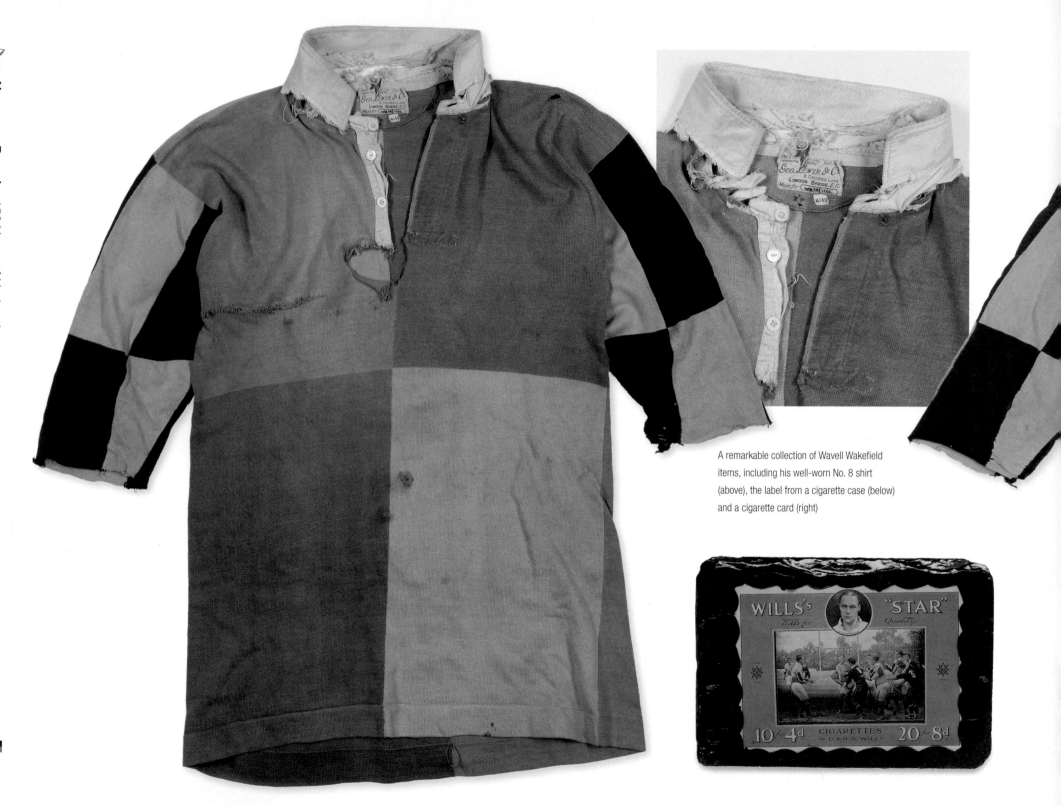

A remarkable collection of Wavell Wakefield items, including his well-worn No. 8 shirt (above), the label from a cigarette case (below) and a cigarette card (right)

WILLS'S "STAR" *Wills for* *Quality*

10 *for* 4ᵈ   CIGARETTES   20 *for* 8ᵈ
W. D. & H. O. WILLS

F. & J. SMITH'S CIGARETTES

2012/1560

PROMINENT
RUGBY PLAYERS
SERIES OF 25.

25
W. Wakefield.

were asked to pick out
ard *par excellence* of
nt day the name of
would almost in-
y be selected. Not
s he tremendous
strength and weight,
exceptional pace and
. He has made a
study of the science
play, every detail of
knows from A to Z.
as a leader, he has
nse influence on his
d as captain of Cam-
e R.A.F. and Eng-
kefield has rendered
service.

W W WAKEFIELD
(HARLEQUINS & ENGLAND)

J. SMITH.

THE IMPERIAL TOBACCO Co
[OF GREAT BRITAIN & IRELAND] LTD

Left: The Wavell Wakefield
Trophy which was presented
– often by the man himself – to
the winners of the Harlequins
Sevens Tournament between
1968 and 1993, although in
1993 it was exclusively an
Under-21 tournament

THE
WAVELL WAKEFIELD
TROPHY

Presented by
THE RT. HON. LORD WAKEFIELD OF KENDAL
President of
HARLEQUIN F.C.
to the Winners of the
ANNUAL HARLEQUIN IMITATION SEVEN-A-SIDE TOURNAMENT
To hold for the Year

Above: The Harlequins team prepare to depart to play the British Army of the Rhine in Germany in 1923, in doing so becoming the first complete rugby team to travel to a fixture by air

Right: A cigarette card featuring Harold Kittermaster

The club continued to break new ground the following year under the captaincy of Davies when it undertook a game against the British Army of the Rhine in Cologne – the real novelty being that it became the first complete rugby team in history to fly to a game, in two chartered planes at £8 per head. At least one young Quin was apparently banned from travelling by his parents because of the perceived danger of such an enterprise.

The mid-1920s were generally a busy period and a successful time, and although the team might have failed to scale the pre-war heights, there was not much in it and Harlequins retained its rather glamorous reputation.

There was also huge progress off the pitch as the club purchased and developed its own ground at Fairfax Road in Teddington, finally giving Harlequins a permanent home. It was an ambitious step in the extreme. The purchase of the plot cost the club £2,125 and a further £3,700 had to be raised by a

debenture scheme – Harlequins Estates Ltd – to pay for the development of the ground, clubhouse and a house on site for the groundsman to live in. These were big sums of money for the time.

Quins' first match at their new ground was duly played against Swindon on 3rd October 1925, although the clubhouse wasn't ready and the teams reportedly changed at Kingston Swimming Baths.

In 1924 one novelty fixture was played against Stanford University, who had taken it upon themselves to represent the USA in the 1924 Olympic rugby tournament in Paris. The Americans organised a three-match 'tour' of England by way of preparation – Plymouth Albion and Blackheath were the other matches – and gave a

PLAYER'S CIGARETTES.

H. J. KITTERMASTER

good account of themselves against a Harlequins XV before losing 21–11 at Twickenham. Given the gala nature of the game, Quins invited the legendary England fly-half 'Dave' (W J A) Davies – more usually a star turn for United Services Portsmouth but a welcome addition to Harlequins' ranks – to guest for the day. While refereeing the game, Stoop was impressed with the Americans and after they had been entertained at the Savoy Hotel that night he organised several extra training sessions before their departure. The visitors certainly benefited from their short stay in England, subsequently travelling to Paris where they defeated Romania and France to take the Olympic title.

It was a good season for Quins under the captaincy of Viv Davies, with victories in 22 of their 31 matches including the pleasure of a double over Blackheath and wins at Cardiff and Swansea on their Easter tour. Pride of place, though, must go to the day earlier in the season when the club contributed five players – four backs and a forward – to the England team that performed admirably against the touring All Blacks before going down 17–11.

Those involved that day were Davies, Hamilton-Wickes, Harold Kittermaster (who scored an outstanding try), and wings John Gibbs and Wavell Wakefield. Gibbs, who was hailed as the fastest player ever to represent England, returned to his first love of football after retiring from rugby. He served in the RAF in the Second World War and is sometimes credited as the man who arranged for Douglas Bader's squadron to drop a spare prosthetic leg close to the prisoner of war camp Bader had been taken to after he was shot down flying over France in 1941.

Dashing fly-half Kittermaster was another exciting product of Rugby School where he captained the school's rugby and cricket teams, scoring a century at Lord's for the latter against Marlborough. While at Oxford he won two rugby Blues and started appearing regularly for Harlequins, his form winning him selection for England against the 1925 All Blacks. His try that day, combining with Quins colleague Hamilton-Wickes, was considered the best of the game despite England's 17–11 defeat and he scored another try in his next international two weeks later to help England to a 12–6 victory over Wales. Kittermaster often produced his best form for Harlequins and only won seven caps for England, a poor return for such a quality player.

Another colourful character who featured around this time was lock Leo Price, also a water polo and hockey Blue, who was once called in to Twickenham on the morning of an England game as a reserve. Later that day, Price was released when the injury crisis was over and then sped to Birmingham to play centre-half for the England hockey team. Centre Geoffrey Huskinson, meanwhile, was possibly better known as a reliable batsman in the Nottinghamshire middle order.

A major development in the 1920s was the establishment of the end of season Middlesex Sevens, which was organised by a London Scot – Russell Cargill – for charitable purposes, but actually became ultra-competitive with a trophy and title at stake during a period when the ubiquitous friendly still dominated. It was a chance for the club to earn bragging rights and it was manna from heaven for Quins given the club's free-flowing style.

Left: The match programme from the historic fixture between Harlequins and Stanford University, who just over a month later represented the USA at the 1924 Olympics in Paris, claiming the title by defeating France 17–3 in the final

Below: Harlequins in action against Old Merchant Taylors' on 9th December 1922. The match took place at OMT's ground in Udney Park Road, Teddington – just a stone's throw from the Fairfax Road site which Quins would move to in 1925

Left: An evocative series of pictures from a foggy fixture against Blackheath in 1925, courtesy of the World Rugby Museum at Twickenham

Right: The proud winners of the inaugural Middlesex Sevens tournament in 1926, one of the strongest Harlequins Sevens sides ever put out. Standing (*from left to right*): John Worton, John Chick, John Gibbs, William 'Horsey' Browne; Seated: Wavell Wakefield, Vivian Davies, Richard Hamilton-Wickes

Below: The base of the trophy showing Harlequins' succession of Sevens triumphs over the following years

included a 500-a-side exhibition game between spectators in the half-hour break before the final, an experiment not continued in future years, much to the relief of the Twickenham groundsman.

That notable win in 1926 was the first of four straight victories for Harlequins at the Middlesex Sevens, a run the club topped in the 1980s when it won five consecutive titles between 1986 and 1990. In total, Harlequins won the title on a record 14 occasions before the competition was discontinued in 2011, and at various times it served as a fine proving ground for emerging players in the Quins camp.

Another notable occasion in 1926 came when Harlequins entertained a strong New Zealand Maori side who were midway through an ambitious 40-match tour of Europe, Australia and Canada. Harlequins prevailed 11–5 in front of 15,000 at Twickenham, comfortably the biggest home crowd during this period. The Maoris had just beaten Yorkshire and travelled on to Wales where they defeated Cardiff, but the touring team found Quins a different proposition. The following month the Maoris returned to France, where they played the majority of their games, and twice defeated the French national team.

Towards the end of the decade, however, it appears that Quins became a much more forwards-dominated team and at the end of the 1928–29 season a slightly irritated Stoop, the club's President at this stage, used his address at the AGM to exhort the Quins backs "to put a bit more into it".

One back who might have contributed handsomely in the years to come was James Reeve – another of Quins' flying hurdlers on the wing – who broke in to the England team

Harlequins took it seriously from the off. In fact, the club's line-up in the inaugural competition in 1926 is probably still one of the best Sevens teams seen at the tournament as the club fielded all its big guns – Wakefield, Gibbs, Hamilton-Wickes, Davies, John Worton, Ireland's William 'Horsey' Browne and John (J S) Chick, another recruit from the RAF who, despite being the only uncapped player in the team, was considered by many observers to be the best Sevens player of the lot.

Quins beat old rivals London Scottish in the quarter-finals and Blackheath in the semis before a 25–13 victory over St Mary's Hospital in the final. The tournament incidentally

in 1929 despite missing out on a rugby Blue at Cambridge where he was best known for his running and hurdling. Reeve scored a spectacular try against Wales in 1929 and amassed eight tries for the Lions on their 1930 tour of New Zealand, but was killed in a motor accident in 1931, aged just 28.

The 1920s had been a mixed bag for Quins as it had taken a mighty effort to regenerate the club after the Great War. Like every other club, it was forced to swallow its pride and shamelessly recruit, but very quickly the club was back on its feet and, miraculously, little had changed. The essential facets of camaraderie, commitment and the ability to think outside the box – the very DNA of the club – remained the same and Quins seemed in good shape as it headed into the next decade.

Left: The New Zealand Maoris perform their haka before the historic match against Quins in 1926

Below: Richard Hamilton-Wickes races down the right during the 11–5 win over the visiting New Zealand Maoris in front of a then club record crowd of 15,000 at Twickenham Stadium

STEPPING UP TO THE MICROPHONE

WILLS'S CIGARETTES

CAPTAIN H. B. T. WAKELAM

■ **Above:** Teddy Wakelam as depicted on a cigarette card in his Harlequins tie

■ **Right:** The *Radio Times* advertises the 1927 England v Wales match at which Wakelam made his commentating debut

An extraordinary number of Harlequins emerged as pioneer sports broadcasters after their playing careers ended, while others turned easily to print journalism. Notable Quins have not only made the news over the years but reported it as well, and certainly Teddy Wakelam – who features prominently elsewhere in these pages – and Howard Marshall are both towering figures in the history of sports broadcasting in the UK.

The remarkably versatile Wakelam was the man who made the first live radio reports of rugby, football, cricket and tennis for the BBC in 1927, while further down the line, in the 1938 Test series against Australia, he also offered up the first live cricket commentary on TV.

Originally a building contractor by trade after serving in the First World War, Wakelam – who would later pen the first official history of Harlequin Football Club, *Harlequin Story* – was approached early in January 1927 by a BBC producer, Lance Sieveking, who had been tasked with investigating the possibilities of live sports commentaries on the radio. It was an inspired punt by Sieveking because not only did Wakelam have a crisp voice and detailed working knowledge of many sports, but he brought a tidy military mind to proceedings and a wealth of contacts through his Quins connections.

For his first assignment, England's Championship match against Wales at Twickenham on 15th January 1927, the duo cleverly thought outside the box. Wakelam seated a former rugby player who had unfortunately gone blind next to him in the stands and set himself the task of simply describing the action as it unfolded. By way of a trial run the duo had done exactly the same thing 48 hours earlier at the traditional Richmond Schools v London Scottish

Schools game, which was effectively a schoolboys international between England and Scotland.

In that single moment of genius they stumbled on a technique that is still considered textbook nearly 90 years later, even if it very quickly became the norm to imagine your conversation with a blind man rather than to invite him along personally.

It was Wakelam and Sieveking who also came up with a way of identifying where the action was taking place by dividing the pitch up into eight numbered squares, with the grid being reproduced in the *Radio Times*. While Wakelam was commentating, in the background Sieveking or the duty producer would quietly read out the number of the square where play was occurring. The phrase 'back to square one' comes directly from this early device for reporting sport on radio – 'square one' covering the centre of the pitch from where a team would re-start the match after conceding.

Wakelam can also probably claim the first live on-air gaffe when, during an England game and unaware the microphone was still on, he turned and said to Sieveking, "What about a beer?"

On a roll, Wakelam completed the first live football commentary in Britain just a week later, a 1–1 draw between Arsenal and Sheffield United, and later that year also undertook the first live radio

Radio Times, January 13, 1933.   SOUTHERN EDITION.

This Issue contains Complete Annotated Programmes for the week JANUARY 15–21

THE RADIO TIMES

THE JOURNAL OF THE BRITISH BROADCASTING CORPORATION

NATION SHALL SPEAK PEACE UNTO NATION

Vol. 38. No. 485. JANUARY 13, 1933. Every Friday. TWO PENCE.

A RADIO REVUE BY ARCHIE DE BEAR ON MONDAY

ENGLAND v WALES
at Twickenham

A running commentary will be relayed on Saturday, January 21

SATURDAY: LAST NIGHT OF D'OYLY CARTE SEASON

Remarkably, throughout a long, hot fortnight, he both umpired in the early afternoon and then commentated on one of the big matches later in the day. Wakelam and Sieveking also trialled commentating at a county cricket match which saw Surrey's Andy Sandham score a particularly dour century to force a draw. The decision was taken that perhaps cricket did not lend itself to commentary. Well, you cannot get it right all the time...

That decision was revisited in the 1930s and it was Marshall, a former Quins captain like Wakelam, who defined the art of ball-by-ball cricket commentary in the UK with his more relaxed, intimate style and rich voice. Marshall probably reached his peak with his peerless radio commentaries of the 1938 Test series against the Aussies, particularly his recording of the moment Len Hutton reached the then record Test score of 364.

His smooth style won many plaudits, not least from poet Edmund Blunden, who wrote: "And then on the air, Mr Howard Marshall makes every ball bowled, every shifting of a fieldsman so fertile with meaning that any wireless set may make a subtle cricket student of anybody."

Marshall, who became known for his catchphrase "Over goes the arm", was the *Daily Telegraph* rugby union correspondent for much of this period and also won much praise for his reports from the Normandy beaches during the D-Day landings.

It might be difficult to match that illustrious duo, but other Quins have stepped up to the microphone with conspicuous success. Scrum-half Nigel Starmer-Smith was for many years one of the leading rugby commentators for the BBC and presented Rugby Special for 15 years, as well as editing *Rugby World* magazine.

Above: Legendary cricket commentator and former Quins captain Howard Marshall

Left: Nigel Starmer-Smith interviews Bill Beaumont

Brian Moore provides expert analysis for the BBC, often working in tandem with Eddie Butler, while Paul Ackford worked as the *Sunday Telegraph* correspondent for the best part of two decades and Will Carling has been a long-time columnist for *The Sun*. Will Greenwood is another member of the press and media crew working variously for Sky TV and the *Daily Telegraph*, while Keith Wood and Ugo Monye have turned their hands to punditry with notable success and long-serving Club Secretary Colin Herridge served as the first RFU press officer. A Harlequin, it would seem, is rarely short of something to say...

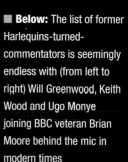

Below: The list of former Harlequins-turned-commentators is seemingly endless with (from left to right) Will Greenwood, Keith Wood and Ugo Monye joining BBC veteran Brian Moore behind the mic in modern times

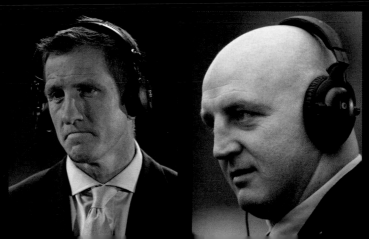

4

Tough Times

1930–1939

4

By any measure Adrian Stoop and Wavell Wakefield were among the most influential players and rugby thinkers in the history of English rugby. Thus it was almost inevitable that Quins experienced an on-field dip in fortunes when these two stalwarts' playing days finally came to a close. That is essentially what happened to Harlequins in the 1930s, which proved to be a challenging decade for the club. Stoop and Wakefield were at the forefront of everything progressive that was going on in the game and left huge shoes to fill.

Title page: The Harlequins 1932 Middlesex Sevens team

Below: The signed silver salver presented to Adrian Stoop in 1930

Opposite: Harlequins v Blackheath at Twickenham in 1930

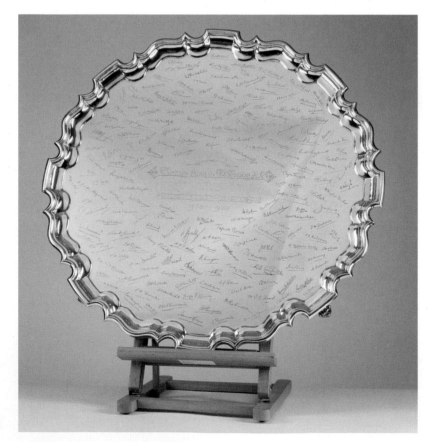

Gates and income declined slowly during this period, with the club recording a small annual working loss for eight seasons on the bounce between 1932 and 1939, mainly on account of falling attendances which perhaps reflected a slight decline in the perceived glamour of the side. Financially, and not for the first time, the club was indebted to those who had put it on such a sound financial footing at the turn of the century. Loyalty among club members was also high: Adrian Stoop was always digging deep into his pockets and the redoubtable Arthur Cipriani left Harlequins £500 in his will. Eventually, careful management by the club's board saw it reach the end of the decade, when all rugby was suspended following the outbreak of the Second World War, with a healthy surplus of £5,363.

In the absence of any organised competition – barring the Middlesex Sevens which Quins won again in 1933 and 1935 – it is difficult to judge the quality of the rugby on offer. That said, the club's representation in international teams offers a rough guide and it is clear that Harlequins continued to provide a haven for talented players who were also very much individuals of considerable character on and off the pitch.

Surely the most famous example of this was Second World War fighter ace Douglas Bader DSO (Distinguished Service Order) and bar, DFC (Distinguished Flying Cross) and bar. Bader had shown prodigious rugby talent at St Edward's School, Oxford – swapping between fly-half and centre – and word of his precocious abilities soon reached the ever-vigilant Stoop.

Stoop promptly made himself known to Bader and persuaded him to join the club in 1929, secretly hoping he had unearthed the next Poulton-Palmer. However, Stoop did

accept that Quins would have to share Bader with the RAF, where many of St Edwards' most glittering alumni gravitated to over the years, including fellow Second World War fighter pilots Guy Gibson VC (Victoria Cross) and Adrian Warburton DSO and bar, DFC and two bars.

Towards the end of 1931 the young Bader was being tipped for an England debut against the touring Springboks after impressing for Quins all autumn and being one of the few successes in the Combined Services XV which lost to the tourists at Twickenham. Stoop was on the England selection panel and argued Bader's case strongly. Bader followed his appearance for the Combined Services with an average game for Quins against Richmond on 12th December, though he was clearly in considerable discomfort from the broken nose he had suffered during the clash with the Springboks.

Nevertheless he was in his usual high spirits when he took off for a flight in his Bulldog trainer on the morning of 14th December 1931 at Woodley Aerodrome, near Reading. The irrepressible Bader indulged in some extracurricular aerobatics when he came in too low on a landing approach and his left wing tip hit the ground. His plane was a write-off and Bader was rushed to Royal Berkshire Hospital where he had both legs amputated.

Right: Legendary RAF war hero and Harlequins player Douglas Bader pictured in 1940, ten years after the accident which cost him his legs and ended his rugby-playing career. Adrian Stoop is credited with playing a large role in Bader's remarkable rehabilitation, including introducing him to the game of golf (far right) at which he excelled despite his disability

There was to be no more rugby for the RAF, Harlequins or anybody else. But the Quins connection did not end with Bader's near fatal crash – far from it. In fact, when Bader was taken to the hospital in Reading Stoop was one of the first on the scene and in the coming months personally paid for the country's top surgeons and medics to attend his protege. They could not save his legs but they probably saved his life.

Then, with Bader understandably depressed at the prospect of a seemingly shattered life, it was Stoop who invited him to stay at the Grange, his magnificent country house, where he personally and energetically supervised his physical rehabilitation. This initially consisted of teaching the stricken Bader to walk again, but he was uncooperative and resentful to start with and it needed a man of Stoop's authority, iron discipline and charisma to persuade Bader that life could still be worth living.

As the hard work progressed the canny Stoop introduced golf to the schedule, which was just about the only sport the prodigiously gifted Bader had not tried and excelled at while at St Edward's or RAF Cranwell. To Bader's surprise he mastered the rudiments and within months was beginning to tackle and beat able-bodied golfers. This was a massive confidence boost and convinced Bader that he might yet continue his RAF career, something which he did to remarkable effect in the Second World War before ending up as a prisoner of war at Colditz where he spent every waking hour dreaming up ways of escaping.

Stoop's role in the remarkable Bader story was fully recognised in Lewis Gilbert's film *Reach for the Sky* (1956), with character actor Jack Lambert playing Stoop, who is also listed in the credits as a technical advisor. Kenneth More played the role of Bader, although both Gilbert and Bader had originally wanted the rugby-loving Richard Burton to take the part.

in the Christian Toc H charity which helped many ex-servicemen who were struggling in peacetime after the horrors of the First World War (Stoop was another ardent supporter of the movement). As a rugby player Dunkley's finest achievement was being a member of the England team which defeated New Zealand at Twickenham in 1936.

Alongside Dunkley in the back row against New Zealand that day was another Quin – flanker Edward Hamilton-Hill – who also shared in the club's Sevens success the previous season. Hamilton-Hill was a Royal Navy man and moved to Malta after the Second World War.

Reg Bolton, a Yorkshireman from Queen Elizabeth Grammar School, Wakefield, was another distinctly useful Quins back row forward who won five caps for England. He became a medic in the Second World War and was injured in an air raid in Naples when serving with the Royal Army Medical Corps.

Ken Chapman, the son of a famous sporting father, was also a much-admired figure at the club. His father, Herbert Chapman, was probably the best-known football manager in England before the Busby and Shankly era, having won league and FA Cup titles with Huddersfield and Arsenal and possessing an attention to detail that set him apart from his contemporaries.

It is not always easy to be the son of a famous sporting father and Ken turned to a different sport

Left: Scrum-half Geoffrey Dean was another Harlequin who served his country with distinction during the Second World War

Below: A 1933–34 RFU fixture list for Twickenham Stadium where Harlequins continued to play the majority of its First XV matches

Rather poignantly, Bader's most frequent half-back partner during his brief Harlequins career also suffered an amputation after being wounded in action whilst fighting for his country. Geoffrey Dean was a very useful scrum-half who was capped against Ireland in 1931 and starred in the team that won the Middlesex Sevens in 1935. He served as a tank officer in North Africa in the Second World War, where he lost a leg after his tank was blown up. He was held in a prisoner of war camp for the rest of hostilities before returning to Quins where, with typical rugby club humour, his artificial limb soon earned him the nickname 'Tinny'.

Flanker and No. 8 Peter Brook, who won three caps for England and was an inspiring presence throughout much of this period, also lined up in the Middlesex Sevens-winning team of 1935. Tall, rangy and athletic, Brook covered the ground exceptionally well and was a player very much in the Wakefield mould. He took Holy Orders in 1936 and moved to Bristol where he became chaplain at Clifton College, later serving as chaplain to the XIV Army in Burma. He always maintained close links with Quins, though, and one of the great advantages of having Brook in the Clifton area was that a good number of their best prospects were rapidly pointed in Quins' direction, including the likes of Roger (R A M) Whyte, David (D G) Perry, the Forbes brothers and Jack (J E) Hutton.

Another to feature in that 1935 Sevens success was No. 8 Philip 'Pop' Dunkley, who captained the club between 1933–35. He was a teetotaller and another man of strong religious conviction, serving as a leading light

RUGBY FOOTBALL UNION GROUND, TWICKENHAM.
SEASON 1933-34.

1933	September.	1934	January
Sat. 16 2.30	HARLEQUIN TRIAL GAMES	*Sat. 6 2.15	ENGLAND v THE REST
Sat. 23 3.15	HARLEQUINS v ROSSLYN PARK	Sat. 13 2.45	HARLEQUINS v BLACKHEATH
Sat. 30 3.15	HARLEQUINS v BATH	Sat. 27 3.0	HARLEQUINS v CAMBRIDGE UNIVERSITY
	October		February
Sat. 14 3.15	HARLEQUINS v UNITED SERVICES	Sat. 3 3.0	HARLEQUINS v NORTHAMPTON
Sat. 28 3.0	HARLEQUINS v GUY'S HOSPITAL	*Sat. 10 3.0	ROYAL NAVY v ROYAL AIR FORCE
		*Sat. 24 3.0	NORTH v SOUTH
	November		March
Sat. 11 2.45	HARLEQUINS v RICHMOND	*Sat. 3 3.0	ROYAL NAVY v THE ARMY
Sat. 18 2.45	HARLEQUINS v OXFORD UNIVERSITY	Sat. 17 3.0	ENGLAND v SCOTLAND
		*Sat. 24 3.0	THE ARMY v ROYAL AIR FORCE
	December		April
Sat. 2 2.30	HARLEQUINS v LEICESTER	Sat. 7 3.15	HARLEQUINS v BRISTOL
*Tues. 12 2.15	OXFORD v CAMBRIDGE	Sat. 21 3.15	HARLEQUINS v LONDON WELSH
Sat. 16 2.30	HARLEQUINS v CARDIFF	*Sat. 28 2.0	SEVEN-A-SIDE FINALS.
Sat. 30 2.30	HARLEQUINS v THE ARMY		

*Tickets for these matches can be booked at ALFRED HAYS, LTD., 26 Old Bond St., 74 Cornhill and Branches.

N.B.—Alterations or additions to the above Fixtures will be notified in the Press.

S. F. COOPPER,
Engineer Commander, R.N., Secretary.

Above: Ken Chapman proved a dynamic presence in the Quins front row following his switch from centre

before the outbreak of the Second World War and then again when the club re-mustered in 1945–46. He later became President of both the club and then the RFU for the 1974–75 season. Ken's brother, Bruce, was also a loyal clubman and promising centre – he appeared in an England trial game – before a particularly nasty concussion forced him to quit playing.

The Chapmans were not the only brothers to join the club, as the talented Tony (A E C) Prescott and Robin (R E) Prescott, who were nephews of the redoubtable Curly Hammond of German beer-drinking fame, also played. Tony was another hard-working front-rower and Robin was a high-class performer at prop, where he won six England caps and toured Argentina with a very English-heavy Lions squad in 1936. He was also a regular in a number of wartime internationals for British Army XVs and later served variously as an England selector, RFU Vice President and then the RFU's paid Secretary.

Meanwhile, despite starring at centre in one of England's best-ever wins in Dublin – a 36–14 thumping of Ireland in 1938 – classy centre Basil Nicolson only won two caps for his country. However, England's loss was Quins' gain and, as well as playing for the club, Lieutenant Colonel Nicolson was subsequently one of the key figures in planning the D-Day invasion in 1944.

Geoff (A G) Butler was another Quin who got surprisingly short shrift from the England selectors. An Oxfordshire farmer, Butler could really move and was frequently the Southern Counties 100 and 220-yard sprint champion, making the Great Britain athletics team in 1937. A regular try-scorer for Quins and a Sevens star, he played just three times for England, including two

altogether and joined Quins as a centre before he started to fill out and enjoy great success in the front row. From there he captained the team for four seasons, three

appearances in their Triple Crown season of 1937 where he scored the winning try in their 9–8 win over Ireland.

England trials prop Chris Thompson was another Quin whose worth was not always fully recognised. A lance corporal in the Federated Malay States Volunteer Force, Thompson was sadly killed while building the Burma–Thailand railway as a prisoner of the Japanese in the Second World War.

Hubert Freakes was a Rhodes Scholar and a very good rugby and cricket player from Durban who played two seasons for Quins when not required by Oxford University. He was capped by England at fullback and on the outbreak of the Second World War served as a flying officer in the RAF Ferry Command which delivered new aircraft being built in North America across the Atlantic to bases around Britain. He was killed when the Hudson Bomber he was delivering crashed at the Honeybourne airfield in Worcestershire in March 1942.

Charles Beamish was one of four Irish rugby-playing brothers who were all aviators of note. He enjoyed one outstanding season with the club in 1935 at the height of his international career, a campaign which also led to his selection for the Lions touring party to Argentina that year.

Fellow Irishman Maurice Daly, always a prolific try-scorer on the right wing, was a major discovery for Quins in the two seasons leading up to the Second World War and he served the club well for a couple of campaigns after hostilities ceased. Daly was yet another RAF type and finished the war as an air liaison officer (North West Europe) before he moved to Kenya where he represented his new country in 1951 against a Combined Varsities XV.

In retrospect there was no single outstanding, talismanic player of this era – there was certainly no Stoop, Poulton-Palmer or Wakefield – although there was every sign at the end of the decade that Royal Marine Mike Marshall might have developed into just such a character for Quins and England. A Yorkshireman who had blazed a trail as a schoolboy at Giggleswick before going up to Oxford University and then joining Quins, Marshall had already won five England caps as a lock by the age of 22 and had shown a rare turn of pace for such a big man by sprinting 50 yards to score a try on his debut against Ireland in 1938.

When war broke out Marshall was soon in service commanding motor gunboats in raids and rescue missions on the Dutch, French and Norwegian coasts. He survived five years of hostilities – and won the Distinguished Service Cross (DSC) and bar – only to cruelly lose his life three days after VE Day on a seemingly routine mission from Aberdeen to deliver three Merchant Navy captains to Gothenburg to assume command of their ships. Somewhere en route his launch, MGB2002, hit a rogue mine and only two of the 28 people on board survived. Marshall was only present because he had volunteered for one last mission when a colleague was called to Buckingham Palace to receive his own DSC that day.

A number of notable players and personalities from overseas also passed through Quins' ranks during this period. Frederick Lawson Hovde was an athletic and formidably bright American chemist at Oxford University who, during his short time at Harlequins, is credited with introducing the American football-style torpedo pass into the game when throwing in at line outs.

He was also remembered for using codenames for certain set piece moves in the backs.

Hovde was largely based in Britain during the Second World War and headed up the government's rocket research department. For his services he received the King's Medal for Service in the Cause of Freedom. He then returned to the USA and had a long and distinguished career in academia.

Another briefly met but never to be forgotten character was a burly German forward called Fritz Grunebaum, who was a student in London and a mainstay of the Harlequins 'A' XV where his impressive drinking feats were recounted with much admiration. When the Second World War began he found himself serving as a major in the German Army and, as VE Day

Above: The Harlequins team that won the 1935 Middlesex Sevens, beating London Welsh in the final. Standing (*from left to right*): Guy Hudson, Edward Hamilton-Hill, Philip Dunkley, Peter Brook, Geoff Butler; Seated: Geoffrey Dean, John Cole

Harlequins 1938–39: Standing (*from left to right*): J L Williams, J G Jenkins, W H Leather, F J V Ford, B H Bowring, J L Crichton, O B Rooney, R F Crichton, B D Napper, H C C Laird; Seated: T H Tilling, B E Nicolson, R B Horsley, K H Chapman (captain), F P Dunkley, R Bolton

approached, was among thousands of German prisoners being marched back to their homeland from the Russian front when he spotted a familiar face among the British escort contingent heading his way.

Fritz promptly halted, saluted smartly and said, "Aren't you Ken Robinson, the Quins centre?" It was indeed he and the two Quins colleagues swapped club gossip for ten minutes before returning to the status of captive and captor. The German national rugby ground in Heidelberg is named in his memory, while he was also a big mover and shaker in the USA Union after he emigrated there. He became a successful businessman in the Boston area where he founded the Boston Rugby Festival, and when he died he was buried in his Harlequins jersey.

One Harlequins voice rather than name many would recognise from this era was centre 'Humphrey' (T H) Tilling, a long-time club member who occasionally got a game for the first team. Tilling was a barrister and amateur actor blessed with a wonderfully mellifluous voice, and for many years he was the MC and narrator at the annual Remembrance Service at the Royal Albert Hall.

As a club, Harlequins has always been so full of rich characters that it is a moot point as to which came first, the chicken or the egg. Did the club attract these maverick individuals or did such outstandingly talented and driven men make the club? It is suspected that the latter is the case, but in a fairly drab decade Harlequins was still a lively place to be even if anxieties over the imminence of war prevailed. After the Munich crisis in 1938 many club members decided to join the Services before the war started – Vivian Davies, George Hayes, Ken Robinson, Jay Gould, Maurice Daly and the inexhaustible Wakelam among them.

Left: Prince Alexander Obolensky – a member of the exiled Russian aristocracy nicknamed 'The Flying Prince' who famously starred for England against the All Blacks in 1936 – fends off a Quins defender in the big derby game against Rosslyn Park in 1939

FRIENDS ACROSS THE WATER

■ Players from the Future Hope Club in Kolkata, India, one of eight Harlequins affiliate clubs around the world

There are thought to be approximately 80 rugby clubs and sports clubs worldwide that now use Harlequins or Quins somewhere in their title, but only eight are recognised as 'affiliate clubs' and officially aligned with Harlequin FC. Those clubs are sanctioned to use the same colours, shirts and branding, and a big effort has been made over the years to promote collaboration between the various clubs through tours, player exchanges and coaching back-up.

Pretoria Harlequins (affiliated in 1906): The original affiliate club started as the Civil Service Club in Pretoria but, with numbers dwindling, elected to reinvent itself as an 'open' club and – a couple of years after its formation in 1904 – decided it had better write to Quins in London to officially request permission to use its name, colours and team emblem. A driving force in the early days was an officer in the Welsh Guards stationed in Pretoria – 'Bird' (J E C) Partridge – who became the club's

■ Pretoria Harlequins in South Africa was the first club to become an affiliate

first Springbok. The club has produced a steady stream of Springboks over the years, notably during the famous 1951–52 tour to Britain when three Pretoria Quins made the trip – Jaap Bekker, Willem Barnard and Fonnie du Toit. World Cup-winning coach Kitch Christie was also a proud Pretoria Quin.

Melbourne Harlequins (1928):

A rugby outpost in a state still largely dominated by Aussie rules, Quins is probably the top club in Melbourne and certainly boasts some of the best facilities in the area at its Ashwood Reserve Ground. In the club's early days membership was restricted to British-born players only, but that was soon dropped. The Melbourne Quins run six senior teams and regularly win the Dewar Shield, the premier local competition. All junior categories from Under-6 to Under-18 are catered for, and a women's section has recently been formed. Interestingly, the club's first official fixture was not a rugby match but rather a game of cricket against Sydney Bohemians, a match which saw the Melbourne team field England Test stars Jack Hobbs, Maurice Leyland and Percy Fender.

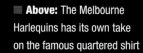

■ **Above:** The Melbourne Harlequins has its own take on the famous quartered shirt

Hobart Harlequins (1933):

Along with the University of Tasmania RFC, Hobart Quins is the oldest rugby team in Tasmania, which is not known as a rugby state. The club is one of ten that contest the Tasmanian State Championship every year, a competition they have won on 12 occasions, the most recent victory coming in 2013. Quins' home ground, Rugby Park on Cornelian Bay, is one of the best rugby facilities on the island and shared with fierce local rivals Taroona Rugby Club and Hobart Lions. Giant lock Adam Coleman, the son of former Tonga captain Pau'u Afeaki, is the club's best-known product, leaving Quins to join the Waratahs and then to play Super Rugby for Western Force.

Hamilton Harlequins (1938): A club founded in New Zealand just before the Second World War, although unsurprisingly it didn't really get going until after hostilities ceased. It differs from most other Quins clubs in that it is more invitational in nature, organising fixtures within Waikato County, and has seen a host of All Blacks stars – Don and Ian Clarke, Colin Meads and Wilson Whineray among them – turn out in its colours. The constitution of the club states that it will "renew and maintain old friendships from playing days; engage in football free from competition for the joy of it; invite promising juniors to play and teach such youngsters the spirit of the game and play friendly games with smaller clubs when such games can conveniently be arranged." The club currently places a big emphasis on organising an extensive programme of matches for its Under-17 team.

Kenya Harlequins (1952): A power in Kenyan rugby ever since it became an affiliated club in 1952, although there was previously a club in Kenya called the Harlequins that could trace its roots back to 1923, but this ceased to exist in 1945. That earlier club had split at one stage, resulting in the formation of the Nondescripts RFC, still one of the bigger clubs in Kenya. In its modern-day existence Kenya Harlequins has won eight Kenya Cup titles – the top competition in the country – including three in a row between 2010 and 2012 and habitually provides a good proportion of players for the Kenyan national team. The Kenya Quins played a huge role in hosting Harlequins' memorable tour to East Africa in 1961, during which Pretoria Quins also visited. The club toured the UK and Ireland in 1986, and has mounted three tours to South Africa, in 1996, 1991 and 2001, the latter of which saw Pretoria Quins host the squad. They also regularly organise tours of Zimbabwe and Uganda.

Dallas Harlequins (1983): The Dallas branch of the Harlequins family was founded in 1971 and became an affiliated club in 1983. It plays in the USA Super League, which it won in 1984 by beating Los Angeles RFC 31–12 in the final. It also plays in the Texas Men's Division and has been the Texan champions on no fewer than 21 occasions. Players who have gone on to represent the USA Eagles include lock Bob Olsonoski, wing Jimmy Aston, hooker Bruce Monroe, scrum-half Greg Goodman, centre Mike Waterman, No. 8 Brannon Smoot, wing Leni Sanf, flanker David Care and wing Justin Boyd. Springbok legend Naas Botha also represented the club during a short stay in the States. Based at Glencoe Park in Dallas, it runs a First and Second XV, a women's team and a junior section. At the last count the club boasted active players from 16 separate nations. In a novel twist on the usual Harlequin figure adorning the players' shirts, the American version brandishes the sword in a Superman pose.

Future Hope Harlequins (2004): A remarkable club based around the Future Hope School and charity in Kolkata, India, which was established by Tim Grandage, a Quins member whose grandfather was a notable forward at the club just before the First World War. Grandage, formerly a banker with HSBC, gave up his job to rescue and educate street children in Kolkata and used his lifelong love of rugby as a major vehicle for restoring their physical health and building a resilient team spirit within the group. A rugby team was formed, Harlequins donated a set of shirts and equipment, and soon the side was playing at the Rosslyn Park Sevens and representing India at the Asia Rugby Under-19 Championship in Sri Lanka – a special set of passports had to be issued because none of the players officially existed. Since then the link has strengthened further with Future Hope Harlequins becoming an affiliated club in 2004. A number of Quins players have flown to India to spend time at the school, helping with general chores as well as coaching the flourishing rugby section.

Abu Dhabi Harlequins (2008): The latest member of the family, having started in 2008, the Abu Dhabi Quins is already a powerhouse club in the region with its senior men's team

competing in the Gulf Top 6. It has also competed with some success on the local Sevens circuit. The club runs three senior men's teams – First XV, Second XV and Vets – a women's team and a flourishing touch rugby section. It is also particularly proud of its junior section, running boys' teams across every age group from Under-9 to Under-19 as well as three girls' teams, Under-12, Under-15 and Under-19.

Above: Youngsters playing for the Abu Dhabi Harlequins play, win and celebrate the 'Harlequins Way'

5

We Go Again

1945–1959

5

The Second World War took a heavy toll on Quins, with 21 club members among the fatalities. Three of the club's pre-war England internationals – Vivian Davies, Hubert Freakes and Mike Marshall – were killed in action, along with Fredrick 'Bunny' Stoop, son of Adrian. Although the club's losses were not as severe as those suffered during the First World War, Quins clearly needed to regenerate itself once again and there was, in many ways, a distinct feeling of *deja vu.* Indeed, three of the leading lights at the club – Holly Ward, Teddy Wakelam and Edward (E M C) Clarke – had been present at the meeting in 1918 when Harlequins set about re-establishing itself in the aftermath of the Great War. Adrian Stoop was also still *in situ* as the club's President and Secretary, although he was looking to step down, and was determined that the club be properly reconstituted.

Title page: The Quins First XV from the 1947–48 season

Club members attended an Extraordinary General Meeting at St Stephen's Tavern on Westminster Bridge on 25th July 1945 and, in sharp contrast to Quins' position after the First World War, found that through the good husbandry of its resources and investments the club was in good shape. The club had over £5,000 in a deposit account and had ownership of their ground at Teddington, although the First XV continued to play the majority of its big matches at Twickenham.

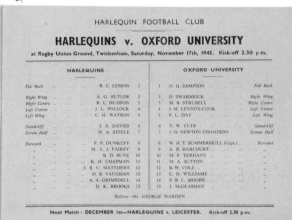

Above and right: The programme from a 1945 match v Oxford University

That geographical split actually became something of a minor issue as the club developed after the war with First XV members missing the more homely comforts and camaraderie of Teddington, although they were always honoured and excited to play at Twickenham. In 1949 the 'A' XV was rechristened the 'Wanderers' and went from strength to strength, developing a unique identity of their own. There was also the experiment of taking some First XV matches to White City – an athletics stadium purpose-built for the 1908 London Olympics – and indeed it was there on 12th October 1954 that Quins beat Cardiff 8–6 in the first senior floodlit match in London.

The matches at White City, though forward-looking and innovative, were not a notable success as its vast open terraces were not conducive to a good atmosphere – as was also the case at an echoing Twickenham – and generally the First XV felt slightly distanced from the club at large. As a result, one of the features of the decade or so that followed was the concerted search for a site that the entire club could enjoy, though that did not come to fruition until the early 1960s.

Meanwhile, at that first meeting after the Second World War the ever-willing Ken Chapman was elected both First XV captain and First XV Secretary and by the end of that first season – when he finally called time on his own playing career – he had also taken over from Stoop as Secretary of the club itself. The succession was complete and Stoop was now free to enjoy his later years in the less onerous role of President, although he still insisted on standing behind the posts on the deserted South Stand terrace at Twickenham – his favoured position for assessing a match.

All things considered, the club was remarkably buoyant on its return to action, even if the make-up of the pool of First XV players was something of a moveable feast (a difficulty shared by all the major clubs at the time). There was still a huge Services contingent whose availability varied while they were either redeployed around the country or awaited demobilisation. Furthermore, a slightly older generation of Oxbridge players – some on shortened degrees – also came into the equation, particularly in the early part of the season and from the Christmas holiday period onwards.

Left: A mixed team photo and action from the first floodlit rugby match ever played in London between Harlequins and Cardiff at the White City Stadium in October 1954. Harlequins played matches at the ground throughout the rest of the '50s, including a further visit from Cardiff in October 1959 (below)

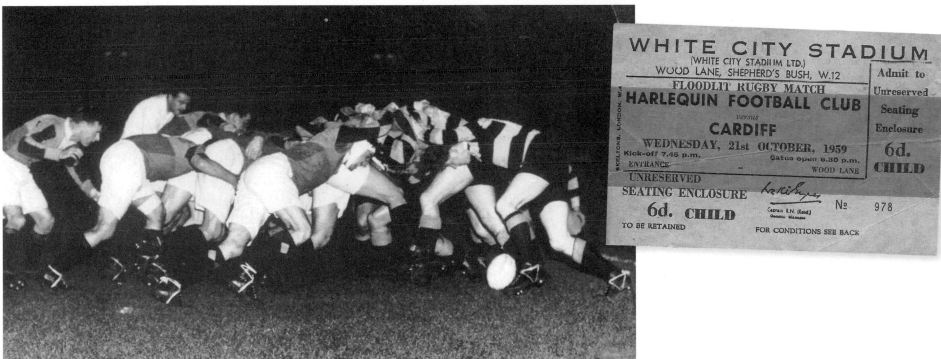

WHITE CITY STADIUM
(WHITE CITY STADIUM LTD.)
WOOD LANE, SHEPHERD'S BUSH, W.12

FLOODLIT RUGBY MATCH
HARLEQUIN FOOTBALL CLUB
versus
CARDIFF
WEDNESDAY, 21st OCTOBER, 1959
Kick-off 7.45 p.m.   Gates open 6.30 p.m.
ENTRANCE   -   WOOD LANE
UNRESERVED
SEATING ENCLOSURE
6d. CHILD

Admit to
Unreserved
Seating
Enclosure
6d.
CHILD

Captain R.N. (Reid)
General Manager

No. 978

TO BE RETAINED   FOR CONDITIONS SEE BACK

HARLEQUIN XV. 1945-46

D.B.Vaughan, D.K.Brooks, C.M.Horner, R.L.Hudson, R.G.H.Weighill, R.C.Lemon, J.M.Lennox-Cooke.

D.G.Barton, H.de Lacy, K.H.Chapman (Captain), A.D.Stoop. F.P.Dunkley, B.H.Birkett.

D.Bulmer, M.Steele-Bodger, A.G.Butler.

One such player was Sydney Dowse MC, who survived the war to enjoy a couple more seasons with the Wanderers and, until the day of his death in 2008, was never seen wearing any other neckwear than his Harlequins tie. Incredibly, Dowse was the man mainly responsible for the construction of 'Harry', the 336-foot long tunnel at Stalag Luft III which featured so prominently in the Hollywood film *The Great Escape* (1963), in which he was portrayed by John Leyton. After masterminding and digging the tunnel, he was captured 14 days following his escape and sent to Sachsenhausen concentration camp where he staged another, albeit unsuccessful, breakout. His escape attempts were put to an end after he was placed in solitary confinement for five months. Back in Britain after the war, Dowse – who went on to become an equerry at Buckingham Palace – was very much the life and soul of most Quins parties. As the great man put it himself: "Once one escapes from Sachsenhausen, life holds no difficulties."

Life wasn't easy in the immediate post-war years with, among other things, petrol rationing making transport for away matches somewhat problematic. Travelling by train was the norm but even that was a fraught process. In 1949 Quins, cutting it a bit fine, headed to Blackheath intending to get the bus from the station to the Rectory Field, only for there to be a bus strike. Skipper Martin

Jackson hailed down an empty coal lorry with the driver agreeing to deliver them to the ground – an image that doesn't quite fit in with the elitist image of the club held by some outside observers.

Around this time many players were bona fide members of two clubs: their home club and their temporary club, which they joined if forced to move around the country with the Services or while seeking work. It was not easy but one way or another Quins started to build a formidable side – with no organised club rugby in England for over six years there was a veritable logjam of younger talent looking to make their mark.

Irishman Maurice Daly turned out for a couple of seasons before he moved to Kenya, and his good offices helped secure the services of Ireland scrum-half Hugh de Lacy, who according to club lore was poached from Rosslyn Park after he impressed in a friendly. De Lacy's smooth passing game was eventually to earn him selection in Ireland's Grand Slam-winning team of 1948.

Centre Jack (J A) Davies starred for Wales in the 'Victory International' matches played in 1946–7 and was another stand-out performer for Harlequins after the war before heading north, but the blow of his departure was softened as a host of outstanding young players began to step into the limelight.

Micky Steele-Bodger – best known as the long-serving President of the Barbarians

– needs little introduction but straight after the war was best known as a revolutionary openside flanker, an early prototype of Neil Back, who made an instant and lasting impression for Cambridge University and Harlequins before furthering his veterinary studies at Edinburgh.

Steele-Bodger was often joined in the back row by an old Oxford opponent, a rumbustious Australian named Basil 'Jika' Travers who arrived in England fresh from the rainforests of Papua New Guinea where he had been fighting the Japanese as a brigade major in the Australian Army. His muscular and forthright presence benefited Quins hugely and, like Steele-Bodger, he soon found himself in the England team. In those dog days of Empire, simple residence in England – temporary or otherwise – was still sufficient qualification for a 'colonial' to play for England. He returned home in 1950 and promptly captained New South Wales to a famous victory over the touring British and Irish Lions.

Opposite: The Harlequins First XV in 1945, the first season after the Second World War

Left: Sydney Dowse MC was responsible for the construction of 'Harry', the POW escape tunnel featured in the 1963 film *The Great Escape*

Below: Post-war Twickenham Stadium fixture cards produced by the RFU

Right: The 1947 Harlequins annual dinner at The Savoy Hotel in London

The duo of Steele-Bodger and Travers sometimes found itself packing down with a third England back-rower named Bob Weighill DFC, who attributed his superlative fitness and mobility to the fact that he had been primarily flying night reconnaissance missions during the war and this had left him most of the day to train. Sleep, it would seem, was considered optional back in those days. Weighill eventually rose to the heights of air commodore in the RAF before serving as an England selector between 1959–64 and becoming the Secretary of the RFU from 1974–86.

For some reason Harlequins has always been blessed in the back row and there were high-quality reinforcements on the way.

Clem Thomas, a future Wales captain, played for a number of seasons while at Cambridge University and won his first caps while at the club. Similarly Cornishman Vic Roberts – who when he joined the club had already been capped 12 times by England and toured Australia and New Zealand with the Lions in 1950 – was a clever and hardnosed presence at flanker who made a huge impact. Roberts later became Harlequins Chairman, a position he held when the club moved to The Stoop in the early 1960s.

The South African-born, English-raised Dyson 'Tug' Wilson missed out on Test honours but was yet another outstanding breakaway who was a member of the Metropolitan Police undercover taskforce.

Wilson returned to normality for 80 minutes every Saturday afternoon with, presumably, both he and the Met Police confident there was no chance of him being recognised by the criminal fraternity at any of the rugby grounds around England. Wilson was selected for the 1955 Lions tour of South Africa and stayed on to run restaurants in Rhodesia before returning to England and Cornwall in 1969 where he became a successful commercial fisherman working out of Newlyn.

Nor should we forget Yorkshire's Brian Vaughan, a Royal Navy officer who even amongst this array of talent proved an exceptional contributor for Quins and produced performances that earned eight

England caps between 1948–50. Vaughan also later enjoyed two successful spells as an England selector, between 1959–62 and again from 1965–66.

Meanwhile another of the many aviators who inhabited the club was Squadron Leader Ted Horsfall, a Yorkshireman who won an England cap at flanker while playing for Harlequins. And Alan Grimsdell, who with those old heavy leather balls used to land penalties from inside his own half, was also a pilot. Like the Chapman brothers, Alan and his brother, Bill, both played for Quins and were the sons of a famous footballer. Their father, Arthur Grimsdell, captained both Spurs and England.

Similarly, Wing Commander John Seldon was a club stalwart for decades, while Ireland centre 'Hex' (R J H) Uprichard was another officer serving in the RAF. Uprichard, an Ulsterman and the youngest of six brothers, was christened Richard John Hexagon – the last name shortened to Hex by which he was known – and later became the RAF's expert on Arctic survival. Roy Austen-Smith and Ken Cross were both loyal club men and rose respectively to the ranks of air marshall and air chief marshall during their military careers. Cross was a member of the aircrew aboard the aircraft carrier HMS *Glorious* when she was sunk at the end of the Norwegian campaign in 1940. He was one of around 40 survivors out of a complement of more than 1,200.

All in all it was a remarkable era, and when everybody was available Quins could be formidable. In the 1952 Probables versus Possibles trial match for England, Harlequins contributed no less than 14 players, while nine players of various nationalities were capped from the club that season.

Left: Former wartime pilot Alan Grimsdell displays his immense power and strength against Richmond in 1954

Right: Harlequins captain Ricky Bartlett exchanges pennants during a tour to Romania in 1956

More often than not the captain of this eclectic bunch was lock Jonny Matthews, who took over from Chapman at the end of the first season. Surgeon Lieutenant Matthews had spent a good deal of the Second World War stationed in the city of Murmansk, north of the Arctic Circle, where he looked after those involved in the Arctic convoys. On returning to civilisation he had much living to catch up on and proved a fine captain for Quins and England, and also notably led London Counties to their historic win over the 'unbeatable' 1951–52 Springboks.

Fellow Quins Albert Agar, Grimsdell and Hugh (H C) Forbes were also involved in that classic 11–9 triumph over the Springboks at Twickenham, with Grimsdell kicking the winning penalty. Playing twice a week was absolutely the norm during the amateur era and Quins also provided the backbone to the Middlesex side which took the County Championship that season.

Matthews had a sure touch as skipper and led the ever-changing cast list at the club with aplomb. One such player was Cornish centre Keith (E K) Scott, who had started playing for the club before the war while studying at St Mary's University, Twickenham, and who was still available for a season or two after hostilities ceased. Scott was a tough and rather inspiring character, as Steele-Bodger recalls in an incident during England's clash with Scotland in 1948:

"We were beset by injuries. Our scrum-half, Richard Madge, departed with torn ankle ligaments and I was standing in at scrum-half when I took a terrific bang on the head and should probably have come off as well. Then Keith Scott sustained a broken jaw in another furious exchange. You could see instantly what had happened. He had a

crack right down the symphysis where the two jaws meet, upper and lower, but for the time being there was no displacement.

"I remember to this day one of our chaps running on with lemons at half-time and Keith calmly asking him to order a taxi to be waiting outside the England changing room on the final whistle to take him directly to Edinburgh Infirmary where he would need his jaw to be wired. And with that he turned back to his team and gave a stirring half-time talk before leading us back into battle. I have to say I was rather impressed."

As the 1950s progressed, a number of other legendary Quins figures came into sharp focus. David Brooks, a Swordfish pilot in the war, took the helm as captain for two years but was never far from the action on and off the field. His bonhomie and administrative talents were much in demand in later years, with Quins, Surrey, England and the Lions utilising his skills. Brooks managed the 1968 Lions tour to South Africa – the so-called 'Wreckers Tour' – and is credited with the famous line "Couldn't have been much of a party" when presented with a £900 bill for damage by a hotel manager after a hectic night in the bar.

Among the star turns who really got Quins buzzing again behind the scrum were a triumvirate of classy backs in Phil (W P C) Davies, Ricky Bartlett and John Young. All three were capped by England, while Davies and Young also went on to become Lions. Young was the AAA 100-yard champion in 1956 and Bartlett, the master of the well-judged chip or grubber, set up countless tries for his speedster teammate on the Quins wing.

Bartlett, who died well before his time aged just 55, was a much-valued club member but another player who was curiously undervalued by England despite being undefeated in seven appearances, including as an ever-present during the 1957 Grand Slam. There used to be a thought, often expressed in the amateur game, that being a prominent player with Harlequins somehow gained you extra purchase with the England selectors, but there is just as much historical evidence over the years to suggest the opposite.

The dashing Davies was another good athlete but a late developer as a rugby player – indeed he did not even get a Blue at Cambridge and was on the point of giving the game up when he impressed playing fly-half during a pre-season Quins trial game at Teddington prior to the 1951 season which he had attended with no great hope or expectation. His progress after that was quick, so much so that he was first capped by England in 1953 and had matured into one of the world's best centres when he toured South Africa with the Lions in 1955. Davies particularly enjoyed playing with the popular Bartlett, who was clearly a players' player:

"Ricky was a wonderful, quietly spoken man and much revered Quins captain, and was the giver of the softest pass I ever encountered, each with just the hint of a break which put the defence on the back foot. Playing alongside him was a joy. I first played with Rick at Cambridge for the LX Club against Oxford. The programme listed six future internationals.

"We played some great rugby at Quins during this period and there was a great spirit at the club. The Wanderers were very strong in their own right in those days and if work commitments were such that you couldn't travel on an away match there was still

Above: David Marques leaps for the ball

always a high-quality game to be had at home with the Wanderers.

"The week before my England 'debut', which was due to be against France in 1953, I couldn't get away from my teaching job at Christ's Hospital for the First XV game – we were in the West Country somewhere, I think – so I played at Teddington for the Wanderers

Right: Harlequins captain Bob Weighill exchanges gifts with his Paris University Club counterpart before a match at Twickenham Stadium in 1949. The pennant he received (below) is still on display at The Stoop

against Coventry. Anyway, I got a painful boot in the stomach and even though I spent half a month's salary for a consultation and treatment with the eminent sports injury physio Bill Tucker in Harley Street, he couldn't work his magic and I had to drop out of England contention."

One of the ablest and most popular members of the Quins team was Sandy Sanders, who had joined the club from Ipswich YMCA and was so proud of his Suffolk roots that when he won his nine England caps between 1954–56 he insisted on being listed as 'Harlequins and Ipswich YMCA' in the match programmes. Sanders was still young in prop terms – 31– when he suffered a terrible motorcycle accident which resulted in the death of a good friend and saw the Quin hospitalised for three months with multiple injuries, including 30 fractures in one leg. His playing career was over but a considerable administrative career was just starting with Quins and England. By common consent Sanders was the most player-friendly and switched-on England selector of the old amateur era and he proved a notably successful tour manager in 1973 when England produced one of the best results in their history – a 16–10 win over the All Blacks at Eden Park, Auckland.

Sanders was by no means the only forward to make a name for himself during this period. By the mid-to-late 1950s David Marques had started packing down at lock for Harlequins when not required by Cambridge University – where he won four straight Blues. His opposite number in all four Varsity matches was the tough Bristolian John Currie, who started his senior career with Clifton but was soon destined to join Harlequins as well. Together they formed one of the best second row combinations in England history – 22 Tests in tandem between 1956–61, including the 1957 Grand Slam – and for four or five seasons Quins also benefited from their presence. The two of them were the classic combination of tall, athletic line out jumper (Marques) and the shorter pusher and all-purpose forward (Currie), and between them they were very difficult to counter.

Marques was the son of an Australian soldier who moved to Britain after surviving the First World War, including the Battle of Gallipoli, and proved an outstanding Lion when touring Australia and New Zealand in 1959. In 1964 he also crewed as a member of the afterguard squad for the Great Britain yacht *Sovereign*, which contested the Americas Cup in 1964. He was involved alongside three other Quins members – David Page, Paul Anderson and John Scott – who, as the programme observed, had been brought in to provide the 'brawn'. Alas it was all to no avail as *Sovereign* – with Marques and Page on board operating the grinder – lost 4–0 to the USA's *Constellation* at Rhode Island.

P.U.C
5 10
1949

Just 11 years after the end of the Second World War, in 1956 Harlequins entertained the German national team at Twickenham Stadium in a truly historic fixture and were presented with a celebratory pennant to mark the occasion

D.R.V.
8.9.1956

Above: The two teams for the Jubilee Match between Harlequins and Richmond in 1959 to celebrate the 50th anniversary of the first ever match at Twickenham. Survivors from the original match are pictured in the middle row

Right: No self-respecting Harlequins anniversary can ever be celebrated without a decent lunch!

HARLEQUIN FOOTBALL CLUB

JUBILEE MATCH LUNCHEON

December 26th, 1959

—

Chairman:
J. G. G. BIRKETT, Esq.

—

TWICKENHAM 1909—1959

Menu

Cream of Mushroom Soup

—

Minute Steak
Roast Potatoes
Vichy Carrots

—

Fruit Salad and Ice Cream

—

Coffee

Toasts

THE LOYAL TOAST

—

THE RUGBY UNION

K. H. Chapman, Esq.

Reply
J. A. Tallent, Esq., O.B.E., T.D.

Currie, whose nickname was 'Muscles', moved back to Bristol at the end of his career and won his last three caps while playing for that famous club. However, he remained a staunch Quins man and, after serving as an England selector, became very involved again during his time as the club's Chairman from 1980–88. He died suddenly aged just 58.

Even though the 1950s were hardly a decade of plenty, Quins managed to retain its rather exotic and outward-looking reputation. For example, on Sunday 23rd April 1950, immediately after the Middlesex Sevens had concluded, a party left for France to play Paris University – a trip that proved so successful that it became a regular fixture.

Meanwhile, in 1956 Quins really got the international bit between its teeth, firstly hosting the German national team, who they defeated 28–6 at Twickenham, before embarking on a short tour of Romania. Very few clubs have consistently attempted to spread the gospel as much as Harlequins.

As the 1950s drew to a close the club was in rude health from top to toe, with the Wanderers losing just three of their 33 games in the 1958–59 season, many of which were against First XVs. They very much ruled the roost at Teddington, which seemed more their domain than the First XV who spent most of their time at Twickenham or on the road.

Such was the strength in depth at the club that some players – notably Scotland centre Micky Grant – were actually capped directly from the Wanderers side. Grant earned his call-up against France in 1955 as a result of a run of fine performances in Quins' second string. By the end of the decade another exceptional player – future England scrum-half Jeremy Spencer – was also forging his reputation with the Wanderers.

It was during this decade that the Wanderers established their own Easter tour to France – mainly the Basque region – in an annual trip that became one of the most sought-after invites on the circuit. At one stage they became victims of their own success with French clubs having no hesitation in promoting their visitors as the Quins First XV to attract a bigger gate. They also tended to put out their strongest teams, which led to some memorably tough games.

The big challenge though, as Quins approached the 1960s, was to find a new home where the entire club could thrive. The committee had been looking at prospective sites for a good while but the search was showing no sign of drawing to a close. The team and club seemed poised to reach for the next level, but as much as players and members had become attached to their Teddington base, Harlequins had outgrown its confines. Rugby's nomads needed to move one final time.

Above: The Harlequins Wanderers, pictured at Teddington during the 1950–51 season

1914–18 • LEST WE FORGET • 1939–45

The Roll of Honour of former Harlequins players who made the ultimate sacrifice during the First and Second World Wars

FIRST WORLD WAR

First name(s)	Surname	Date of Death	Age	Rank	Branch of Service
Thomas	Allen	26.02.1915	27	2nd Lieutenant	Irish Guards
George Gaylor	Barnes	16.07.1916	25	Lieutenant	Worcestershire Regiment
George Norman	Berney	06.11.1917	25	Captain	Hertfordshire Regiment
George Howard	Bickley	04.10.1917	25	Captain	Machine Gun Corps
Richard Coore	Blagrove	12.08.1915	24	Lieutenant	Duke of Cornwall's Light Infantry
Lawrence Cave	Blencowe	29.06.1917	29	2nd Lieutenant	Royal Sussex Regiment
Cuthbert Everard	Brisley	13.07.1918	32	Major	Royal Air Force
Robert Bucknall	Bowker	05.09.1917	37	Major	Royal Engineers
Edward Fenwick	Boyd	20.09.1914	24	Lieutenant	Northumberland Fusiliers
Frank Arthur	Brock	23.04.1918	29	Wing Commander	Royal Air Force
Henry	Brougham	18.02.1923	34	Major	Royal Field Artillery
Frederick Derick Edwin	Buller	25.09.1914	22	Trooper	East African Mounted Rifles
Reverend John Garrett	Bussell	28.06.1915	33	Captain	Royal Sussex Regiment
Ken McLeod	Carnduff	11.01.1916	25	Captain	Royal Engineers
George Martin	Chapman	30.05.1915	28	Captain	Royal Army Medical Corps
Charles Isaacs	Coburn	31.07.1917	32	2nd Lieutenant	Kings Royal Rifle Corps
Jessel ('Jay')	Crawford-Kehrmann	24.01.1915	28	Lieutenant	Rifle Brigade
Raymond Vivian Leslie	Dallas	13.04.1918	25	Captain	Northumberland Fusiliers
Frank Maturin	Davenport	22.11.1915	27	Captain	Oxfordshire and Buckinghamshire Light Infantry
Fairfax Llewellyn	Davies	08.07.1917	26	Lieutenant	Norfolk Regiment
Walter Melbourne	Dodds	14.10.1918	33	Captain	Northumberland Fusiliers
Sydney Earnest	Dove	16.08.1916	28	2nd Lieutenant	Queen's Own Royal West Kent Regiment
Frank Oswald	Eiloart	03.05.1917	24	Captain	London Regiment (Royal Fusiliers)
Kenward Wallace	Elmslie	04.11.1914	27	Lieutenant	4th Royal Irish Dragoon Guards
Errol Russell	Garnett	18.10.1916	25	2nd Lieutenant	Wiltshire Regiment
George Maurice Gerald	Gillett	26.09.1916	33	Captain	Leicestershire Regiment
Roby ('Ronnie') Myddleton	Gotch	01.07.1916	26	Captain	Sherwood Foresters
William Briggs	Grandage	14.05.1917	37	Lieutenant Colonel	Royal Fleet Auxiliary
Geoffrey Stewart	Grundy	14.04.1915	28	Private	Honourable Artillery Company
Arthur John Shirley Hoare	Hales	06.07.1916	34	Captain	Wiltshire Regiment
Arthur ('Fatty') Claude	Hammond	12.01.1916	21	Private	Norfolk Regiment
Ralph Escott	Hancock	29.10.1914	26	Lieutenant	Devonshire Regiment
Arthur Hensley	Hudson	31.07.1917	25	Captain	Royal Berkshire Regiment
Thomas Heylyn	Hudson	13.10.1915	25	Captain	Royal Berkshire Regiment
Thomas Roland	Juckes	09.05.1915	19	Lieutenant	Royal Sussex Regiment
Douglas ('Dan')	Lambert	13.10.1915	32	2nd Lieutenant	The Buffs (Royal East Kent Regiment)
George Aubrey Kennedy	Lawrence	28.01.1917	25	Lieutenant Colonel	Royal Flying Corps
Ralph Hawksworth	Legard	09.08.1915	40	Captain	Durham Light Infantry
Gwion Llewellyn Bowen	Lloyd	11.08.1915	27	Captain	Dorsetshire Regiment
Frank Augustus	Lowe	04.06.1915	32	Lieutenant	Royal Naval Reserve
Alfred Frederick	Maynard	13.11.1916	22	Lieutenant	Royal Naval Reserve

First name(s)	Surname	Date of Death	Age	Rank	Branch of Service
William Cattell	Morton	22.07.1917	25	Lieutenant	Royal Field Artillery
Geoffrey Dorman	Partridge	03.11.1914	23	Lieutenant	Welch Regiment
Arthur William	Passmore	04.04.1916	27	2nd Lieutenant	The Queen's (Royal West Surrey) Regiment
Ronald ('Ronnie') William	Poulton-Palmer	04.05.1915	25	Lieutenant	Royal Berkshire Regiment
Kenneth	Powell	18.02.1915	29	Private	Honourable Artillery Company
John Haughton	Rohde	28.10.1914	26	Lieutenant	Royal Engineers
Alan Percy	Rosling	04.03.1917	20	2nd Lieutenant	Worcestershire Regiment
Douglas George	Rouquette	26.09.1917	26	2nd Lieutenant	Royal Flying Corps
George Amelius Crawshay	Sandeman	26.04.1915	33	Captain	Hampshire Regiment
Frank Guy	Shackle	21.11.1917	27	Captain	Middlesex Regiment
Charles Owen	Spencer-Smith	03.08.1917	38	Captain	London Regiment (Queen's Westminster Rifles)
Gerald Cameron	Southern	21.07.1915	23	Lieutenant	53rd Sikhs (Frontier Force)
William Beverley	Surtees	28.09.1916	21	Captain	West Yorkshire Regiment
Cornelius	Thorne	30.09.1916	24	Captain (Temp)	East Surrey Regiment
Donald ('Dolly') Owen Howard	Tripp	18.08.1916	26	Captain	Loyal North Lancashire Regiment
Montague Dalston	Turnbull	27.04.1918	31	Lance Corporal	Queen's Own Royal West Kent
Lancelot Andrewes	Vidal	25.09.1915	28	2nd Lieutenant	Oxfordshire and Buckinghamshire Light Infantry
Clarence Ernest	Wand-Tetley	22.08.1915	26	Lieutenant	Lancashire Fusiliers
Robert Oscar Cyril	Ward	20.11.1917	36	Major (Temp)	Tank Corps
Arthur Pelham	Webb	09.04.1917	32	2nd Lieutenant	King's Shropshire Light Infantry
Henry Montague	Whitehead	14.04.1915	24	Lieutenant	East Surrey Regiment
Cyril William	Winterbotham	27.08.1916	29	2nd Lieutenant	Gloucestershire Regiment

SECOND WORLD WAR

First name(s)	Surname	Date of Death	Age	Rank	Branch of Service
Francis Victor	Beamish	28.03.1942	38	Group Captain	Royal Air Force
Michael Brooke	Crickmay	19.09.1944	24	Captain	Royal Engineers
John Louis	Crichton	11.11.1942	26	Captain	Parachute Regiment
Harvey ('Tough') Alexander	Dawson	06.06.1942	52	Major	Royal Canadian Engineers
Vivian ('Bobby') Gordon	Davies	23.12.1941	41	Captain	Royal Artillery
Hubert Dainton	Freakes	10.03.1942	28	Flying Officer	Royal Air Force
Clarence Phillip ('Bunny')	Goulding	18.12.1941	29	Flight Sergeant	Royal New Zealand Air Force
Cecil William	Haydon	01.06.1942	46	Brigadier	Middlesex Regiment
Patrick Stuart	Hutchinson	25.07.1941	27	Squadron Leader	Royal Air Force
Maver Llyall Palmer	Jackson	22.03.1943	38	Lieutenant Colonel	Green Howards
Ranulph	Lumgair	03.03.1943	32	Captain	Seaforth Highlanders
Michael Charles Xavier	Mack	24.08.1943	32	Squadron Leader	Royal Air Force (Auxiliary Air Force)
Robert Michael	Marshall	12.05.1945	27	Lieutenant Commander	Royal Naval Reserve
Peter Thurston	Medhurst	01.10.1942	25	Lieutenant	Royal Naval Reserve (Fleet Air Arm)
Aeneas Frank Quinton	Perkins	10.05.1940	47	Colonel	Royal Engineers
Oliver Raymond	Seligman	04.09.1944	28	Captain	Royal Artillery
Howard Phillips	Skinner	30.10.1942	30	Major	Duke of Wellington's (West Riding) Regiment
Charles Lionel	Sparke	11.12.1942	27	Flight Lieutenant	Royal Air Force
Adrian ('Bunny') Frederick	Stoop	09.02.1944	24	Lieutenant	Royal Hussars
Christopher	Thompson	16.06.1943	32	Lance Corporal	Federated Malay States Volunteer Force
Eric Sudely	Unwin	05.10.1941	47	Colonel	Royal Army Service Corps

6

Centenary Celebrations
1960–1969

6

The 1960s proved an extraordinarily busy and exciting decade for Harlequins, with a Centenary to celebrate – which the club did on the grandest of scales – and a number of demanding overseas tours taking place. The ambition and scope was startling considering the amateur ethos of the club and at times Quins stretched its resources to the very limit. Rarely has the club motto 'I Never Sleep' been more apt.

Title page: Scrum-half Johnny Dougall in action against a President's XV at Twickenham Stadium in 1963

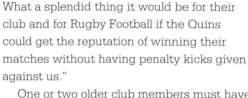

Above: Wavell Wakefield was no less combative a character as Harlequins President than he had been as a player

The decade started with pep talks all round after a 1958–59 season which included just 12 wins in 32 matches. The *Playfair Rugby Annual* reported that Harlequins 'went to pieces after a promising start to the season' and club captain David Marques warned all prospective first-team players that he expected a marked improvement in pre-season summer training ahead of the 1959–60 campaign. Club President Wavell Wakefield was coming off his long run when he also issued a stern rebuke to playing members in a stinging editorial in the May 1960 edition of the club magazine, *Harlequinade*:

"Whenever I see a penalty awarded against the club I am ashamed," wrote Wakefield. "It means a Harlequins player has been fouling or cheating and if that is the case the sooner he stops playing Rugby Football the better. Or it means that the player is ignorant of the laws of the game and that, for a Harlequin, is no excuse at all.

What a splendid thing it would be for their club and for Rugby Football if the Quins could get the reputation of winning their matches without having penalty kicks given against us."

One or two older club members must have spluttered over their pints on reading this critical outburst as they would have remembered Wakefield giving more than his fair share of penalties away during his mighty shifts at the coalface for club and country. But the great man was on a roll, and next he turned his anger on club members for not supporting the Adrian Stoop Memorial Fund which had been established to raise money for the redevelopment of the club ground at Teddington, notwithstanding the fact that Harlequins was still looking for a new ground altogether.

"The officers and committee are disappointed at the response that has so far been made by members," commented Wakefield, "… we can never repay the debt we owe to Adrian Stoop for all he did for all our club."

What Wakefield's forthright comments do indicate is that rugby in the 1960s was on the move. The game, and the attitudes of those who played it, had not altered much during the 1930s, '40s and '50s but the sporting landscape was changing rapidly and a new generation, perhaps unaware of the full history of Harlequins, was upon the club.

Maybe these new players were galvanised

by such straight talking among the club's senior statesmen and there was a flurry of activity at Harlequins in the early 1960s, with one of the most notable events being a first ever tour to East Africa (primarily Kenya) at the end of the 1960–61 season. The trip was timed to coincide with a tour by Pretoria Harlequins and was hosted by Kenya Harlequins RFC, the first example of affiliated Quins clubs around the world combining in this way. Maurice Daly, the Ireland centre who had emigrated to Kenya, was on hand to ensure that things went smoothly.

After landing at Entebbe, Kenya on 4th May 1961, Quins opened up with a 44–13 win against Uganda at Kampala on 6th May before beating West Kenya 24–6 at Kitale and Pretoria Harlequins 13–11 in Nairobi. By now the tourists were into their stride and firmly established in the Kenyan capital, where they beat Kenya Harlequins 16–0 and drew 9–9 with an unexpectedly strong Kenyan Central Province XV, although the rigours of a tough schedule might have been kicking in by then.

The players roused themselves one final time after a hectic but fun-filled 18 days to win the unofficial 'Test' against Kenya 8–0 in the pouring rain at Nakuri before departing for home. According to contemporary reports the large crowd serenaded Quins with a heartfelt rendition of 'Auld Lang Syne'.

The conveyor belt of talent certainly did not seem to lessen in this decade, although availability was not always guaranteed and

PRETORIA HARLEQUINS versus LONDON HARLEQUINS
NGONG ROAD, NAIROBI, KENYA
13 MAY 1961

BACK ROW: R.B. MARSON (LONDON, LINESMAN); DAVID WRENCH** (LONDON); SIR RICHARD LUYT (KENYA, REFEREE); HANS EERENSTEIN* (PRETORIA, FRONT RANK); FRED SWART* (LONDON, FRONT RANK); MIKE MARTIN (PRETORIA); LEON COETZEE (PRETORIA, LOCK); NIC LABUSCHAGNE** (LONDON, HOOKER); JAN O'CONNELL* (PRETORIA, FRONT RANK); DEREK MAGUIRE (PRETORIA); LUKAS KLOPPER (PRETORIA); FRANS HOLTZHAUSEN (PRETORIA); OCKIE DE WIT (PRETORIA).

THIRD ROW: T.I. EVANS (LONDON); M.J. WHITESIDE (LONDON); DUDLEY HOLTON* (PRETORIA, FLYHALF); H. EDEN (LONDON, WING); EWALD BRUNE (PRETORIA, CENTRE); MIKE WESTON (LONDON, FLYHALF); DAAN BEKKER* (PRETORIA, LOCK); M.R.M. EVANS (LONDON, FLANK); COEN GROENEVELD (PRETORIA, FLANK); G.C. MURRAY (LONDON, FRONT RANK); JAN RHOODIE (PRETORIA, FLANK); J. MALLET (LONDON, LOCK); ROBERT TWIGGE** (PRETORIA, WING); JOHN YOUNG** (LONDON, WING).

SECOND ROW: W.M. PATERSON** (LONDON, CENTRE); ROBIN HUTCHINSON* (PRETORIA, CENTRE); JOHN CURRIE** (LONDON, LOCK); DAAN RETIEF** (PRETORIA MANAGER); DAVID MARQUES** (LONDON, LOCK) CAPTAIN; DAN NESER (PRETORIA, LOCK) CAPTAIN; DEREK WHITING (LONDON MANAGER); JOHN MAYNIER (PRETORIA, HOOKER); R.A.M. WHYTE (LONDON, FLANK); TOMMY SLABBERT* (PRETORIA, WING); AUBREY LUCK*** (LONDON, SCRUMHALF).

FIRST ROW: M. HARDWICKE (LONDON, FULLBACK); HANS STRAEULI* (PRETORIA, SCRUMHALF); R.J. READ (LONDON, CENTRE); WILLIE LATEGAN (PRETORIA, FULLBACK).

* Represented NORTHERN TRANSVAAL; ** INTERNATIONAL; *** WESTERN PROVINCE

Left: The Harlequins of London meet their South African counterparts during the ground-breaking tour to Kenya in 1961

Harlequins mid-1960s: Back row (*from left to right*):
J Bazalgette, J J McPartlin, A Prosser-Harris, G C Murray,
A J S Todman, J R L Adcock, R B Marson, J T Cox, R B Lloyd,
D R Trentham; Middle row: V R Marriott, D K Brooks (Chairman,

known to everyone at the club as 'Brookie'), C M Payne (captain),
W Wiggins, (Team Secretary), J E Williams, F D B Wrench; In front:
B J Bennet, R F Reed

some players continued to hop between clubs as their job commitments demanded. John (J G) Willcox, who also won a boxing Blue during his time at Oxford, was a considerable talent at fullback who not only forced his way into the England team but played in three of the four Tests for the 1962 Lions in South Africa.

Colin Simpson, from Ipswich School, proved a powerful wing and went on to win his single cap for England while technically still a cadet at Sandhurst, whereas Bob Lloyd, a young centre fresh out of Cheltenham College and headed straight for the top, made his debut in 1963. Stoop himself would have approved of the classic lines Lloyd cut in midfield and he quickly became a key man behind the scrum for Quins, although England took a while to be convinced before he made his Test debut in 1967, scoring two tries against New Zealand at Twickenham. The Lions wanted Lloyd to tour South Africa the following year, but he was tied up completing his civil engineering exams and thereafter England seemed reluctant to trust his sumptuous skills (in fairness, John Spencer and David Duckham offered viable alternatives in Lloyd's preferred position).

Lloyd was recalled to the England squad touring the Far East in 1971 and captained his country in a non-capped Test against Japan in Osaka in 1971 when his team scored five tries en route to a 27–19 win. He was, however, criticised by coach John Burgess for encouraging England's fast and loose running approach and was dropped for the second Test. In Tokyo, England adopted a much more pragmatic style under returning skipper Budge Rogers and only scraped home 6–3. Lloyd was another Quin whose club colours and general approach probably

worked against rather than for him at international level.

The intriguing Jeremy Spencer was still a livewire at scrum-half who spent two or three seasons with Quins' powerful Wanderers team before earning regular first-team rugby from 1964 onwards, and though he may have been small and frail-looking he was in fact as tough as old boots, attributing his wiry frame to his love of gymnastic ballet. Spencer was unlucky to get dropped by England after his one international in 1966, an 11–8 home loss against a Welsh side whose pack dominated proceedings, although England would have won had Don Rutherford kicked his goals.

Spencer was an educationalist, an artist who has since exhibited with Juan Benito, and a talented weaver, and before settling on rugby he had trials with Tottenham Hotspur and Surrey County Cricket Club. He lived in a converted bus but, although he was considered a scruffy beatnik figure at the time, he invariably had the prettiest debutante on his arm at social events.

Soon after being rejected by England, Spencer moved to France – the scene of a number of happy Easter tours with the Wanderers – and started playing and coaching for St Jean de Luz in the Pays Basques. He then coached at Bayonne and Perpignan and, after moving to Spain, worked with the Spanish Federation to help promote the game in schools.

In 2007 he published a paper on introducing young children to rugby in conjunction with the RFU. Spencer was an unconventional but very 1960s figure who slotted in perfectly to the Quins changing room.

Three stalwarts in the pack of this era were prop David Wrench, second row Colin Payne and flanker Vic Marriott. Wrench, a schoolteacher, arrived via Leeds University and a post-graduate degree at Cambridge, while the raw-boned Payne, a television executive, was a high-quality player up front and became England's first-choice second row from 1964–66.

Marriott, meanwhile, was another Quin held in higher regard by his peers and England fans than the selectors. An outstanding performer in England's two Tests during their inaugural tour of New Zealand in 1963, when England could arguably have won both clashes, Marriott surprisingly only ever played two more internationals before he was considered surplus to requirements.

There was a lot going on at Harlequins in the 1960s, and Saturday 16th November 1963 was a very notable day indeed as the club moved from their old ground in Teddington just across the A316 from Twickenham to their new home – The Stoop Memorial

Below: Changing room door signs which were used at Twickenham when Harlequins were at 'home'

HARLEQUIN FOOTBALL CLUB

NUNQUAM DORMIO

Official Opening of
The Stoop Memorial Ground
Twickenham Sports Stadium, Craneford Way, Twickenham

by

Mrs. Audrey Stoop
H.W. The Mayor of Twickenham
The President of the R.F.U.

On Saturday, 16th November, 1963

Right: An invitation to the grand opening of The Stoop includes a detailed list of the facilities that would be available at the club's brand-new ground

Far right: Mrs Audrey Stoop addresses the assembled guests

The opening of our new ultra-modern headquarters should be a red letter day for all Harlequins. Your Committee hope that from this day onwards you will use the Clubroom as much as possible and that, if you are watching a match at the R.F.U. Ground, you will use the amenities of your own Clubroom both before and after the game, for your own entertainment and for any friends you care to bring with you.

Like all new ventures we aim to improve the amenities as time progresses and we hope that all Members will let the Committee have any ideas which they think could be usefully and economically introduced for the greater comfort and enjoyment of Members.

At this time the following facilities can be made available, providing they are well supported.

1. The Bar and Clubroom will be open every Saturday from 12 to 2 p.m. and from 4.30 p.m. to 11 p.m.

2. From the Saturday after the opening, hot meals will be available to Members and guests in the smaller Clubroom. We are hoping to offer quite a variety—from sausage and mash to lobster thermidor.

3. Tea can be provided on Saturdays by the public caterer in the tearooms on the first floor of the Pavilion, but it would be appreciated if Members would indicate their tea requirements to the caterer as early as possible.

4. The Clubroom can be used by Members for special dances and social receptions as long as these can be fitted in at hours other than the ones in which the Clubroom is required for the general use of Members, and providing that application is made to the Committee at least one month before the required date.

5. On each Saturday there will be an official of the Club on duty and the name of the person concerned will be on the Notice Board by the entrance. Any complaints or suggestions regarding the Clubroom services should be made to the Duty Officer and the Committee asks all Members to support this officer in ensuring that the Clubroom is kept to its present high standard. Remember that this is your Clubroom and be proud of it.

Ground, which was soon shortened to 'SMG' by most club members. The stadium, technically on a 999-year lease from the local council, boasted a 600-seater stand and a clubhouse within its confines, while there was also room for a Second XV pitch and ample parking – an increasingly important consideration for a club situated on London's western fringes.

As early as 1960 club officials, headed up by Sir Patrick Meaney, the future Chairman of the Rank Organisation, had entered into negotiations with the local authorities to buy the plot that was the home facility of Twickenham Athletics Club. The local council were keen that it continued as an athletics facility, which it did for a while despite the track having lain unused and covered up for many years. It was finally dug up in 1990 and the pitch moved nearer to the main stand.

The actual unveiling of the new ground was essentially a dummy run, as while the Quins First XV played Oxford University 400 yards across the road at Twickenham, a Harlequins 'Veterans XV' captained by the sprightly 55-year-old Peter Brook took on a combined veterans team from near neighbours Richmond and London Scottish. The game was brilliantly captured by the *Sunday Telegraph* and, although the report was not by-lined, the dry wit of a certain John Reason is unmistakable:

"Soon after 11am Gordon Carey, who kicked off the first match at Twickenham, obliged again 54 years later. It must be recorded that he sacrificed length for accuracy. The match was between 15 Harlequins stalwarts, whose combined ages totalled 580, and a fifteen of combined London Scottish and Richmond descent who could only muster a mere 500. The match was drawn 5–5 and the younger side were finishing the stronger.

"Both teams made their well strapped way onto a greasy pitch in a cloud of embrocation. The first scrum produced a creak audible from the stand and the second a grunt which slowed the traffic down on the Chertsey by-pass. There were moments when it was hard to say whether players were falling on the ball or collapsing with exhaustion. It was all good fun and, contrary to expectations, all ancient muscles stood up well to the end. I feel however that today might be the judgment day in this respect.

"Architecturally the style of the new clubhouse is early Festival Hall with more than a hint of White City. However the bars and changing room are palatial to the point of opulence. In addition to a fine playing area there is a running track for those who need to exercise with their drinks."

The Harlequins First XV duly made their much-anticipated debut at The Stoop the following week when they played Cambridge University. The club still retained the right to stage up to 13 matches per season at Twickenham and for a large part of the 1960s, '70s and even into the early 1980s Quins often exercised its right to play at the home of English rugby, certainly before Christmas in the days when there was often just one

autumn international at the ground.

What with that first ever tour of East Africa and the tumultuous move to The Stoop, it is hardly surprising that some members – with jobs and families also requiring their attention – began to flag a little. Certainly there is evidence of a sagging in energy levels at the end of the 1963–64 season, which is when skipper Colin Payne famously admonished his players for a lack of spirit and commitment, again using the club newsletter to make his views known:

"The time has come for a few harsh words in public. What has happened to the playing strength of the club in the 'A' echelons? There is a spirit of malaise which, in my opinion, is only in the mind. Let us just stop and consider for the moment why things are not what they ought to be. First and foremost I get the impression from the team captains that there is a complete lack of spirit and lack of pride in the jerseys you are wearing. Secondly, and as important, there is a general lack of fitness. Players are not even fit enough to stay and drink after the game.

"Thirdly, and this is tied in with the team spirit, three-quarters of you couldn't really care less whether you played or not. I put it to you that just a small sacrifice for the club will repay itself in results. If a team is not winning nobody enjoys themselves. If a team is not winning it is not good enough just to

Left: Skipper Colin Payne demanded that his teammates upped their game to match the new facilities

Right and far right: The former site of an athletics club, The Stoop came complete with a cinder running track and raised grass banks which were perfect for picnicking

Below: The new ground was conveniently located just a stones-throw from rugby's HQ

walk out and give up. I am convinced that everybody is playing at least 50 per cent below his capabilities merely because there is a general air of 'couldn't care less'. Snap out of it gentlemen and live up to the name of the club."

Having realised that perhaps he was sailing close to the wind – after all the Quins First XV had still won 17 of its 36 games, including a notable triumph over Coventry and a rare double over Leicester – Payne then modified his comments a little. But only a little:

"Let's be more cheerful. The scene is not as black as all that. Much of the trouble stems from the fact that, at the time of going to press, the Quins have something like 15 out of the top 45 players injured or unavailable through business and work. Also the fixture list has been considerably strengthened and has taken one or two of us

by surprise. Let us surprise somebody else for a change!"

Payne was perhaps fretting too much as another wave of players strengthened the Quins cause midway through the decade, and they were certainly needed because – with a Centenary season to celebrate in 1966–67 – the fixture list and demands on members were to reach a new intensity.

Nigel Starmer-Smith was a lively scrum-half who came down from Oxford in 1966, while Quins' reputation for fielding international quality locks continued despite the retirement of David Marques. Following his graduation from St Luke's College, Exeter, Quins saw more and more of Mike Davis, and his second row partnership with Nick Martin became one of the best around – again the tried and tested combination of quality athlete and jumper (Davis) and willing grafter (Martin) proved most effective.

Davis won 16 caps between 1963 and 1970, though by common consent it should have been at least double that total but his world-class talent was often distrusted by England. Meanwhile Nick Martin had to wait until 1972 for his solitary cap, which he won when coming on the field as a replacement for the injured Tony Neary against France at the Parc des Princes. England were a badly demoralised team at that stage and were hammered 37–12, although nothing should detract from Martin's fine career with Quins.

Another underrated player from the era was centre/wing Paul Parkin who, as well as being the youngest ever Harlequins player, would not have been far behind Andrew Harriman and John Young in a footrace between the fastest ever Quins. Parkin was 16 years and six months old in October 1963 when he was summoned from his biology

lesson at Fortescue House School in Twickenham by his headmaster. Harlequins had just been in touch – they were a man short for a game against the Army at Fairfax Road that afternoon, did he have his boots with him? Parkin did, and in no time was heading for the match.

The young Parkin had impressed with his blazing pace at the Quins trials a month earlier and had played for the 'A' XV against Eastbourne College in a recent game, so he was already on the radar when the summons arrived... just.

"It all happened so quickly that I didn't have time to worry," recalls Parkin. "One minute I was studying biology and the next I was in the dressing room changing next to Ricky Bartlett and Micky Grant. My first action was trying to bring down Army lock Mike Campbell-Lamerton who had just returned from captaining the Lions."

Parkin, who logged a time of 9.9 seconds in the 100 yards as a youngster, went on to enjoy a fine career. He played for England Schools against Wales at Cardiff Arms Park, where he marked opposite centre Gerald Davies, scored 64 tries in 146 first-team games for Quins, was a regular partner in the centre for Middlesex with John Dawes – "The best I ever played with or against" – and earned a final England trial.

"They were great days, there was so much talent around the club you struggled to always get a game," says Parkin. "I remember once I touched the ball three times in a match against Llanelli at Twickenham and I scored two tries and kicked a drop-goal. We won 9–0 but I was dropped for the next week!

"Bob Hiller, Bob Lloyd, Roger Lewis and John Cox were great guys to play with and,

for a couple of seasons, Tim Rutter and John Novak, a big, fast wing from Guy's Hospital. I attended a players' reunion back in 2014 and Bob was back from Hong Kong and John had flown in from Texas. Forty-five-odd years on and it was just like we were having a chat in the changing room after a game.

"I suppose pace was my biggest asset, I was pretty quick at one time. I'd have to say John Young was probably quicker than me but I did beat him once over 100 yards at training in a race the boys set up when we were down in South Africa on tour. But I was still a youngster then and he was at the end of his career."

The 1966–67 Centenary season was celebrated long and hard and started with a six-match summer tour of South Africa, mainly organised through the good offices of the Pretoria Harlequins club who really excelled themselves. The Pretoria Quins had to raise £8,000 – a huge sum 50 years ago – to cover the expenses but pulled together a strong fixture list which attracted good crowds to ensure the tour broke even with more than enough left over to celebrate properly. Harlequins played four provincial sides, a strong South African Universities XV and the Quaggas – the South African equivalent of the Barbarians – and a record of three wins, one draw and two defeats was a decent effort. Then in the autumn came a rush of celebratory matches, beginning with an 11–6 victory at Twickenham against a powerful French Select XV gathered by France's former captain Jean Prat, with Parkin and John Adcock scoring Quins' two tries. Quins also recorded a win over an East Africa XV but lost to a Wellington side from New Zealand as the celebratory games continued.

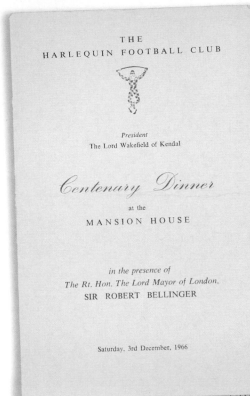

THE
HARLEQUIN FOOTBALL CLUB

President
The Lord Wakefield of Kendal

Centenary Dinner

at the
MANSION HOUSE

in the presence of
The Rt. Hon. The Lord Mayor of London,
SIR ROBERT BELLINGER

Saturday, 3rd December, 1966

A 2.11.66

The President and Committee of the Harlequin Football Club
request the pleasure of the company of

Mr A.R.F. Wright

at the Dinner to celebrate the Centenary of the Harlequin Football Club
to be held at the Mansion House
on Saturday, 3rd December, 1966
in the presence of the Rt. Hon. the Lord Mayor, Sir Robert Bellinger

R.S.V.P. D. A. Whiting
Griffin Cottage, Mop End
Amersham, Bucks

7.15 for 7.45 p.m.
Black tie

Above: Happy birthday! Harlequins reached the ripe old age of 100 in 1966 and celebrated in the manner to which the club was accustomed

Kreuznacher Bruckenhaus
Deinhard 1964

Chambolle Musigny 1959

Martinez Old Crusted Port

Brandy:
Croizet V.S.O.P. Cognac

Taramasalata

Turbot Dieppoise

Saddle of Lamb
Redcurrant Jelly
Mint Sauce
Rissolée Potatoes
Petits Pois a la Française

Harlequin Gateau
Petits Fours

Canape Raucher Kase

Coffee

Liqueurs

Toasts

THE QUEEN

THE RIGHT HON. THE LORD MAYOR,
THE CORPORATION OF LONDON AND THE SHERIFFS

Proposed by The Lord Wakefield of Kendal
Response by The Rt. Hon. The Lord Mayor

THE RUGBY FOOTBALL UNION

Proposed by T. H. Tilling, Esq.

Response by The President of the R.F.U.
D. H. Harrison, Esq.

THE GUESTS

Proposed by K. H. Chapman, Esq.
Response by The Rt. Hon. Edward Heath, M.B.E., M.P.

On the domestic front the club rose splendidly to the occasion with a host of outstanding wins against most of its traditional rivals – Northampton, Llanelli, Leicester, Oxford and Cambridge Universities, Newport, Bath and Swansea – and draws against London Welsh and Cardiff. Given the strength of their fixture list and all the other activities inevitably surrounding the Centenary year, Quins' record – played 36, won 22, drawn 3, lost 11, points for 409, points against 288 – was certainly more than acceptable.

Away from the pitch the social side of the club's Centenary was hectic to say the least. There was a cocktail reception at the House of Commons on 9th November, which was attended by Leader of the Opposition Edward Heath; a reunion day on 16th November to coincide with the club's game against Oxford University when all Quins past and present were invited down to the ground; and a Centenary Dinner at the Mansion House on 3rd December.

Nevertheless, the highlight for all those who survived this social marathon was the grand Centenary Ball on Friday 12th May 1967 when a massive marquee – reportedly 120 yards in length – was erected at Twickenham to cater for nearly 1,200 guests. No fewer than four bands were on hand to provide the necessary music to keep the guests entertained, and on the official invitation carriages were ordered for 4am. It was certainly not a quiet affair.

Harlequins even boldly ventured into the forbidden world of sponsorship and persuaded cigarette manufacturer Wills to underwrite the publication of their Centenary booklet, which included a particularly glowing tribute from Welsh legend Cliff

Morgan, who admitted that he held a natural prejudice against such a very English and seemingly Home Counties club until he played them and immediately fell in love with the Quins approach:

"Time, thank goodness, has destroyed my immature image. Now my appreciation is realistic. Few club matches in which I played for Cardiff provided as much fun as the Harlequins fixture. Absent was the inevitable tension of the close club rivalry of Welsh football, indeed there was a genuine desire by the Harlequins to attack the opposition with all the facilities available.

"It was the dignity on and off the field that made the Quins boys I know first-class company," continued Morgan, who then singled out Bartlett for particular praise.

"It's not until another fly-half makes you look second best that you really respect him. Ricky did this to me on two memorable occasions. I respected and still respect him for, apart from his playing, his approach epitomises what a rugger man should be."

One direct result of such a high-profile and enjoyable social season was that Harlequins decided to dispense with the strict ruling that only players and former club players – albeit of whatever level – could be club members. It had become apparent that others, who were now too old, injured or simply unable to play, wished to be closely associated with the club,

offer their support and enjoy whatever festivities were afoot. Henceforth the rules for membership were amended.

On the pitch, the Centenary season built to a crescendo at the end of April 1967 when the club managed to win the Middlesex Sevens for the first time since 1935, and in so doing broke the dominance of London Scottish and Loughborough College who between them had won the previous eight tournaments. Harlequins, characteristically, had to do it the hard way though, coming from behind to win all four games on the day.

Harlequins opened up with a 15–10 win over London Scottish and then beat Headingley 16–13 after extra-time before accounting for Northampton 16–8 in the semi-final. Come the final itself Quins proved just too good for a Tommy Bedford-inspired Richmond, winning 14–11. Bob Hiller captained the team and scored 40 of its 61 points on the day, while Bob Lloyd and Tim Rutter helped to provide a cutting edge and Roger Lewis, Mike Mason, Pat Orr and Colin Payne made up the rest of the successful squad. Helpfully, the exact same squad had warmed up for the Middlesex Sevens in the preceding weeks by winning the Surrey and Esher tournaments.

But Quins' unexpected Sevens success gave rise to a rather amusing sequel. To round off the Centenary festivities a quick-

fire end of season tour to France had been arranged, with the first match kicking off the day after the Sevens tournament. Having not won the Middlesex Sevens for 32 years – and having appeared in only one final since the war – the Club Secretary felt confident in booking the touring party on the 8pm flight from Heathrow to Toulouse that day.

However, come the mighty Sevens triumph it just so happened that the majority of those involved were also meant to be bound for France and a farcical scene ensued as the players dashed for Heathrow in a fleet of taxis clutching their champagne bottles immediately after the hurried presentations. Somehow they talked their way on board the flight – which had mercifully been delayed a little – after being initially told the doors had been closed and they were too late.

A strong France Select XV – bristling with various illustrious Camberabero and Spanghero brothers – won the first game 29–21 but Quins recovered to defeat Brive the following night, even though the French side claimed that they would be fielding a few guest players as a result of reaching the final stages of the French Cup. Cue the Camberabero and Spanghero brothers again.

In the third and final match Harlequins defeated old rivals Paris University and by this time, rightly guessing that the opposition would once again be bolstering their team with high-quality ringers, Quins had astutely phoned home and flown in a few replacements themselves.

It is certainly a marvel that the players were able to fit in the breathless Centenary schedule during the very height of the amateur era. Presumably they all had indulgent, rugby-loving employers!

HARLEQUIN FC CENTENARY 1866-1966

RUGBY FOOTBALL UNION

Right: Harlequins continued to play some home fixtures across the road at Twickenham, including this 1966 encounter with Newport. Scrum-half John Gronow kicks to touch while (*from left to right*) Colin Payne (*behind Gronow*), Paul Harris, Rhys Williams, Grahame Murray and Humphrey Mains look on

Far right: Bob Hiller was a hugely influential player for Quins in the 1960s, eventually becoming captain

Hiller, Lloyd, scrum-half Lewis, wing John Coker and club captain Grahame Murray were also heavily involved with Surrey in a remarkable County Championship – most matches were midweek – with Surrey eventually reaching the final where they shared the title with Durham after first the final at Twickenham and then the replay.

Surrey's route to the final had been extraordinary, requiring a play-off against Middlesex to win the South East Group after they had finished level on points after five games, and then three matches to progress past Cornwall in the semi-final. "It was a financial bonanza for the Counties and they would gladly have kept the final going until late May I suspect," recalls Hiller. "But the players were out on their feet. It was time to

call it a day. Quite a few of us didn't look at a rugby ball for a couple of months after that season ended."

One way or another Hiller, who became Harlequins President in 2002, has been a fixture at the club since the late summer of 1962 when, as a schoolboy who had been playing for Bec Old Boys, he made a considerable impression at a First XV trial.

Studies at Birmingham University and then a year at Oxford, where he was a double Blue, restricted his availability, but as the 1960s progressed Hiller was to become a massively influential player and then captain at Harlequins. He became known worldwide for his metronomic goal-kicking, but in the early years of his career his attacking flair was much to the fore and he emerged as the

key man in the club's Sevens team which reached the semi-finals of the Middlesex Sevens in 1966 and then won the tournament the following year.

Hiller had been earmarked by England's first coach Don White as the man to take the Red Rose forward after years of frustrating underachievement, and Hiller takes the plaudits for a tale concerning England's first squad session under the new regime one misty Sunday morning at Welford Road as they prepared to tackle the Springboks:

"Don was very well respected from his time at Northampton and on that first Sunday he drew us all around in a circle and gave us a rousing team talk about how we were going to be fitter, stronger and better from this point onwards," Hiller explains with a smile. "The bad days were over and England were going to stop being the big under-performers of international rugby and become a real force. He finished by saying 'let's go to work' and ordered us to take up our normal positions. At which point we all went and stood under the posts. A sense of humour always helps in rugby."

While at Harlequins, Hiller not only earned England recognition but he was also selected for the Lions tour of South Africa in 1968 and then, after taking the England captaincy in 1969 and being involved alongside Starmer-Smith and Davis in England's first win over South Africa, an 11–8 victory at Twickenham, he toured Australia and New Zealand in 1971. After his England career ended in 1972, the redoubtable fullback continued playing for the Harlequins First XV for another four years before dropping down to the junior sides where he played regularly until his late 40s.

Overall, the Centenary celebrations had been a triumph, but there had to be a reaction to all the excess – rugby and social – and to the surprise of nobody Harlequins struggled terribly at the start of the 1967–68 season, losing nine of the first 10 games as the club suffered a vicious post-Centenary hangover. The quality players remained, however, and once they regained their fitness and form Quins proved much more formidable, winning 17 of the remaining 24 games, including a rare double over Cardiff and Swansea on the Easter tour of Wales.

The 1960s had been a rollercoaster ride but the club had proven itself as adaptable and resourceful as ever. All looked set fair as the next decade approached, but the 1970s was to prove much more difficult than had been anticipated.

 in the right margin:

Left: Hiller – who became Club President in 2002 – is introduced to RFU President Bill Ramsey. Also pictured are (*from left to right*) Nick Martin, Mike Davis, Nigel Starmer-Smith and Bob Lloyd (*immediately behind Ramsey*)

Centenary Celebrations 1960–1969

CLOSE QUARTERS

HOME SWEET HOME

It might have taken the best part of a century for Harlequins to lay down permanent roots, but the result was definitely worth the wait. The bustling Twickenham Stoop Stadium has become one of the best rugby 'days out' in the country.

With an official capacity of nearly 15,000, The Stoop never lacks for atmosphere. Fans invariably arrive early and leave late and the noise levels match any ground in the game. Adding to the cacophony at

regular intervals is the club's theme tune – *The Mighty Quinn* – played at full volume over the PA system. A number one hit in Britain in 1968 for Manfred Mann, it was originally written and performed by Bob Dylan the year before during his famous Basement Tapes sessions.

The food outlets are many, varied and well-positioned, with a couple of familiar Quins names in evidence – former lock Olly Kohn's delicious 'Jolly Hog' stalls do a roaring trade while Chris Robshaw's coffee shop dispenses welcome cappuccinos and flat whites. The drinks stalls are all easily accessed and the giant public bar

Right: Another packed house at The Stoop

under the East Stand provides a natural gathering spot after a match, with a variety of live bands regularly helping supporters get into the party spirit.

For younger supporters there is a range of activities on offer at the Mighty Quins Village, including face-painting stalls, bouncy castles and giant games, while pupils from nearby schools and community clubs are regularly invited to form the pre-match guard of honour, waving Quins flags when the teams run on to the pitch before kick-off. The club mascots, Harley Bear and Charley Bear, are also much in evidence and love to encourage the crowd.

Of course, a rugby stadium is only as good as its playing surface and The Stoop's all-grass pitch is one of the very best around, draining quickly and efficiently in order to assist Quins' expansive game. While some clubs such as Saracens and Newcastle Falcons have elected to install artificial 4G playing surfaces, given the consistent excellence of The Stoop pitch Harlequins have no current plans to follow suit.

It all adds up to an ideal place to enjoy rugby, with plenty to keep fans of all ages entertained. If you haven't sampled the matchday atmosphere at The Stoop, then there's no time like the present…

Left: There is always a great atmosphere at Harlequins' home ground

Above: Wearing the colours – no mistaking who this fellow supports!

Right: The Stoop has become one of the liveliest matchday venues in the Premiership

Above and left: Some warm up with a lunch and drink in the Players' Lounge, others work up a sweat on the pitch

Opposite: Immovable object meets irresistible force! A young Quins fan tackles the club mascot Harley

Harlequins
Harlequins
Harlequins
Harlequins
Harlequins
Harlequins

Kids of all ages can enjoy their big day at
The Stoop

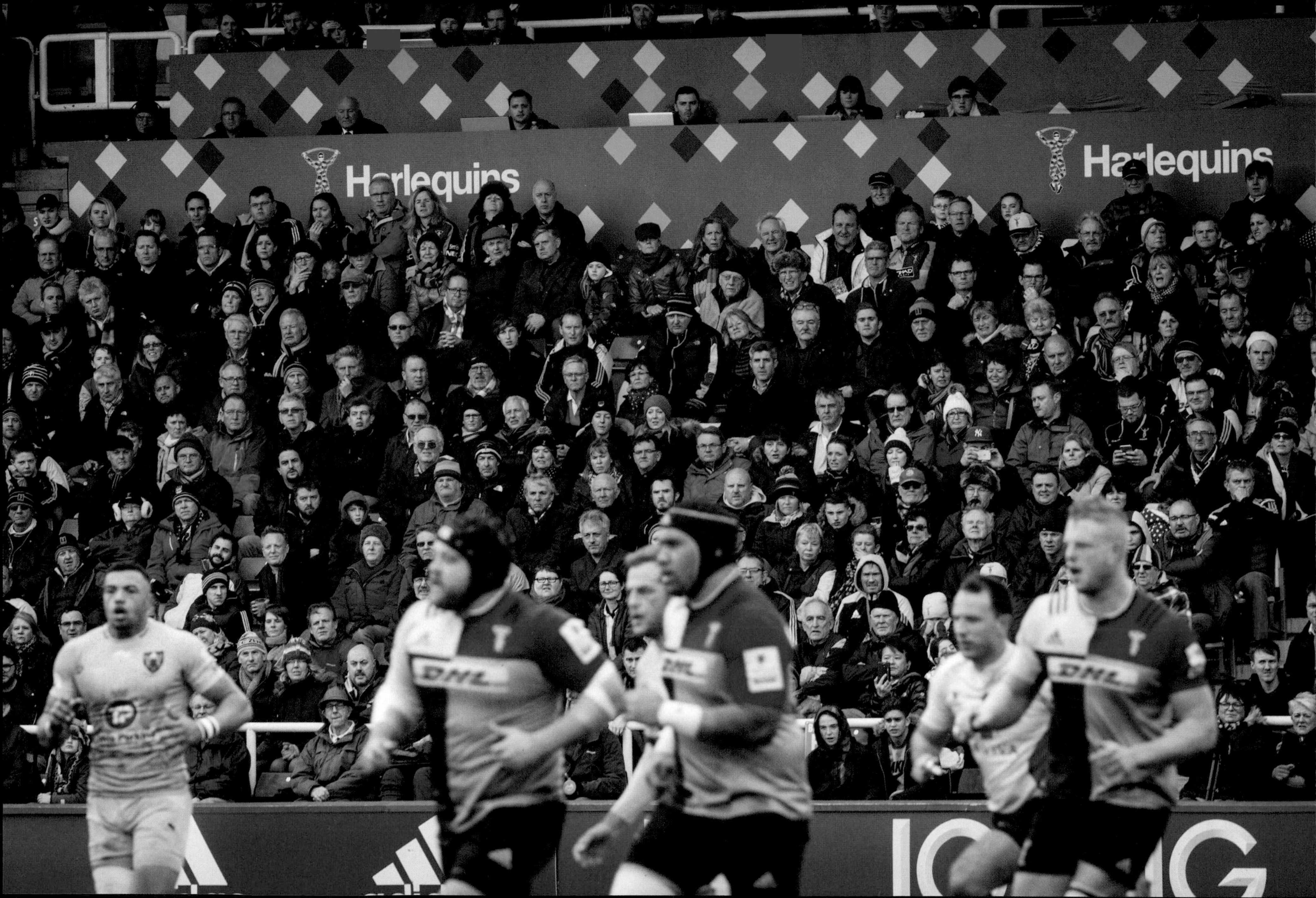
Harlequins
Harlequins
DHL
DHL
DHL

'Oh come all without, come all within, you'll not see nothing like the Mighty Quins!'

123

7

Up for the Cup

1970–1979

7

It is possible to look back at the 1970s with rose-tinted glasses as a golden era for British rugby, and certainly in terms of the British and Irish Lions – with their successes in 1971 and 1974 – and the all-conquering Wales team that is the case. That buoyancy, however, was not reflected in the English club game which was struggling more than a little with Harlequins no exception. This was a fraught period for the club with player availability changing significantly, and although in retrospect the introduction of the RFU cup competition was a huge development for the game at the time, its general reception was initially lukewarm and its impact limited.

Title page: Andre Dent surges forward with the ball, with Everton Weekes in support

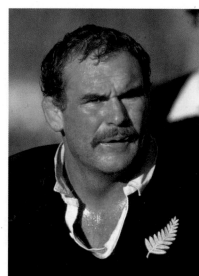

Above: All Black Andy Haden's stint with Harlequins featured a regular commute to Rome

Right: Now Club President, Wavell Wakefield continued to keep a very close watch on proceedings at Quins

The British economy was in a mess for much of the period and harassed employees were much less inclined to take liberties in terms of time off to either play or train. For example, the Armed Forces were contracting and it was not easy for rugby-loving servicemen to make themselves available. Getting leave or fellow officers to cover for you on a Saturday proved much more difficult. Similarly teachers – another rich source of rugby talent over the years – were under increasing pressure with less time to pursue what was still their hobby. The end result was that playing squads fluctuated in strength dramatically and this inevitably bred inconsistency.

However, Harlequins still seemed to possess an X factor. Two big name All Blacks – Peter Whiting and Andy Haden – parachuted in for short but enjoyable periods at the club, with the latter somehow managing to play for Quins on Saturdays and Algilda Rome on Sundays during a stay in Europe after the 1978 All Blacks tour. It is not entirely certain whether his club in Rome were ever fully aware of this arrangement, but Haden managed to avoid injury and the British European Airways service from

Heathrow to Rome on Saturday evenings fortunately never let him down.

A more permanent Kiwi presence came in the shape of former All Blacks fly-half Earle Kirton, who joined the club when he settled in England to study dentistry at Guy's Hospital in London and then set up his practice after retiring from international rugby. Kirton's influence came first as a player, then as the club captain in 1972, and finally as Harlequins' first appointed coach in 1974.

Of course, up until that point the players received coaching but it was generally left to the club captain to organise it himself or delegate the task to one of the physical education graduates in the side. Bob Hiller, having seen how the likes of Don White operated with England, was in effect Quins' quasi-coach for a number of seasons before Kirton's formal appointment, and among other things Hiller introduced prolonged pre-match warm-up routines.

For a while the club managed to hold its own but there was, however, a notably poor run of form between 1972–76 when Quins averaged just over 13 wins a season – not impressive in a fixture list that regularly consisted of 36 or more First XV games.

Generally Harlequins proved lacklustre during this period, although it was still capable of fielding strong teams and there

were occasional outstanding results to set against the general trend. For example, in the 1974–75 season there was a double over Leicester and an unexpected home win over a strong Cardiff side – and yet Quins often managed to lose to lesser teams. In the same season there was also a 10-try victory at Stade Toulasain over a Toulose side which contained Rives, Skrela and Noves amongst its numbers.

Hiller was still a prolific goal-kicker and class act at fullback, and he scored one of the best tries ever seen at Twickenham in the Calcutta Cup game of 1971. Sadly, as England succumbed to a last-minute defeat, Hiller's rounding off of a superb team try is often forgotten. A man who always called a spade a spade, Hiller recalls an amusing shot across the bows around this time from the Club President Wavell Wakefield, who was taking a keen interest in his Harlequins and England career.

"My wife and I were invited to dine – just the two of us – with Wakefield and his wife at their London residence, and very nice it was too," Hiller explains. "Then at the end he extravagantly motioned the ladies to go through into the sitting room and rather conspiratorially pulled the double doors together. He clearly had something to say and eventually he came out with it. The England selectors and certain committee men at the RFU had expressed concern at my rather colourful language on the field of play and this was not befitting the England captain. He himself had also occasionally noticed this tendency with Harlequins. Could I desist? Of course I could. I was guilty as charged. Having got that assurance we re-joined the ladies for coffee."

Nigel Starmer-Smith was still playing at this time, although his availability lessened as a result of his television duties, and Harlequins' well-founded connections with Oxford University had also reaped a rich reward when Peter Dixon started playing for the club. Dixon's form for Oxford and then Quins was such that it earned him a place on that 1971 Lions tour – and three Test starts – before he was capped by England. He briefly succeeded Hiller as the England

Left: Peter Whiting (*centre*) was another All Blacks star who wore the Harlequins shirt during the 1970s

Above: Nigel Starmer-Smith continued to play when his television duties allowed

Right: Peter Dixon briefly captained the club before moving north to Gosforth

Far right: Former Harlequins forward Maurice Trapp went on to become one of the most successful coaches in rugby history with Auckland

captain in 1972 and was a huge loss to Quins when he moved back to the north of England and joined Gosforth, where he was a mainstay and continued playing Test rugby until 1978.

Powerful prop Grahame Murray's playing career for Quins straddled three decades as a first-team regular, and his influence was immense during the 1970s. Murray made his debut at the Recreation Ground in March 1959 on the Easter tour and, with a nice symmetry, bowed out 14 years later against the same opponents at the same ground. In total he made 307 appearances, captaining the side on 80 occasions, including throughout that exhausting 1966–67 Centenary season, and even helped himself to 25 tries en route. Murray was considered very unlucky not to earn an England cap by all his contemporaries (he was actually invited to both England and Scotland trials

on the same day and chose the former, so who knows what might have happened), but such was his impact on the club that Quins members petitioned the committee in 2010 to drop its 'guideline' that indicated that only capped players could be included in the Harlequins Hall of Fame.

Another interesting character in the Quins pack around this time was Maurice Trapp, an honest trooper rather than a stand-out performer in the back five for a number of seasons. Trapp had a considerable rugby brain and had been a member of the fabled Loughborough University team of 1970–71 which provided nine of the England Universities team that thrashed Welsh Universities 33–3 in Cardiff, and as such sat at the feet of revered Loughborough coach Jim Greenwood, who himself had Quins connections having played for the club while doing his National Service with the RAF.

Trapp eventually emigrated to Australia and then New Zealand, where he found himself much in demand as a coach, and by the end of 1986 he was one of three contenders for the prime appointment as Auckland's Head Coach – a young schoolteacher named Graham Henry, later of All Blacks fame, was one of his rivals.

However, Trapp eventually got the nod and the next four years saw him mastermind one of the most successful runs in rugby history, with his all-conquering Auckland side winning 86 and drawing one of their 90 games – a run that included a record 38 consecutive Ranfurly Shield defences. Furthermore, in 2015 he was elected as Vice President of New Zealand Rugby.

Another future Greenwood disciple who was also seen at The Stoop for a year or so while he worked as a local bank clerk before going to Loughborough University was Clive

Woodward, who debuted for the club in 1974. Woodward was mainly a jinking fly-half in those days before he switched to centre.

The big on-going story that provided the narrative for most of the 1970s was the revolutionary introduction – from the 1971–72 season onwards – of an RFU club knockout competition. This became known as the John Player Cup in 1976 when the cigarette manufacturers were prevailed upon to support the competition financially and provide a little profile.

The competition – which later morphed into the Pilkington Cup (1989–97), Tetley's Bitter Cup (1998–2000) and the Powergen Cup (2001–05) – was ultimately to prove a big driver in the modernising and commercialisation of the English club game, although it was a slow burn. Remarkably, even five seasons into the tournament only 7,500 fans turned up at Twickenham for the final between Gosforth and Rosslyn Park, although, as we will see in the next chapter, Harlequins proved supportive right from the off and played a huge role in glamorising the competition in the following decade.

Outwardly the competition seemed to go against the long-held Quins tradition of playing just for fun but the club committed to the tournament from the get-go, as travelling to far-flung destinations and making new rugby friends was definitely part of the Harlequins DNA.

The club was experiencing a reasonable season – 17 wins and 18 defeats – when the cup first started in 1971–72 and could even boast a third 1971 Lion, after Hiller and Dixon, in their ranks. Prop Brian 'Stack' Stevens is a legend of Cornish rugby but had reached a time when he was probably not getting his just rewards in terms of England

caps, so with the blessing of all concerned he started making the 500-mile commute from Penzance to the capital. This was on the not unreasonable assumption that the England selectors would be more likely to pop in at The Stoop or Twickenham than the Mennaye Field in Penzance.

It was only for a year or so but the ploy seemed to work and for three or four seasons he was an England regular, earning 25 caps which included famous home and away wins over South Africa, a victory over the All Blacks in New Zealand and a Test win over Australia.

It all started very encouragingly for Quins in that first cup competition with an impressive 18–4 win down the road at London Scottish, followed by a 12–4 victory over Blackheath in the second round. Suddenly the club was in the quarter-finals and the competitive juices were beginning to flow. Next up was Wilmslow and Quins switched the match to Twickenham to underline the importance of the clash.

Wilmslow were something of a mystery to most rugby fans in the south-east, but not for Quins as the Wanderers side had been playing them for some time. Packed full of Cheshire County players and with future England scrum-half Steve Smith among its ranks – playing whenever he was not needed by Loughborough University – the club was enjoying a golden period in its history and had already beaten Liverpool and Birkenhead Park en route to the quarter-finals. Come the big day Wilmslow duly won 17–6 at the home of English rugby, which was a chastening experience for Harlequins and a wake-up call for English club rugby in general. Hiller remembers the day very well:

"The result was bad enough but after the game I was buttonholed by a lady member of

TWICKENHAM

SEASON 1975-76

1975				Kick-off
Sat.	Sept.	13	Harlequins v. Northampton	3.00
,,	,,	20	Harlequins v. Llanelli	3.00
,,	,,	27	Harlequins v. Leicester	3.00
,,	Oct.	4	Harlequins v. Swansea	3.00
,,	,,	11	Harlequins v. Gloucester	2.45
,,	,,	18	Harlequins v. Rosslyn Park	2.45
,,	,,	25	Harlequins v. Cardiff	2.45
,,	Nov.	1	Harlequins v. Bristol	2.30
,,	,,	8	LONDON COUNTIES v. AUSTRALIA	2.30
,,	,,	15	Harlequins v. Oxford University	2.30
,,	,,	22	Harlequins v. Cambridge University	2.30
,,	,,	29	Harlequins v. London Welsh	2.15
Tues.	Dec.	9	OXFORD v. CAMBRIDGE	2.15
Sat.	,,	13	Harlequins v. Waterloo	2.15
,,	,,	20	ENGLAND v. THE REST	2.15
1976				
Sat.	Jan.	3	*ENGLAND v. AUSTRALIA	2.15
,,	,,	17	*ENGLAND v. WALES	2.30
,,	,,	24	Harlequins v. Royal Air Force	2.45
,,	,,	31	Harlequins v. London Scottish	2.45
,,	Feb.	21	THE ARMY v. ROYAL AIR FORCE	3.00
,,	Mar.	6	*ENGLAND v. IRELAND	3.00
,,	,,	10	Universities Athletic Union Final	3.00
,,	,,	13	ROYAL NAVY v. THE ARMY	3.00
,,	,,	27	ROYAL NAVY v. ROYAL AIR FORCE	3.00
Wed.	Apl.	7	R.F.S.U. (19 Group) England v. Japan	3.00
Sat.	,,	24	R.F.U. Club Competition Final	3.00
Sat.	May	8	Middlesex Seven-A-Side Finals	12.40

Wilmslow in the committee lounge at Twickenham, who explained at great length how unjust was the reputation they – Wilmslow – had of being a rather snooty and aloof club on the northern circuit. I was rather conscious of the irony of the situation in view of the circumstances in which the conversation was taking place.

"My initial sympathy was tempered somewhat, however, when we went back to The Stoop Memorial Ground only to find one of the Wilmslow committee had parked his helicopter on the running track right in front of the clubhouse. Later that evening several of our opponents' officials downed their beers and took off in the helicopter, with lights flashing, directly past the noses of the

Above: The background to this picture of Clive Woodward in action for Harlequins in 1975 sums up how far rugby has come, due in no small part to what he would later achieve in coaching England to World Cup glory in 2003

Opposite: Harlequins take on London Welsh during the mid-1970s at a packed Old Deer Park

dejected Quins supporters drinking in the upstairs bar. That was certainly a black day for the club as we were forced to concede we had been out-Harlequinned in every department."

Furthermore Quins did not even qualify for the John Player Cup the subsequent year – in those early experimental seasons clubs were required to win the County Cup tournament to qualify for the following campaign's RFU club competition. This was an unsatisfactory arrangement as not all clubs entered their respective County Cup, while counties with a large number of senior clubs, such as Middlesex or Surrey, could still only qualify

one team. It was abolished a few seasons down the line when the so-called 'big clubs' were given a bye into the third round in the same way as the FA Cup is run in football.

However, Harlequins found itself back in action in the 1973–74 competition and once again the victim in a famous David and Goliath victory, with Orrell administering a painful 25–7 drubbing at Edge Hall Road in the first round. At the time Orrell were possibly even less well known than Wilmslow, but the Lancastrians were at the start of a dramatic surge that for a brief period would make them one of the strongest clubs in Britain. Victory over Quins was very much a

taste of things to come and, in fact, was a huge part of the process as it put the club on the map and made it easier to attract quality players in the north-west. Hiller again takes up the story:

"The introduction of the John Player Cup proved to be a considerable culture shock to many of the major clubs, who found themselves travelling to previously unvisited parts of the country to play against teams they had barely heard of. Many of these new encounters proved to be humorous or catastrophic, and sometimes both.

"Our trip to far-flung Orrell needed to be planned with the precision of an overseas tour and taxed our administrators to the limit. My off-the-cuff, supposedly humorous, comment about their ground being situated on a lay-by off the M6 came back to haunt me over the years and it certainly did much to galvanise the efforts of the Orrell players. The outcome was almost inevitable, a heavy defeat, and many of our players claimed their poor performance was due to jetlag.

"The result was obviously a great disappointment to us but the hospitality was wonderful and we made new friendships at an amazing club and rugby community in a part of the world where we didn't normally play. The day was enjoyed by all, irrespective of the result, and to my generation at least that was what rugby was still all about."

Quins continued to endure very mixed fortunes in the cup throughout the decade and it was not until the 1976–77 season before they featured again, this time losing 17–9 to Gloucester at Kingsholm. But the following season the club finally got another run together under the captaincy of David (D A) Cooke, a very useful centre who won four England caps.

Right: A match ticket from Gosforth v Harlequins in 1979

GOSFORTH FOOTBALL CLUB

John Player Cup - 2nd Round
Gosforth v. Harlequins

SATURDAY, 24th FEBRUARY, 1979
Kick off 2.30 p.m.

New Ground, Great North Road, Gosforth

Admission to Ground & Stand £1.50

Below: Terry Claxton (*far right*) in action for London

This time Quins made a good start by winning 19–6 at United Services Portsmouth before overcoming a strong London Irish outfit 17–15 at home, followed by an 18–6 victory over Liverpool at The Stoop. The club had reached the semi-final for the first time, but that is where the run sadly came to an end following another tough visit to Kingsholm to play Gloucester. This time the Cherry and Whites won 12–6 and subsequently went on to win the cup a couple of weeks later after defeating Leicester 6–3 in the final at Twickenham.

The following season was less successful as Quins tumbled out in the second round at Gosforth after beating Plymouth Albion in the first round. However, 12 months later the club mounted another stern challenge, this time under the determined captaincy of prop Terry Claxton.

The appointment of a lorry driver as captain at Quins seemed to tickle the fancy of the media, which had always liked to pigeonhole the club as toffs, but Claxton and his brother, Micky, were hardcore and much-respected Harlequins members along with a third brother, Gary, who also played for the club. Terry took over a couple of months into the season when the elected captain Adrian Alexander suddenly turned professional with rugby league club Oldham after six seasons' hard work in the Quins back row. Alexander later enjoyed a brief spell with the ill-fated Kent Invicta.

This move, it has to be said, had its occasional diehard critic. Former Club Secretary Major Jay (H J) Gould would sit on his own in the North Stand at Twickenham Stadium rather than sit with the committee in the main stand as a protest at Claxton's appointment!

Under Claxton Quins put a useful run together, beginning with a 23–6 win over near neighbours Esher, followed by another 23–6 victory away to Nottingham and an immensely satisfying 9–3 win over Gosforth in the quarter-finals. A final at Twickenham seemed within the club's grasp but again it was thwarted, this time by Leicester who went on to win the competition. It was a disappointing but positive end to a decade of fluctuating fortunes.

Historically, an upswing in Quins' fortunes is often mirrored by the club doing well in the Middlesex Sevens, and thus their was much delight when, after an 11-year gap, the club won the Russell Cargill Trophy in 1978.

Cambridge University Blue Gordon Wood was the flyer in the side, captained by Cooke, and the powerful Alexander was a key man up front – in fact it was probably his performances in the Sevens that alerted the rugby league scouts. The very solid Colin Lambert, a former schoolboy Sevens star with Normanton, was another very quick man but opted to play in the front row rather than his usual position out on the wing, a decision that paid dividends. At the time of writing, Lambert still holds the club record for the number of tries (eight) scored in a single match.

Local rivals Richmond had won the trophy in three of the preceding four years, but Harlequins proved imperious and, after accounting for London Irish, Hawick and London Welsh, scored eight tries in the final to hammer Rosslyn Park 40–12.

Sadly, this Middlesex Sevens win, unlike some in the club's history, did not herald a new golden era with an accompanying wave of exciting talent waiting to come through. Instead, though the club always retained its ability to have fun and be happy in its work, the 1970s had been a struggle and something of an eye-opener. There were ambitious so-called 'junior' clubs out there who had sensed the sea change that the cup had brought into the game and were getting stronger with each season. Quins was still a senior club and a name that resonated throughout the game, but from this point onwards rugby was changing so quickly that nothing could be taken for granted.

Left: Defeat to Leicester in the 1979–80 John Player Cup semi-final at Twickenham, captured on a set of photographic contact sheets and including a fly-past by Concorde as it comes in to land at nearby Heathrow

TROPHY CABINET

Historically Harlequins rugby has never been just about winning trophies, but a tangible reward for effort expended is certainly always welcome!

For decades it was success in the Middlesex Sevens that seemed to inspire the club, then came the John Player and Pilkington Cups, the latter a rather diminutive if hard-earned glass trophy.

The European Challenge Shield in 2001 is comfortably the biggest trophy the club has ever won, while the most recent was the LV= Cup in 2013, but pride of place definitely goes to the 2011–12 Premiership trophy.

MIDDLESEX SEVENS
1926, 1927, 1928, 1929, 1933, 1935, 1967, 1978, 1986, 1987, 1988, 1989, 1990, 2008

JOHN PLAYER CUP
1988

PILKINGTON CUP
1991

**EUROPEAN CHALLENGE
SHIELD**
2001

PARKER PEN & AMLIN
CHALLENGE CUP
2004, 2011

NATIONAL LEAGUE
DIVISION ONE
2005–06

POWERGEN NATIONAL
TROPHY
2006

AVIVA PREMIERSHIP
2011–12

LV= CUP
2013

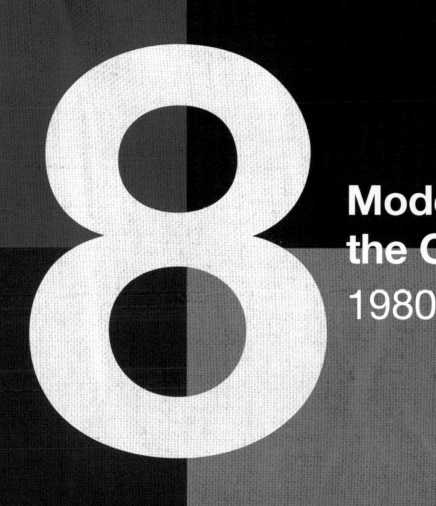

8

**Modernising
the Club**

1980–1989

8

The 1980s were a decade of great change in English rugby, as not only did the John Player Cup gather momentum as an event but the game itself also moved inexorably towards the establishment of a league system. And with each campaign growing increasingly competitive, the debate about whether elite players should turn professional or not began in earnest.

Title page: Paul Jackson dives over for a try against Leicester in 1986

Above: Roger Looker (top) and Colin Herridge saw the club through a crucial period

There was a lot going on as the biggest clubs in the land tried to deal with the shifting landscape, and Quins undoubtedly owe a huge debt to Roger Looker and Colin Herridge for their work in modernising the club throughout the period. Without their timely arrival and monumental input the modern-day history of Harlequins might have been significantly different.

Looker – an England prospect at prop in his playing days – retired from rugby at the age of 24 to pursue a career as a lawyer and businessman, but he never lost his love for the game and brought considerable business and legal expertise during his tenures as Honorary Secretary and Club Chairman. Likewise Herridge, another businessman who has served in many roles at Harlequins including Chairman of Rugby, Club Secretary, Vice Chairman and Chairman of the Trustees. He was also an RFU member and, for the best part of seven years, the RFU's press liaison man – an unpaid job in those days! Sadly, Looker died of cancer in 2014 but Herridge remembers those tumultuous and turbulent years at Harlequins:

"I was the Team Secretary at Surrey and John Young, the famous Quins wing, was Chairman and recruited me while we were accompanying a Surrey tour of South Africa and Rhodesia. Ricky Bartlett had sadly died and in 1979 Harlequins needed a chairman of their Rugby Playing Committee and I was very happy to oblige. I had always liked Quins and their approach to the game and life. In no time at all they also needed a new secretary when Roger [Looker] had to move to the USA for a year or so with his job, and that was a big undertaking – the equivalent of the CEO's job these days.

"I decided to accept that job in 1981 and it proved a very enjoyable, if occasionally stressful, 13-year stint before I stepped down as Secretary in 1994. Luckily when Roger returned from New York he was installed as Chairman and was a huge influence as we tried to drive through a few changes.

"We tried to sharpen up on a number of fronts. With Earle Kirton in the vanguard we became very proactive in recruiting from junior clubs in Surrey and Middlesex. It was Earle who had brought Adrian Alexander and the Claxton brothers – Terry, Micky and Gary – to the club. The steady drip-feed of talent from the Services and Oxbridge was beginning to dry up and it was time to get out there and sell ourselves to talented players. The team started to take on a much more egalitarian look.

"Alongside that we made it easier to become a member; it would take just two to three weeks instead of two to three months to join. All members were allowed to wear a tie, whereas in the past only players and former players enjoyed that privilege.

"We started to take a serious look at merchandising – jerseys, jumpers, tracksuits and memorabilia – and over the years that has become a significant factor in the club's finances. With the famous club colours and club logo we had plenty to work with and the former Quins wing Hugh Forbes did a good job of building this up when he came back from Malaysia, where he had settled and captained the national rugby team.

"Another issue was that the First XV were still playing a good proportion of their games at Twickenham, especially before Christmas, which was a two-edged sword. The prospect of playing at 'HQ' was quite useful in recruiting, but it fostered a 'club within a club' scenario with players and some fans staying over at Twickenham for a drink. We were very keen to totally eliminate that and make The Stoop the focus for everybody.

"To do that we really had to improve the ground and facilities. We fought a 10-year battle with the local council to get permission to take up the athletics track which had lain dormant for a long time and had weeds and plants growing up through the surface.

"By installing temporary stands we could get the capacity up to 3–4,000, but we needed more than that and, finally, early in the 1990s, we got permission for the East Stand to go up."

Harlequins had held their own for a couple of seasons in the early '80s but were poor in the 1984–85 season, losing over half of their games. Happily there was an upswing in fortunes after that, which was just as well because the advent of professional rugby was just around the corner and a long-term dip in form could well have seen the club miss the boat altogether.

At one stage former Quins lock Mike Davis, who had masterminded England's Grand Slam in 1980, took up the role of honorary coach after he had stepped down from international duties in 1982.

"In retrospect it wasn't my wisest decision," recalls Davis. "I was too stretched in various directions to do the job justice, but I was keen to help out if possible. I had just taken on a house mastership at Sherborne and I would drive up from Dorset for training on Monday and Wednesday nights and get back just before midnight and still have a fair bit of paperwork to do with the school. I was burning the candle at both ends.

"It was still tremendously enjoyable, though. The club was making big efforts to move with the times and

was recruiting good players, but it had retained a great family atmosphere and there was still that tradition of at least trying to accomplish things with a healthy dose of style and panache.

"Quins was, and always has been, a really good place to play and watch your rugby,

Left: Graham Birkett lifts the Wavell Wakefield Sevens Trophy while sporting the new-style Harlequins shirt, complete with Bukta logo and cross-stitching (below)

Right: Mike Davis showing the passion that made him a top coach, albeit only briefly for Harlequins

and although I reluctantly concluded that I couldn't have my cake and eat it, I continued to help out with the U21s, Wanderers and even the Firsts occasionally on a more ad hoc basis.

"We did have patchy results but you could see the potential and you could also see that Dick Best was in the pipeline, so to speak, and would soon be a very good coach indeed.

"The role of the coach was becoming more important and this contrasted hugely with my playing days. When I was packing down for Quins we didn't have a coach, but Bob Hiller did a very good impression of one and introduced the dreaded warm-up out there on the pitch. Like all us schoolmasters, Bob enjoyed nothing more than getting people running around, and some of our warm-ups seemed to last 30–40 minutes. I treasure one dressing room conversation before a match when our prop, Grahame Murray, told Bob: 'Skipper, I can give you the warm-up and the first half, or I can give you the first half and second half. I could even give you the warm-up and the second half. But there is no way on this earth I can give you a warm-up, first half and second half!'"

The big debate in the early-to-mid-1980s was whether the RFU would introduce leagues or not. There was much instinctive opposition within the RFU, yet even a conservative union like Scotland had long since organised its top clubs into a league structure. It was what the players and the fans wanted, but initially the RFU came up with a horrible halfway house: Merit Tables.

Merit Tables were a curious compromise whereby top clubs – or at least clubs considered to be elite by the RFU – were grouped together in Merit Table A, which took in southern England, and Merit Table B,

which incorporated the top teams in the Midlands and North. The results of their traditional fixtures were recorded and positions within the table were decided on a percentage basis because invariably teams finished the season having played a different number of fixtures.

The Merit Tables were unnecessarily complicated and much derided but were important in one key respect – when the quantum leap was made in the 1987–88

season to form a properly constituted 'Courage League', the top six teams in Merit Table A and B were lumped together to form 'Courage National League One', in effect what we would consider to be the modern-day Premiership.

It was a big moment in rugby union history and it was Quins, who had never taken the Merit Tables particularly seriously, who argued successfully with the RFU that the top six positions that would determine

the clubs going into the Courage League should be computed using the results across the last three seasons. Everybody knew the situation going into the final season before the foundation of the league and Quins just made the top six ahead of London Welsh – in retrospect, a hugely significant moment in the history of both clubs.

The original 12 teams to form the league were Bath, Bristol, Coventry, Gloucester, Harlequins, Leicester, Moseley, Nottingham,

Above: The Harlequins squad assemble for the first ever Courage League season in 1987–88

Above: Leicester's Dean Richards outjumps the Harlequins pack during the 1985–86 John Player Cup quarter-final

failed to complete all their fixtures, while both Quins and Bristol asked for their 1988 John Player Cup Final at Twickenham to count as their league match.

Quins finished third in that inaugural campaign, a fine performance, but the following season proved less successful, finishing eighth with five wins out of 11 games as Bath claimed the title. It was much the same in 1989–90 as Quins recorded six wins out of 11 to finish seventh, with Wasps clinching the silverware. Relegation was never an issue but after that initial season Quins quickly gained a reputation as a solid mid-table team.

It was left to the John Player Cup to deliver Quins' moment of glory during the '80s, albeit success certainly did not arrive overnight. In the 1980–81 season the club suffered the disappointment of losing 20–9 at home to old rivals Rosslyn Park, although Park were a very strong side during this period. The following season was a little more encouraging, although it ended with a 24–12 quarter-final defeat at Coventry, still very much a power in the land at the time.

Revenge was sweet in the 1983–84 competition, though, when Harlequins beat Coventry 24–16 at Coundon Road in the quarter-final. At the time this felt like a breakthrough performance, but Quins subsequently came up against a gnarly Bristol side at the Memorial Ground in the semi-final and, although the team performed well, slipped to an unlucky 21–18 defeat. Close but still no cigar.

The barren run continued for a few more seasons, with a 31–12 quarter-final pounding at Gloucester in 1984–85 and a 15–8 quarter-final defeat at home to Leicester the following year. Worse was to follow in 1986–87 as the

club was knocked out early after a 12–10 defeat to old northern rivals Orrell. The result was frustrating, but there were reasons for optimism emerging around the club – Orrell away was always going to be a massive test and a young and maturing side would undoubtedly profit from the experience.

The 1987–88 season saw that impression confirmed. It started with a comfortable but low-key 40–0 win over junior club Maidenhead and ended in triumph with John Olver lifting the trophy high at Twickenham after a thrilling 28–22 victory over Bristol – Harlequins' first 'national' trophy of any description in the club's history. (The Middlesex Sevens is not considered to be a 'national' competition as it was essentially based in London, with a couple of invitees from the regions or Wales and Scotland.)

Although 1987–88 was the first season of the Courage League, the John Player Cup had been identified as a key target for Harlequins from the start of the campaign – the club clearly believing that it was high time it stamped its mark on the competition. After their initial win over Maidenhead, the team faced a tricky visit to Berry Hill, renowned cup fighters from the Forest of Dean who had pulled off an impressive 13–10 win at London Welsh in the previous round. It was a tough assignment but Quins had experience of away trips to previously unknown clubs by now and produced a rock solid performance at the Recreation Ground in Coleford, advancing to the next round thanks to an impressive 17–4 win.

Next came the quarter-final against a powerful-looking Waterloo team stacked with Lancashire players, but Quins really moved up through the gears and enjoyed a crushing 37–4 win with Jamie Salmon – the team's

Orrell, Sale, Wasps and Waterloo. The first season proved somewhat haphazard – there was no structured league fixture list and clubs were expected to arrange matches, both home and away, themselves. The results were unsurprising – four teams, champions Leicester, Gloucester, Bristol and Waterloo,

first-choice goal-kicker – amassing 23 points. The joy after the final whistle was accentuated later that evening with news of Bath's shock 4–3 defeat to Moseley. Bath had won the competition the previous four seasons and this surprise result gave hope to the remaining clubs in the competition.

Nevertheless, Wasps away in the semi-final was a very tough prospect indeed. Coach Dick Best had decided that the way forward was to dominate their old rivals up front because Wasps, losing finalists in the previous two seasons, had gathered a back division capable of cutting teams to shreds. At Monday night training before the match the Quins pack did nothing but live scrummaging practice for the best part of 90 minutes – one survivor of the session reckons the official count was 70 scrums – and come match day Quins certainly dominated in that department. Wasps' runners were still extremely dangerous, however, and at the end of 80 minutes at Sudbury the scores were level at 16–16.

Extra-time and the drama of knock-out rugby was the competition's *raison d'etre*, and in the case of Andrew Harriman and Richard Moon it was cometh the hour, cometh the men. Wasps were attacking and, with a two-man overlap, looked certain to score when Harriman went for broke and flung out an arm. The ball stuck and he set sail up field, and although the scrambling Wasps defence managed to block his way, a well-timed pass to Moon saw the speedy scrum-half sprint in for the decisive score.

Elsewhere, Bristol had made its way to the final via wins against Bedford, Richmond, Sale and Moseley, and boasted a formidable pack in addition to dangerous outside runners such as Ralph Knibbs, John Carr and

Jonathan Webb – the latter a very accomplished goal-kicker. The match certainly caught the imagination of the public and the 37,000-strong crowd was a considerable increase on any previous cup final. In retrospect, this was the match and occasion that elevated the cup competition to an entirely different level.

The two sides seemed evenly matched on paper, and so it proved on the pitch. Quins came tearing out of the blocks and raced into a seemingly unassailable 18–0 half-time lead with two sumptuous tries. Will Carling scored the first after great attacking work from Everton Davis and good handling from the two locks, Neil Edwards and Paul Ackford, with the latter giving the scoring pass. The second try came from a scrum, with Salmon running a loop in the centre for Harriman to score.

These were halcyon early days for Carling who had joined the club 18 months earlier, initially on the recommendation of Mike Weston, the England Chairman of Selectors, while studying at Durham University on an Army scholarship. During his last year at Durham, Carling regularly attended at least one midweek training session at The Stoop, getting back to Durham at 3am the next morning on the milk train before repeating the 500-mile round-trip at weekends to play. Despite missing out on the 1987 World Cup, Carling's career was accelerating and in January 1988 he made his England debut. Following the John Player Cup triumph he toured Fiji and Australia with England before being appointed England captain for the autumn international against Australia.

At 18–0 the match looked well won, but Bristol – in their centenary season – had no intention of quitting and fought back

superbly with a try from Huw Duggan and a penalty try. With just 15 minutes left the score was 21–19. Bristol also had a 40-metre drop-goal attempt by Simon Hogg unluckily disallowed by referee Fred Howard which just about everybody else on the pitch, including the Quins players, thought had probably squeezed over.

Then came the moment of the match, a brilliant 80-metre counter-attack from Harlequins with Stuart Thresher, Harriman, Davis and Salmon all handling before Carling sprinted over. It was a spectacular way to round off a cracking game and in no time a beaming Olver was walking up the steps to the Royal Box to receive the trophy.

"I always look on that cup success in 1988 as a big milestone in Quins history," reflects Herridge. "It was a validation of the way the club had been progressing, but it was also a calling card if you like. It said we intended to be a big factor in this evolving modern game. Club membership went up, merchandising increased again and it was also easier to recruit top players because they could see what was happening and also liked the brand of rugby the team was playing. It was a thrilling game and we won playing the Quins way.

"It all nearly ended in tears though. After the match and the initial celebrations at Twickenham, the RFU Secretary, Dudley Wood, asked me to be responsible for the cup over the rest of the weekend, thinking that perhaps I was a sober and upright citizen. A long night followed and we ended up in the Albert pub near my home in Esher, celebrating until late. It all got very hazy but after getting home I woke up in a cold sweat at 3am. Where was the cup? I hadn't brought it home. It had to be at the Albert, surely?

I couldn't sleep and at 7am I was back at the Albert banging loudly on the front door. I'm not quite sure what the neighbours made of it but eventually the landlord, Bruce, appeared brandishing the silverware and said, 'I think you are looking for this, Colin. Come in and have a coffee, you look dreadful.'"

> ### JOHN PLAYER SPECIAL CUP FINAL 1988
> ## Harlequins 28 Bristol 22
> ### (Twickenham)
>
> **Harlequins:** S Thresher; A Harriman, J Salmon, W Carling, E Davis; A Thompson, R Moon; P Curtis, J Olver, A Mullins, N Edwards, P Ackford, M Skinner, T Bell, R Langhorn
> **Tries:** Carling (2), Harriman **Conversions:** Thresher, Salmon **Penalties:** Salmon (3), Thresher
>
> **Bristol:** J Webb; R Knibbs, D Thomas, H Duggan, J Carr, ; S Hogg, R Harding; C Phillips, D Palmer, R Doubleday, N Pomphrey, A Blackmore, A Dun, W Hone, P Collings
> **Tries:** Duggan, Penalty Try **Conversion:** Webb
> **Penalties:** Webb (3) **Drop-Goal:** Knibbs
>
> **Referee:** F Howard (Liverpool)
> **Attendance:** 37,000

It has previously been mentioned what an important showpiece occasion the now-defunct Middlesex Sevens competition provided for Harlequins. This was definitely the case between 1986–90 when the club won an extraordinary five Russell Cargill Trophies on the bounce. Training for, winning and then dominating the competition became a big focus during this era and an important component in the development of the club.

Opposite: Andy Harriman races clear of a despairing Bristol dive to score during the 1987–88 John Player Special Cup triumph

Left: The club's first major cup final proved to be a great day out for the Harlequins supporters

Above: John Olver lifts the cup but, typically, Micky Skinner takes centre stage

Right: Rob Glenister was a key cog in Quins' Sevens machine, the club winning the Middlesex Sevens in 1989 and 1990

The modern-day rugby fan might be tempted to dismiss the Sevens tournament as a bit of a sideshow, but for decades the competition was much more than that. Before leagues and cups became the be-all and end-all, the Middlesex Sevens was the one chance for senior clubs to compete for a trophy, and off the back of that it became a

gala occasion that attracted 60–70,000-strong crowds to Twickenham on the last Saturday of the season. It was a long time before the John Player Cup, in its various guises, ever matched these audiences, with 30,000 more fans watching Quins beat Bristol in the 1988 Middlesex Sevens Final at Twickenham than had watched the two sides contest the John Player Cup just seven days earlier at the same venue. The competition also commanded long hours of live TV coverage during an era when that was still comparatively rare for rugby.

"For a group of us who enjoyed Sevens, the toughest training of the entire year came in April when we used to have a Sevens session with Dick Best every Wednesday night," recalls Peter Winterbottom, who played in two of those Middlesex winning teams in 1989 and 1990. "Some of those sessions were murderous and we would play three or four warm-up tournaments before Middlesex.

"Dick was unusual in that not only was he a very good Fifteens coach but he also 'got' Sevens. He had played for Quins at the Middlesex Sevens in years gone by, so he knew what was required and what positions you needed your athletes in. And he was always happy to experiment. We used to play our tall fullback from Fifteens, Stuart Thresher, as a prop to give us a line out presence in the forwards, and I seem to remember that Craig Luxton, normally a scrum-half, hooked for us one year.

"Adrian Thompson was the ringmaster, along with Rob Glenister, and speed men like Andrew Harriman and Everton Davis were untouchable. Simon Hunter had wheels as well. I think Andrew was clocked at 20.9 seconds for the 200 metres one year. He was our real cutting edge and players like him made it worth your while grovelling around

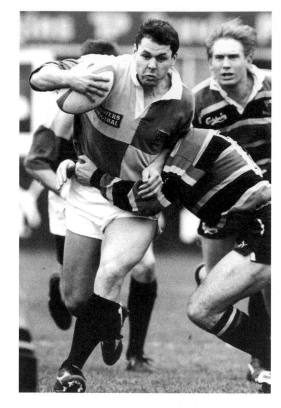

the park trying to win some ball. John Olver was very good with the ball in hand and a great Sevens player. Will Carling gave it a good rip one year and was very impressive, Micky Skinner as well. I don't think we ever got Jason Leonard involved though.

"I probably wasn't the most natural Sevens player in the world but I enjoyed the way Quins made a virtue of them. It was never a chore. I benefited from the extra fitness work and even in the latter stages of my career I definitely felt my handling skills improved as a result of playing Sevens, which was a vital ingredient, I believe, in prolonging my England career. They were great days and a good opportunity for Quins supporters to wear the club colours and make some noise over at Twickenham."

Quins' historic run started in 1986 when they defeated Nottingham 18–10 in the final and Micky 'The Munch' Skinner announced himself to the rugby world with a couple of big hits and barnstorming runs. Skinner might have started his career at Blaydon and finished at Blackheath, but for six seasons he was a galvanising force of nature at Quins with his hard-edged Geordie approach adding real steel to the club's effort up front. His tackling was often off the Richter scale and he was a much better ball player than he is given credit for.

Skinner was known for his trademark loud waistcoats off the pitch and often wore a bespoke Quins version displaying the club's many colours. Away from rugby he was – and remains – a computer wizard and was prone to be called in by the Met Police at ungodly hours to fix the latest glitch in their equipment. He earned 21 England caps in his career, but Skinner is not a player you remember by statistics; he is an individual you always recall by the impact he made on and off the field.

In 1987 Skinner was again a force to be reckoned with up front, while Hunter enjoyed a big day and Harriman was again unstoppable. A crowd of nearly 70,000 stayed on to watch the final and were keenly anticipating the head-to-head between Harriman and Rosslyn Park quick man Martin Offiah, who many claimed was just as fast. Alas both went off injured early in the game and Quins went on to win 22–6.

The following year Quins won a second final match-up against Bristol, with captain Andre Dent's side clinching a thrilling spectacle 20–18. To the delight of the fans, this was the tournament when, for the only time ever, Quins featured all three fliers –

Harriman, Davis and Hunter – in their starting line-up. In 1989, with Best choosing to spread the workload around, Quins fielded an entirely new squad and still won, beating Rosslyn Park 18–12 in a tense final. Winterbottom was fully on board now and packed down alongside Chris Sheasby, who went on to become a prominent member of the England Sevens squad that won the inaugural World Championship Sevens a few years later. Harriman was another Quin who starred for England in that competition at Murrayfield.

Finally in 1990, with Carling in the squad, Quins swept everybody aside en route to the final. Here Quins met old rivals Rosslyn Park, a side augmented by a good contingent of former Quins Sevens stars such as Dent, Thompson, Hunter and Alex Woodhouse. Carling was in exceptional form all day and scored two tries in Quins' 26–10 victory in the final, although there was a comic moment much enjoyed by all and sundry when Hunter and Woodhouse held the England centre up in the deadball area, preventing him from going to ground and scoring a try.

Save for a win in 2008 that was pretty much the last hurrah for Quins as the tournament suffered with the onset of professionalism, eventually ceasing to exist in 2011. However, it was magnificent while it lasted. The Sevens consistently provided a focus for the club over nine decades and an outlet for their promising youngsters before academies had ever been dreamt of, while the club's array of naturally gifted and extrovert players relished the chance to shine with the extra space available. All in all, the Middlesex Sevens served Quins – and the wider game – very well indeed.

Victorious! Richard Lawrence (*left*), John Olver and Simon Hunter (*right*) lift the trophy following another Middlesex Sevens triumph in 1986

CLOSE QUARTERS

ALL THE PRESIDENT'S MEN

As part of the 150th anniversary celebration of Harlequins players past and present, the club's President Bob Hiller has selected a Quins team of the ages – a fantasy XV to take on the world and win in style.

"As hospital passes go this is right up there," says Hiller. "Selection is always difficult enough as it is, but where do you start when you have got 150 years' worth of players to choose from? Some will have been professional, many amateur, some long-term club members, while others will have made a big impression in a short space of time before moving on.

"In the end I gave myself some strict guidelines. For the starting XV I've limited myself to England-qualified players who represented Harlequins over a considerable period of time and who contributed significantly to the club. On the bench I've widened the net and considered the many brilliant overseas players who have passed through our ranks for shorter periods of time, some fleetingly during the amateur days and others as contracted professionals.

"You will notice that, with the cunning that all selectors are known for, my self-imposed guidelines enable me to pick Nick Evans at fly-half in the starting XV as he became a British citizen some time ago and could theoretically have put himself forward for international consideration for England – although, of course, as a proud All Black he would never do that!

"Like most selectors I will have undoubtedly made a massive howler somewhere by missing a glaringly obvious candidate, and for this I apologise in advance. And like many selectors – certainly England selectors in the '60s and '70s – I would possibly pick a very different XV next week. Anybody who needs to discuss this selection further during our 150th anniversary season can find me at the bar after most home matches!"

BOB HILLER'S HARLEQUINS TEAM OF THE AGES

15. Mike Brown

There have been some pretty good fullbacks at Quins over the years and for a long time I had Ireland's Jim Staples and England's John Willcox on level pegging. But then Mike Brown came along. I love Mike's aggression and passion for the game, whether that be playing for Quins or England. He's got a massive left boot, is brilliant under the high ball, brave in the tackle and a natural try-scorer. Furthermore, Mike came up through the Quins academy and is a credit to the club.

14. Dan Lambert

We used to moan about England selectors in my time but spare a thought for Dan Lambert, who was dropped after his debut in 1907 despite scoring five tries against the French. A big, strong, fast man, Adrian Stoop plucked Dan from the Wanderers' pack and converted him into a winger, one who was clearly a formidable opponent in full flight and a good goal-kicker as well. J C Gibbs and J R C Young were also both serious speed merchants who only narrowly miss out.

13. Will Greenwood

I'm completely spoiled for choice at centre with Bob Lloyd, Jamie Salmon and Will Carling to name just three prime candidates, but I've opted for Will Greenwood. A World Cup winner in 2003 who was a sumptuous player in midfield, he always had time on the ball, was very creative and capable of scoring a try for himself. Playing outside him would be a joy.

12. Adrian Stoop

Stoop could play anywhere in the backs, although fly-half was his preferred position and from where he was capped and revolutionised the game. Everything I have heard about Stoop, and from what he wrote himself, leads me to think he would be a sensational modern-day 12, the second playmaker and alternative kicker from hand. Wakefield would captain the team but Stoop would definitely 'run' the backs!

11. Ronnie Poulton-Palmer

One of the immortals of English rugby, Poulton-Palmer could just as easily be picked at centre, but with the creativity of Greenwood and Stoop inside him he would cause carnage on the wing. Reading his father's wonderful biographical tribute to him – published following Poulton-Palmer's death on the Western Front – it's clear that he was an exceptional bloke as well as a brilliant rugby player.

10. Nick Evans

Just squeezes in ahead of Ricky Bartlett, one of the most underrated England players of his era and a wonderful clubman. Nick has been a class act from the moment he arrived after the 2007 World Cup and immediately bought into what Quins is all about. A superb fly-half with all the skills, he would have won many more New Zealand caps had he not been a contemporary of Dan Carter.

9. Danny Care

Jonny Williams was a very fine scrum-half indeed and Rob Glenister was a great clubman who was involved in multiple Pilkington Cup and Sevens successes, but Danny is the pick of the crop – good pace, a nose for the break, a natural try-scorer, a nice pass and a good kicking game. When Danny is buzzing he plays the game at great tempo and energises everybody around him.

1. Grahame Murray

A great friend and colleague from my days, Grahame was an incredibly dedicated clubman, inspiring captain and a very fine prop who was famously unlucky to miss out on the England cap he surely deserved. His 307 appearances is a club record and will probably stand forever, although Mike Brown and Chris Robshaw could go close if they stay injury free.

2. Brian Moore

A terrific hooker and one of those characters like Peter Winterbottom who somehow managed to combine a demanding full-time job with almost incessant playing demands on the eve of the game turning professional. Joined the club from Nottingham and was a key player during a very successful period for Harlequins.

3. Jason Leonard

An extraordinarily durable and talented prop who won a record 114 caps for England and served Quins superbly from the moment he joined the club from Saracens early in his career. Always ensured that traditions were observed off the pitch and pints were drunk with the opposition no matter how heated the game. Heads up a long line of Quins front row 'characters' such as Curly Hammond and the Claxton brothers.

4. David Marques

It's a toss-up at second row where we have an absolute embarrassment of riches. Mike Davis was another hugely underrated player, while Paul Ackford was a mighty performer during his spell with the club and John Currie also served Quins so well on and off the pitch. In the end, though, I've opted for David, an incredible athlete and player, a former club captain and a character who was much admired around the rugby world.

5. Wavell Wakefield

I got to know him very well in his later years and he was an amazing character and player. Like Stoop he revolutionised the game with his approach to fitness and modern outlook. Best known, of course, as a back row player, he was a big guy and an exceptional athlete so I see him as an ultra-mobile, rampaging lock. Wakefield enjoyed three spells as Quins captain, and also captained England to back-to-back Grand Slams.

6. Chris Robshaw

Chris has been a magnificent club servant after coming up through the academy and captaining our Premiership-winning side in 2011–12. You get everything for the full 80 minutes from him – he's a grafter but is also much more skilled than he's given credit for. Chris played the vast majority of his rugby at openside but started his Quins career at blindside and is back there again this season. It's possibly his best position and I would pick him just ahead of Mickey Skinner.

7. Peter Winterbottom

'Winters' is one of the greats of English rugby and an automatic selection in this team. He arrived here quite late in his career but his impact was massive. He was totally dedicated to the cause in every way and was incapable of giving less than 100 per cent, playing or training. He took other players in our squad to a new level in that respect. His five seasons or so with us, three as captain, were amongst the most successful in our history.

8. Nick Easter

Nick would have been outstanding in any era. He's got that raw strength – 'man strength' as Conor O'Shea calls it – at close quarters to have excelled years ago on those quagmire pitches of the '60s and '70s. But he also has the ball handling and offloading skills that you need in the modern game. A very loyal and popular Quin, as was Colin Payne who – like Nick – could play second row or No. 8 with equal facility.

Replacements:

Keith Wood
(Ireland)

Iain Milne
(Scotland)

Andy Haden
(New Zealand)

Andre Vos
(South Africa)

Zinzan Brooke
(New Zealand)

Jonny Williams
(England)

Ricky Bartlett
(England)

Bob Lloyd
(England)

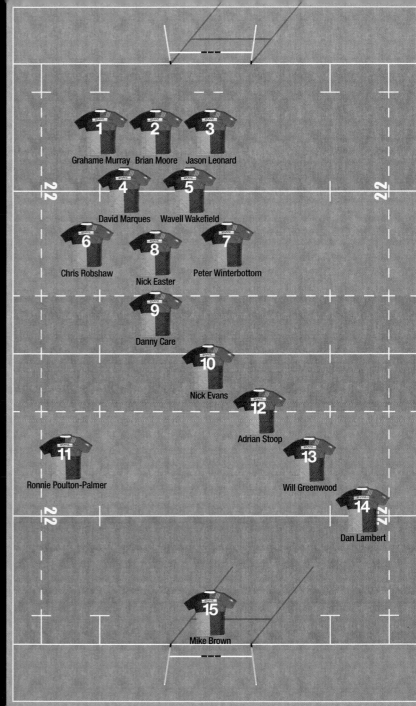

1 — Grahame Murray
2 — Brian Moore
3 — Jason Leonard
4 — David Marques
5 — Wavell Wakefield
6 — Chris Robshaw
8 — Nick Easter
7 — Peter Winterbottom
9 — Danny Care
10 — Nick Evans
12 — Adrian Stoop
11 — Ronnie Poulton-Palmer
13 — Will Greenwood
14 — Dan Lambert
15 — Mike Brown

9 The Glory Years

1990–1995

9

As English club rugby became more and more competitive and headed rapidly towards professionalism, Harlequins entered into what we should now recognise as another golden era that saw the club boast an array of players of world renown. Having acquired a taste for knockout rugby with that groundbreaking victory over Bristol in 1988, Harlequins continued to chase cup glory during the first half of the '90s, and the upsurge in media interest in rugby union saw the Harlequins name – and that of the club's stars – to the forefront.

Title page: Paul Ackford lifts the 1991 Pilkington Cup

Below: The combative Brian Moore was a key member of the Quins side

Right: A thank you note from the RFU following the 1991 World Cup

In five seasons, from 1990–91 to 1994–95, Harlequins reached the final of the cup (renamed the Pilkington Cup in 1989) on three occasions and lost in the semi-finals in the other two seasons. This period may only have resulted in one more trophy, coming when Peter Winterbottom's side memorably beat Northampton in extra-time in the 1991 final, but Quins had confirmed itself as a force to be reckoned with and contributed more than its fair share of the epic ties which helped the cup competition outshine the emerging league.

The demands on amateur players during this period were immense, and perhaps the cup suited Harlequins' temperament rather better than the league. In 1991, for example, eight of Quins' Pilkington Cup-winning team – Winterbottom, Will Carling, Simon Halliday, David Pears, Micky Skinner, Paul Ackford, Brian Moore and Jason Leonard – were also involved in England's Grand Slam-winning squad. The same octet also toured Fiji and Australia with England that summer and were key members of the team that reached the 1991 World Cup Final. A ninth player, lock Troy Coker, also played for Australia in the 1991 World Cup and earned a winner's medal with the Wallabies.

Such year-long commitment can come at a price though, and the excessive workload for some players inevitably caused a degree of inconsistency. Riding on the crest of the wave in the 1990–91 season, Quins

actually performed well in the Courage League, winning eight out of 12 games and finishing a very creditable third. For the next four seasons, however, during which time Quins took centre stage in the Pilkington Cup, the club's league position – eighth in 1991–92 and 1992–93, sixth in 1993–94 and eighth again in 1994–95 – left room for improvement.

"They were great days in the cup – we played up to our champagne image a little," recalls Winterbottom, who captained Quins in all three cup finals during this period. "It suited us for the opposition to think that was what we were about, but the reality is that there was an incredible mix of people, with a lot of northerners like myself, Micky Skinner, Brian Moore and David Pears, and carpenters

Rugby World Cup 1991

Presented to

Harlequins F.C.

in recognition of your contribution to Rugby World Cup 1991

Your assistance and service throughout the Tournament has been much appreciated

On behalf of Rugby World Cup we should like to thank you for all your efforts

Monsieur M. M. Martin,
Chairman, Rugby World Cup BV.

Mr. R. W. Thomas, CBE,
Chairman, Rugby World Cup Limited

Sir Ewart Bell, KCB, MA,
Director, Rugby World Cup.

like Jason Leonard playing alongside the City and Oxbridge types.

"The truth is that we worked bloody hard at our rugby and were very passionate about it. We more than earned the occasional big night out. Dick Best's beastings on the training field were legendary and when push came to shove we were very fit and tended to get stronger as the game progressed.

"As a team we trained every Monday and Thursday and there was a track session at Tooting Athletics Club most Tuesdays which you were 'encouraged' to attend. They were very focused sessions – speed or endurance – and I got a lot from them. You were also expected to put in a couple of lunch hours down the gym every week. Friday was about the only day of the week I remember not training or playing. Even Sundays you would be either recovering with a jog or meeting up with England."

The 1991 Pilkington Cup campaign began with a resounding 56–4 home win over Clifton in round three, but the stakes were immediately raised in the next round when Quins escaped with a 15–13 win in a cliffhanger against old cup foes Gloucester – the kind of victory that makes a team think that it might just be their year.

Next came a solid performance to beat Rosslyn Park 21–12 in the quarter-final, before another nail-biter in the semi-final against a Nottingham team with England goal-kicking machine Simon Hodgkinson in its ranks. This time Quins squeezed through 22–18 after extra-time, with an opportunist try from Andrew Harriman doing the trick – a testament to the fitness work put in by the coaches and players on the training pitch.

The final against a Northampton team now captained by former Quins favourite John

Left: Peter Winterbottom captained the club in three Pilkington Cup Finals in a row between 1991 and 1993, although he only lifted the trophy once

Right: The programme and team line-up for the 1991 Pilkington Cup Final against Northampton

RUGBY FOOTBALL UNION

THE **PILKINGTON** CUP

FINAL

HARLEQUINS v NORTHAMPTON

TWICKENHAM
SATURDAY 4 MAY 1991

THE **PILKINGTON** CUP

Official Programme
£1
(including 20p
contribution to
the Wavell Wakefield
Youth Trust)

RFU CLUB KNOCK-OUT COMPETITION

Secretary R.F.U.

25 – 13.

| NORTHAMPTON | | | HARLEQUINS |
| Black, Green & Gold Jerseys | | | Light Blue, Magenta, Chocolate, French Grey, Black and Light Green Jerseys |

13-25

Referee:
Ed Morrison (Bristol Society)
Touch Judges:
Fred Howard (Liverpool Society)
Colin High (Manchester Society)

NORTHAMPTON			HARLEQUINS
15	I. HUNTER	FULLBACK	S. E. THRESHER 15
		THREE QUARTERS	
14	F. PACKMAN	RIGHT WING	†A. T. HARRIMAN 14
13	J. THAME	CENTRE	†W. D. C. CARLING 13
12	P. MOSS	CENTRE	†S. J. HALLIDAY 12
11	H. THORNEYCROFT	LEFT WING	E. G. DAVIS 11
		HALF BACKS	
10	J. STEELE	STAND-OFF	†D. PEARS 10
9	R. NANCEKIVELL	SCRUM HALF	R. J. GLENISTER 9
		FORWARDS	
1	G. BALDWIN	PROP	†J. LEONARD 1
2	C. J. OLVER†	HOOKER	†B. C. MOORE 2
3	G. S. PEARCE† (Captain)	PROP	†A. R. MULLINS 3
4	C. HALL	LOCK	†T. COKER 4
5	J. ETHERIDGE	LOCK	†P. J. ACKFORD 5
6	P. ALSTON	FLANKER	†M. G. SKINNER 6
7	P. PASK	FLANKER	†P. J. WINTERBOTTOM (Captain) 7
8	T. RODBER	NO. 8	R. S. R. LANGHORN 8

Replacements:
16 D. Elkington
17 B. Ward
18 M. Ebsworth
19 P. Roworth
20 V. Pocklington
21 D. Newman

† International

Replacements:
N. J. Killick 16
T. C. Luxton 17
G. J. Thompson 18
A. P Challinor 19
M. P. Russell 20
M. J. Hobley 21

| HT | |
| FT | |

KICK-OFF 3.00pm

The RFU gratefully acknowledge the support of Pilkington plc

RULES FOR FINAL:
If, after 40 minutes play each way the scores are level, there shall be an immediate period of replay between the same teams of 10 minutes each way, with a one minute interval. If the scores are then still equal the team that has scored the most tries shall be the winner. If this does not produce a result, the team that has scored the most goals from tries shall be the winner. If no result is then achieved the match shall be adjudged a Draw.

Olver was another exciting affair, and with English rugby on a high after the Grand Slam just over a month earlier there were 53,000 fans at Twickenham to watch the game.

With 11 capped players in the starting XV, including seven in the pack, the bookies had Harlequins down as 2/5 favourites and Winterbottom's side certainly monopolised the possession and territory as expected. Quins scored an early try through Richard Langhorn, but Saints proved in trenchant mood defensively and made life very difficult. Eventually it required a 74th-minute try by Harriman to level the scores at 13–13, and that is how they remained as the referee blew the full-time whistle.

In extra-time however – perhaps as a result of Best's fitness regime – Quins pulled ahead decisively thanks to well-taken tries from Halliday and Rob Glenister. It was a record-breaking sixth appearance in a final for Halliday, who had played five times for Bath before his work in the City persuaded the England centre to join Harlequins.

"That was one of the really great days for the club and it was a proud moment lifting the cup," reflects Winterbottom. "We had to dig very deep and there were some very tired bodies out there after a long season, but again we demonstrated that we could usually find an extra five per cent in the cup."

Here it is poignant to mention one of the game's try-scorers, Richard Langhorn, who tragically died, aged 29, during a back operation in November 1994. Educated at

Sevenoaks School and employed as a City trader, Langhorn was a vital member of the Quins team in the late 1980s and early '90s, playing in three of the club's four cup finals at Twickenham and switching from lock to the back row with ease. On a number of occasions during his career he was the only non-international in Quins' all-star pack, although he did play for England in a non-capped series against Canada in 1993.

In his memory, family, colleagues and friends founded the Richard Langhorn Trust, which raised the best part of £1 million for nominated charities – such as wheelchair basketball – during its 20-year existence. He was a wholehearted clubman who made a massive contribution on and off the field.

The following season featured another tumultuous campaign for Harlequins which ended in the most dramatic way with an extra-time defeat against Bath in front of a then club world record crowd of 60,500 at Twickenham. Cup rugby had become the centrepiece of the developing club game and Quins had taken its place right at the heart of that process.

Harlequins' progress to the final looked simple enough on paper, but the journey was not without its moments. After winning 33–3 at Bedford, the next match was a tricky trip to Wasps, and on the appointed day a difficult decision had to be made over a frosty pitch that was not thawing as quickly as hoped. Wasps were keen to play but Quins objected and the game was postponed – a decision that caused some criticism.

Harlequins revealed that it had spent £1,500 gathering the team in a hotel the night before by way of preparation and so were just as disappointed that the game could not go ahead. The club also pointed out

that it would have been heavily criticised if any of its seven England regulars had picked up an injury on account of the conditions ahead of the following week's Five Nations game. As a result there was a fair bit of feeling when the rearranged tie was finally played, which Quins went on to win 20–9.

The momentum was building and Rosslyn Park were impressively dispatched 34–12, followed by a hard-fought 15–9 victory over Leicester in a tense semi-final. Cup kings Bath awaited Quins in an eagerly anticipated final, but as the day approached the club found itself beset with injury problems up front, compounded by the unavailability of Skinner and Langhorn who had both been sent off on the stroke of half-time in a Courage League game against Gloucester at The Stoop the week before. It should also be mentioned that Quins had slumped to an 18–9 deficit prior to that double sending off, and it was indicative of the spirit of the team during this era that the 13 men remaining started running from all positions and scored two late tries to record one of the most memorable victories in the club's modern history.

Despite these setbacks, the spirit in the squad remained high and all was not lost for the final. But the squad did need some back-up, and quickly. At which point the retired Ackford, who had originally been booked for a speaking engagement at a pre-match lunch at Twickenham before the final, takes up the story:

"I had decided that the 1991 World Cup would be my last hurrah and I would stop playing completely after that. And that's exactly what I did. Not only didn't I play a single game of rugby after the World Cup Final on 2nd November, I didn't do any fitness work or anything remotely athletic.

Opposite: Harlequins players celebrate Rob Glenister's crucial try in the 1991 Pilkington Cup Final victory over Northampton

Left: Will Carling takes his turn at lifting the trophy

Richard Langhorn, a Harlequins stalwart who tragically died during a back operation aged just 29

Police inspector Paul Ackford was hauled out of retirement by coach Dick Best to play in the 1992 Pilkington Cup Final

I immersed myself full-time in my job as a police officer and was thoroughly enjoying not being a rugby player.

"Then Bestie [Dick Best] phoned towards the end of April. There were serious injuries [within the squad]. Neil Edwards was the only lock still standing and he had ricked his neck, while Andy Mullins, Brian Moore, Chris Sheasby and Nick Killick all had knocks and were only 50/50 for the match. Meanwhile Micky Skinner and Richard Langhorn were unavailable after their spot of bother against Gloucester. It was a bit of a doomsday scenario that Dick painted and he asked could I at least come down to training and see how I felt. Dick had been my coach throughout my Quins career, which is when my England career took off, and we got on. Eventually I agreed, although not without reservations. I was in no condition to play any sort of competitive rugby match.

"Training didn't go well. I needed a warm-up match, and quickly. Hurriedly we made a few calls and on the Tuesday before the final I found myself playing No. 8 for the Met Police against a London Welsh XV. Out of position, unfit and trying too hard, I had my worst match in years, which was exacerbated by the fact that most of the rugby correspondents had got a whiff of a decent story and descended on Imber Court to report on my very average efforts.

"Even then Dick wasn't dissuaded, he still wanted me to play. On the day, I decided I had to be smart about this or else I would make a fool of myself. Quins needed me for one thing and that was my line out work. Every ounce of my energy had to be directed getting from one line out to the next. Nothing else mattered, there was no point in me trying to be a factor elsewhere."

The final itself was more of an intense affair than the free-flowing classic some had hoped for, but the weakened Quins pack, with Ackford and Edwards providing a constant stream of line out possession, were at their dogged best and made Bath work very hard indeed. In fact, the *Rothmans Rugby Union Yearbook* records that the Quins duo won no less than 14 Bath line outs between them. Quins led 12–3 at half-time with skipper Peter Winterbottom scoring from a rolling maul following yet more line out possession and David Pears adding the conversion and two penalties. Could Quins' patched-up side do the unthinkable and win the unlikeliest of victories?

Alas, it wasn't to be. Bath, who registered a solitary Jonathan Webb penalty before the break, started to claw their way back in the second half with another penalty from the England fullback before a well-worked try for Phil de Glanville, converted by Webb, equalled the scores and sent the match into extra-time. For Quins, with their large England contingent scarcely having had a week off – one way or another – since the summer of 1990, it was a bridge too far.

Quins did have chances in extra-time, with Pears and Paul Challinor both sending drop-goal attempts wide of the posts, but eventually it was the Bath skipper, Stuart Barnes, who clinched the issue with a

Above: The Harlequins team celebrate Peter Winterbottom's try in the 1992 Pilkington Cup Final, although Bath went on to triumph 15–12

40-yard drop-goal. It was certainly not the most elegant kick, with Barnes admitting afterwards that it was a mishit, but it did the job and Bath once again lifted the trophy.

"It haunts me a bit to this day," continues Ackford. "Despite my misgivings it had gone very well in the line out, but extra-time was my worst nightmare and I began to struggle badly in the last 10 minutes or so. At that final line out from which Barnsie kicked the drop-goal, I was so knackered I couldn't even get off the ground, let alone challenge Ollie Redman for the ball. That evening the club had booked a nightclub or something down in Fulham for an end of season party and by the time I got there I was so sore that I sat in a chair in the corner for four hours and didn't move. When I got home I slept for 24 hours solid.

"My other memory from the day is a strange one. Jonathan Webb is one of my best mates in rugby – then and now – but having been parachuted in so close to the final I wasn't in that zone that clubs go into before a huge match. So when I walked out in my posh Quins cup final blazer and slacks to sniff the air and stroll around Twickenham before the kick-off, I wandered over to Jonathan full of the joys and wanting to shoot the breeze. Bad call on my part. It was a Quins versus Bath cup final and for the next couple of hours we couldn't be mates. He cut me dead. During my retirement I had completely forgotten how close-knit teams become and the intensity of these big occasions."

The final was the last day of Best's first spell as Harlequins coach – he was going to devote himself full-time to the England job – and in retrospect that first period under his charge was an outstanding era for the club. Best was a formidably hard taskmaster but Winterbottom believes Quins has a lot to thank him for.

"As captain I had a lot of dealings with Dick," Winterbottom explains. "He was, and remains, a forthright character and so am I, and I wouldn't deny we had words on occasions, but they were always aimed at making Quins a better and more successful team and we enjoyed some pretty good years in tandem. As a coach, pure and simple, he was very good indeed.

"Dick also imposed some great attitudes on the club that were ahead of their time – hardcore professional attitudes in terms of total commitment to training and punctuality. That didn't always make him popular, but

when the game went professional a few years down the line the club, on the pitch, wasn't far off the levels required."

The following 1992–93 season Harlequins, with Jamie Salmon now installed as the manager and Australia's Bob Templeton helping out with the coaching, started the new campaign extravagantly as it homed in on a third Pilkington Cup Final in successive years. Blackheath were routed 72–3 and Wakefield dismissed 47–18 before a testing encounter at Blundellsands against a Waterloo team featuring a young Austin Healey. In the previous round the Liverpool-based side had pulled off one of the biggest shocks in the tournament's history by edging past reigning champions Bath 9–8.

Quins knuckled down to win 21–14 thanks to a peach of a try from wing Mike Wedderburn and another from Kent Bray. In the semi-final, a late try from Gavin Thompson after good work by Jeff Alexander and Chris Madderson

Below: In 1992 the club celebrated its 125th anniversary with a suitably stylish and well-attended dinner at Skinners' Hall

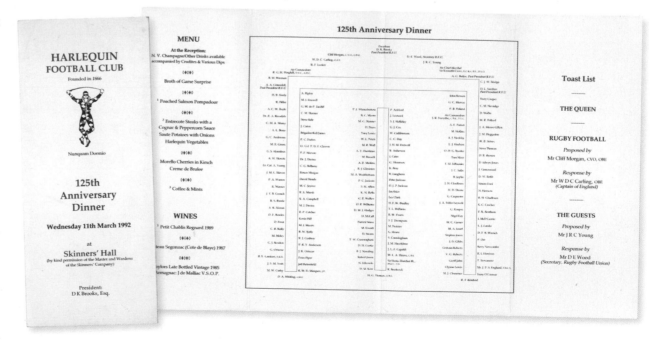

was enough for Quins to again nick a win at Wasps, this time 14–13, to tee up a final against an in-form Leicester Tigers.

Alas it was one of those finals that failed to live up to the high expectations as a spectacle, which was a shame for the 54,000-strong crowd (Twickenham at the time was undergoing renovations that limited its capacity). It became a battle of the packs from which Tigers eventually emerged victorious.

Quins had led 13–10 at half-time through a converted try by Glenister and a brace of penalties from Challinor, but Leicester turned the screw after the break and it was a try from a promising young second row called Martin Johnson that saw Tigers clinch the win. It was a disappointing end to the season, especially for Quins skipper Winterbottom who finally called time on his illustrious career after the match.

Winterbottom's dedication to the cause at Quins in the previous five seasons had been nothing short of immense, despite various other commitments and honours. On one famous occasion he played a Courage League game on the Saturday, then flew to South Africa to play for the South African Barbarians on the Monday night against Transvaal at Ellis Park, Johannesburg – where he was voted man of the match – and as Quins skipper was the first man at training on the Tuesday night ahead of an important match against Leicester the following Saturday. Another time, in his final season, he flew straight from a tough England game against Scotland to play for Harlequins in a stunning midweek victory against the Orange Free State in an M-Net Challenge game at Ellis Park, before then returning home to be at his desk in the City at dawn on the Thursday morning.

Left: Lock Alex Snow soars above a young Martin Johnson in the 1993 Pilkington Cup Final which the Tigers won 23–16

Right: Chris Sheasby makes a break with the ball during the 1994 Pilkington Cup semi-final defeat to Bath at The Stoop

Below: In 1992 Harlequins signed a £350,000 five-year sponsorship deal with Flowers Bitter, at the time the biggest sponsorship deal in British rugby

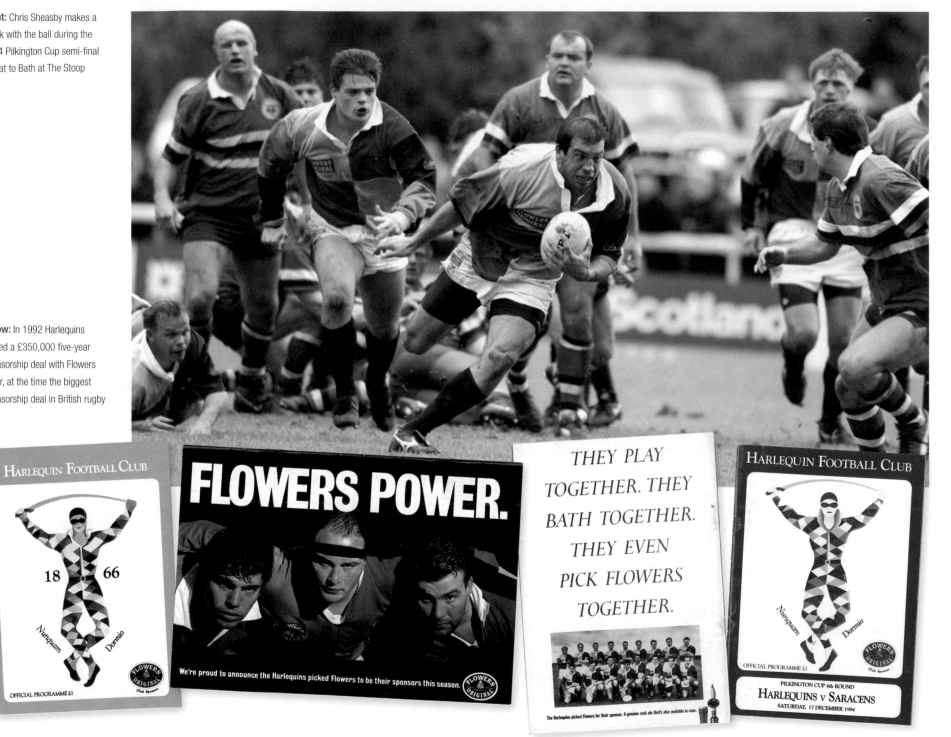

"Harlequins is not a club I would ever have thought of joining when I was younger, to be honest," says Winterbottom. "I had played at Headingley for years and been happy there, but after a 'gap year' playing for Transvaal following the 1987 World Cup I was coming back to England and thinking a change might be good. I had become friendly with Chris Butcher and John Olver and they suggested I try Quins, so I made myself known and immediately felt at home.

"The club had entered a successful phase under Dick Best on the field, and Roger Looker and Colin Herridge were matching that off the pitch with their organisation. But there was still a definite emphasis on having fun once the rugby was over, which I very much enjoyed.

"Quins did give me a few introductions to people in the City – the club was proactive in trying to help in that way as it looked to recruit players – but actually, despite reports to the contrary, I fixed myself up with a job through another rugby contact – Jeremy Hughes – who played at London Welsh and also worked in the City. It was a great phase of my life, working incredibly hard on and off the field during my time at Quins, and with the co-operation of both the club and my employers I was able to enjoy the best of both worlds, for which I am eternally grateful."

Winterbottom might have gone but the club's cup tradition soldiered on into the 1993–94 season. Quins, with Keith Richardson from Gloucester now installed as coach, looked set to add another cup final appearance to the list the following year only to narrowly go down 26–25 against Bath in an exhilarating semi-final.

However, Harlequins' domination of the Pilkington Cup was coming to a close and a

31–13 thumping at the hands of Bath in the semi-final the following season signalled that the end of an era was at hand.

It had been a successful period for Harlequins and the team had done the club proud, but a new challenge was about to confront the game. On 26th August 1995, IRB

Chairman Vernon Pugh emerged from a smoke-filled room in Paris at the IRB General Meeting to announce that his committee had voted to declare the game 'open'. Rugby union was free to be an openly professional sport. But what did that mean in practical terms? Quins, and others, were about to find out.

Above: Jason Leonard (*right*), with Andy Mullins in support, leads the charge but Quins lost this Pilkington Cup semi-final against Bath in 1995

CLOSE QUARTERS

TRUE COLOURS

The famous four-quartered Harlequins jersey is the most iconic kit design in club rugby and, according to a recent survey, the third most recognisable shirt in the whole of rugby after those of the All Blacks and the British and Irish Lions.

■ **Below right:** Following the somewhat controversial introduction of an away shirt in 2007, the club has produced an array of eye-catching designs

■ **Below:** The strict guidelines for 'Club Colours' as outlined in the 1920–21 season ticket book

Ever since Hampstead Football Club became Harlequins in 1869 and the colours of magenta, chocolate brown, French grey and light blue (with green and black quartered sleeves) were decided upon to match the club's new name, the distinctive colours have set Quins apart. They serve as a statement that says this is no ordinary club – it is a maverick, a pioneer. The shirt represents the spirit, style and, last but not least, sense of fun that has always underpinned the Harlequins ethos.

From the end of the 19th century through to the 1950s and '60s the players' jerseys barely changed. Originally supplied by Saville Row tailors and later by bespoke sportswear suppliers, they were made from heavy cotton – which became even heavier, of course, with the addition of mud and rain – with long sleeves and traditional white collars. But with the advent of sponsorship in the 1980s and '90s, and then the professional era and the adoption of lightweight, high-tech fabrics and designs for rugby shirts, numerous variations of the famous colours have now adorned the Harlequins heroes.

For the first 141 years of the club's history, so unusual were its colours that no change, or 'away', design was ever needed. However, the commercial pressures of professionalism meant that in 2007 Harlequins played in a second strip for the first time ever. Initially meeting with disapproval amongst traditionalists, this move has since allowed the kit designers to get creative with the club colours and in recent years – especially since the tradition of having a bespoke 'Big Game' shirt began in 2008 – really let their imaginations run wild.

Since 2014, the task of designing and supplying the famous colours has fallen to sportswear giants adidas, who have taken the strip to a whole new level with their high-performance team kits as well as a stylish range of accompanying training and leisurewear. Designing the jersey for the historic 2016–17 season, however, presented adidas with its biggest challenge yet.

---

21. That notice be sent to each Member on his election, with a copy of the rules, and a request for payment of his entrance fee and subscription; such payment to be held as a submission to the Rules of the Club.

22. That the proposer of a new Member shall in case of that Member's default, be liable for his annual subscription and entrance fee.

Club Colours

23. That the Club colours be light blue, chocolate, French grey and magenta, reversed on back, sleeves light green and black reversed, white knickerbockers and dark stockings; and that all Members wear the same; and that it be at the option of Members to wear a dark blue blazer with the club badge and monogram thereon.

24. That there be a Club Cap, dark blue in colour, having a device worked upon the front; such device to be :—

For the first Team, the figure of a Harlequin worked in colours.

For the "A" Team, H.F.C., A XV.

For the Extra "A" Team, H.F.C., Extra A XV.

and any member who has played two-thirds of the Saturday matches in any Team in one season shall be entitled to purchase a cap of the pattern as arranged for the Team for which he has played the required number of times A match played in a higher Team to count as one in the lower Team for the purpose of qualifying for the cap of such lower Team.

GROUND :

THE RUGBY FOOTBALL UNION,
TWICKENHAM,
Dressing accommodation in Stand "A."

———

Members are particularly requested to play in Club Colours, which can be obtained at
STOKES & CO., LTD.,
46, Cornhill, London, E.C. 3.
C. LEWIN & CO., 8, Crooked Lane,
Cannon Street, E.C. 4.

———

Members wishing to play are requested to write to the Secretary.

———

Members are particularly requested to answer Notices as soon as possible, and give notice of change of address.

———

Each Member is entitled to introduce two Ladies to the Members' Enclosure on "A" Stand free of charge.

———

Tickets admitting Non-Members to the Members' Enclosure, which are available for the day of issue only, may be purchased by Members at the entrance gate.

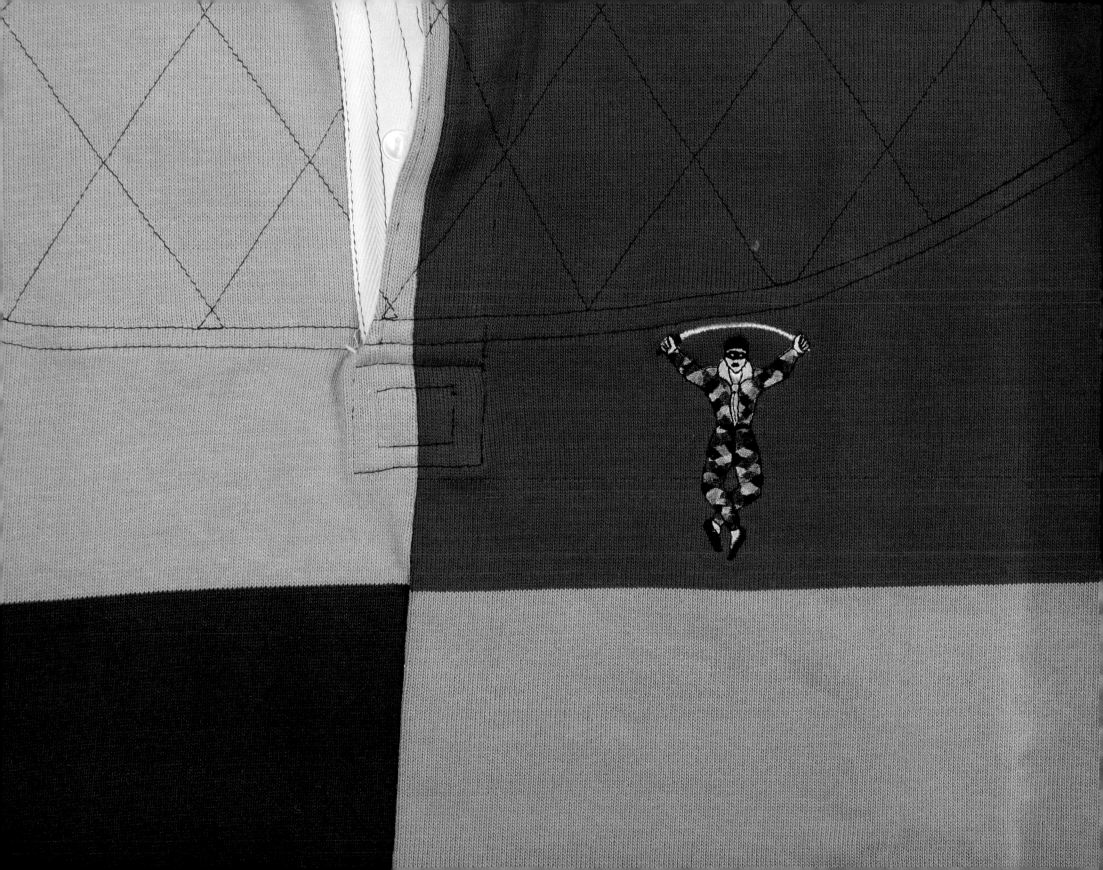

The Evolution of the Harlequins Shirt

1890–1960

1980s

1996–2000

2005–07

2010–12
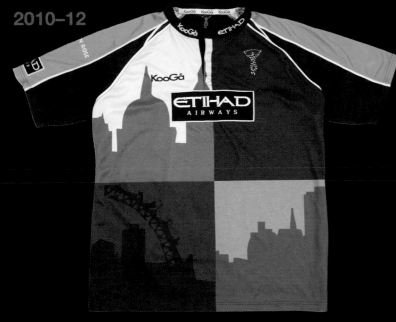

2012–14

2014–15

2015–16

■ **Opposite:** The 'retro' adidas shirt designed to mark the 150th anniversary

■ **Below right:** The design for the 2016 'Big Game' shirt

■ **Below:** A graphic produced by adidas to explain the creative process behind the 2016–17 shirt

"For the 150th anniversary we set ourselves the task of producing a modern high-performance series of shirts – Home, Alternate, Big Game and Training – that incorporate all the historic developments in that shirt," explains Alex Hinde from the adidas design team. "To do that we went back to the archives and the rugby museum at Twickenham to study the jersey throughout the ages.

"Historically the basic colours – magenta, chocolate brown, French grey and light blue – started to develop early on once the new name of the reconstituted club was decided, but the classic tones seem to have become standardised by 1902, which is the earliest confirmed date we have a jersey to work from. That shows the light blue to be slightly darker than is sometimes depicted, and by then the white collar and white shorts had already become standard.

"Then between 1905 and 1908 we noticed the shielded crest of the famous Harlequins starting to feature on caps, so we have incorporated that classic design in the top left-hand quarter of the shirt. By the mid-1980s, diamond stitch was being introduced in performance jerseys to prevent ripping and, although we don't need them as such due to the strength of modern-day fabrics, we have represented that look as well. Half sleeves came in about 1998 so we have also added these. Other design features include having the club's Latin motto *Nunquam Dormio* – 'I Never Sleep' – on the inside of the collar and the year 1866 on the back of the socks."

The classic 'Home' shirt is the centrepiece of the 150th anniversary collection, but the other versions each have their own unique characteristics. Alternate, or 'Away', shirts are meant to have a 'different' look but care has been taken to incorporate the historic club colours, although the focus is on blue and magenta. The link with the past is also maintained with the club motto again printed on the inside of the collar and the club crest on the top left-hand side of the shirt.

There will also be a very special 'Big Game' jersey for the fixture against Gloucester on 27th December 2016, as Hinde explains: "We are producing a one-off for the Big Game, with French grey being the predominant colour but with all the other club colours incorporated on the shoulders and sleeves. The particular feature of this shirt is that the interlocking design down the front features the name of every Harlequins captain since 1866 and, as the designated charity for the game, there will also be the Great Ormond Street logo on the bottom right-hand corner."

Finally, mindful that a huge number of the images required and used by the media tend to be taken at training these days, adidas has also produced a striking shirt for those occasions. In a nod to their roots in the captial, the designers of the training kit have taken the London coat of arms and given it a Quins twist by adding the Harlequins diamonds, sword and the rather striking mask that the famous Harlequin always wears.

Whatever direction the kit designers take the Harlequins shirt in over the next 150 years, you can be guaranteed that it will continue to turn heads, raise a smile and symbolise everything that is so special about Harlequin FC.

1866	1890	1902	1905-8	1956	1985	1998	2015
WHITE COLLAR	WHITE SHORTS	YESTERYEAR TONES	SHIELDED CREST	DIAMOND SOCKS	DIAMOND STITCH	HALF/HALF SLEEVES	QUARTER COLS. INTO SLEEVES

A CELEBRATION THROUGH THE AGES

10

The Arrival of Professionalism
1996–2004

10

The question was simple: should rugby union be a professional sport? And after 130 years of proud amateurism, struggling through the early years and two World Wars, would Harlequins be prepared to make the quantum leap into professional rugby, or would it leave other clubs to step into the darkness and, instead, content itself with simply playing for the love of the game?

Title page: Could the promotional demands of professionalism be making Keith Wood a little weary? The Harlequins hooker takes a moment out from the new season photocall in 2000 to have a quick yawn

Below: Donald Kerr played a huge role in easing the club into the professional era

"It was a very big moment in August 1995 when news of the game being declared 'open' reached us from the IRB meeting in Paris," recalls Colin Herridge, who was Vice Chairman of the club at the time. "It was an odd feeling. Personally I wanted it to happen, it needed to happen, but I didn't think for one minute that it would because, as a member of the RFU, I knew the entrenched views they held on the issue and also those of the other home unions in particular. And no matter what some people may tell you now, the decision to go fully professional caught just about everybody by surprise.

"I got into quite a bit of trouble with the RFU when I reacted to the news by saying that some clubs would thrive, because they wanted the change and would embrace it, and others – including some big names – would struggle and possibly disappear from the top echelon and never come back. The bottom line is that money talks."

Given Harlequins' perceived status as an archetypal amateur club – with the ingrained ethos that winning, although important, was not everything – a big decision loomed. After all, despite being looked on as amateur, Quins had embraced the John Player/Pilkington Cup and appeared in four finals, winning two of them. The squad was also packed full of internationals who, for a while now, had been training and playing with the intensity of professionals. It would not be overstating the case that others were waiting to see which way Harlequins jumped.

Harlequins had never been a club frightened of innovation. Famous Quins had been at the root of the development of the game and its tactics, while the club had helped to get Twickenham up and running and been amongst the first to tour abroad and play under floodlights. Furthermore, in Will Carling and Brian Moore the club boasted two current high-profile players who had been at loggerheads with the RFU over payments for 'non-rugby related activities' such as personal appearances and product endorsements. It was obvious that Harlequins had long been at the cutting edge of rugby union's evolution – would it take that final leap into the unknown?

The RFU, taken aback by the IRB's decision, declared a season-long moratorium on payments being made to players in an attempt to pave the way for a more orderly transition. Even at this stage some at the RFU hoped that, at worst, rugby union would merely become a semi-professional sport with, in effect, generous expenses being officially sanctioned. But in reality that was never an option – the genie was out of the bottle.

"Off the back of a golden era in playing terms we were actually in better shape than many, although it was still a pretty fraught time," continues Herridge. "In the 1980s and the first half of the '90s we had also undergone a big shake-up off the field and were much more streamlined than we had been.

"Our starting point was a question: if you could transport Stoop and Wakefield – two of the most progressive brains in English rugby history – into the modern era, what would they do? Both were incredibly competitive and devoted their sporting lives to trying to be the best, and we took the view that they would be appalled if Harlequins missed the boat, or at least made no attempt to get on board, so that's the route we went down.

"Roger Looker was Chairman at the time and took the lead in trying to make it work. He was an absolute tower of strength and the club will always be in his debt. I think he might have even taken a sabbatical off work for a while to concentrate purely on getting Quins into the professional era. There was no template and, looking back, it would be easy to pinpoint one or two mistakes, but it was a case of trying to make something new and very big happen in a short period of time. Neither clubs, nor indeed investors, really knew what was required of them.

"Donald Kerr was another who worked tirelessly to get things underway. I was very tied up with the RFU and getting the rugby museum at Twickenham underway, but I helped when I could. Roger and I used to meet regularly to review the situation at our 'office' – the George and Dragon pub in Thames Ditton, which was halfway between our two houses.

"We realised straight away that the immediate future was all about money. We tested the water and spoke to many potential investors, although it soon became evident that many were interested for reasons other than rugby. Eventually Roger felt he had found somebody who fitted the bill and the three of us – Roger, Donald and I – produced a document which we presented to members on 14th May 1996 entitled 'Harlequin Football Club: Proposed Capital Reorganisation' with Roger's 'business proposition' the nub of it."

The document outlined the need for a minimum budget of £3.7 million the following season, to contract approximately 35 players with a minimum salary bill of £1.5 million, to increase the number of home games and gate receipts, the urgent necessity to develop the East Stand and, rather optimistically, hopes of a £500,000 profit.

The document also outlined that Riverside PLC, a property investment company owned by the Beckwith brothers, were the preferred investors and that the Harlequins Trust would be set up to oversee both Harlequin Football Club Ltd, the general committee and the club. Various terms and conditions would be put in place, notably that the investors should own no more than 40 per cent of the shares and the introduction of a 'golden share', owned by the club, which was essentially a failsafe mechanism. The golden share was intended to ensure that the club itself had the final say on any significant proposed changes, such as the sale of the club, ground developments or any proposed merging with another club, which was a possibility that had been discussed by many within the game given the cluster of senior clubs in south-west London.

So, at the dawn of professionalism the Beckwith brothers became the first investors in Harlequins but, although they undoubtedly pumped a considerable sum into the club, it quickly became clear that they and the club were not an easy match. The maths simply did not add up after professional rugby started to prove much more expensive than originally envisaged. There was no immediate prospect of breaking even, let alone of short or even medium-term profit. In fact, for the club to remain solvent it probably needed a minimum investment of £2 million immediately, over and above that which Riverside PLC and the Beckwiths had already put in. Again Colin Herridge takes up the story:

"We had appointed Simon Halliday as a trustee, mainly on account of his recent playing experience and affinity with the new professional squad, but of course Simon also had many City contacts via his then job at UBS [Union Bank of Switzerland].

Left: At the start of professional rugby in 1996 the club was rebranded as NEC Harlequins, with the telecommunications company's logo adorning programmes – with this example featuring French international prop Laurent Benezech on its cover – and shirts, as worn by rugby league convert Gary Connolly (right). The relationship between the club and the company lasted for 12 years

Opposite: Laurent Cabannes, the great French back row forward, looks up at the back of the Quins scrum to gauge what Bath are up to. Note the soccer-style squad numbers and names on the backs of the players' shirts

Below: In 1997 the new East Stand was completed at The Stoop, adding covered seating for a further 4,200 spectators as well as executive suites, bars, restaurants and conference facilities

"Fortunately he was talking to a colleague in Hong Kong one night about something completely different when the subject of Quins came up, and to cut a long story short we quickly made contact with Duncan Saville, a businessman based in Australia, and his British-based business partner, Charles Jillings.

"Duncan flew in from Australia about two days later to visit the club and was immediately very keen indeed. We shook hands there on the deal with the usual caveats about due diligence. Although there was some urgency, everything had to be finessed properly and Roger and Donald negotiated our way out of the Beckwith deal.

"Since then, Duncan and Charles have invested heavily in the club. I won't embarrass them by estimating how much, but we are talking very considerable sums. Their support has never wavered – they have been rock-solid and grasped immediately what the club stood for and its ethos. They have stuck with the club through thick and thin, when Quins were relegated in 2005 and again during 2009 after the 'Bloodgate' affair. They have continued to invest throughout. Duncan travels a lot but Charles lives locally and is a very visible supporter. The club voted to do away with the golden share arrangement in 2014, so since then it would be accurate to describe them as owners rather than investors."

The very early days of professional rugby were a rocky ride for clubs throughout the land, who all worked frantically to come up with an arrangement tailored to their needs. Alas there were casualties as well as success stories and as professionalism matured a number of big clubs, respected opponents all, ran into difficulties – Coventry, Orrell, West Hartlepool, Richmond, London Scottish and Bedford to name just a few. For the time being it was enough that Quins had kept their heads above water and been bolstered by loyal and long-term investors. Others, unfortunately, were not so lucky.

Inextricably linked with rugby union going professional was the appearance of the European Cup, sponsored by Heineken, which was seen – correctly, as it eventually proved – as the best way of giving the game more profile and income. It certainly

achieved the former immediately, although the latter was often a bone of contention as clubs initially felt they were not benefiting financially as much as they should have been. It was not so much to do with gate income and prize money, which was a useful addition but hardly a game-changer, but rather it was TV's instant infatuation with the competition and the money that would eventually flow into the game via the RFU – which insisted on remaining as the conduit for all related sponsorship and TV income.

Ultimately, financial incentives aside, Harlequins loved cup rugby and, after virtually pioneering rugby tours abroad in its earliest days, relished the thought of playing big matches overseas. What was there not to like about European Cup rugby? If only it was that simple.

Over the years, Harlequins has enjoyed great success in Europe's secondary cup competition in its various guises – the European Shield, Parker Pen Shield, Parker Pen Challenge Cup, Amlin European Challenge Cup and the European Challenge Cup – but it has conspicuously failed to shine in the main competition itself, and this has been a source of deep frustration for successive coaches, captains and players.

Harlequins' earliest forays into the Heineken Cup were considered to be a little disappointing at the time, but actually represent something of a European high point. Like all the English teams, the club was forced to sit out the inaugural competition by the RFU, but when it joined the party in 1996–97 it opened up with a notable win over Ulster at Ravenhill and qualified from its pool in second place behind eventual winners Brive, thanks in part to a riotous 56–35 win over Caledonia at The Stoop.

Above: Dick Best (top) and England captain Will Carling were big personalities and figures at the club at the dawn of professionalism

The Quins' match away at Brive was the undoubted highlight of the pool, the first big 'European' weekend in France for many Quins supporters who were greeted by a beguiling sunny Sunday October afternoon at a packed Parc Municipal des Sports. The welcome had been hospitable in the extreme – the church bells never stopped ringing – but on the field it was absolute carnage.

Harlequins, unbeaten in all competitions up to this point, had the temerity to take an early lead, which was like a red rag to a bull for opposition fly-half Alain Penaud, who launched three successive 'bombs' in the direction of Quins' fullback Jim Staples. But after bravely climbing to gather all three, as soon as his feet touched the ground he was clattered, taken out and then ruthlessly rucked off the ball by the rampaging Brive pack. Rarely has any individual so effectively been singled out for treatment and the Irish international, as brave as you like but dazed and not knowing what day of the week it was, literally had to be led to a place of safety. European Cup rugby was certainly a different proposition. However, despite Quins' eventual 23–10 defeat to that year's champions, many consider it to be one of the club's better early European performances.

Quins went on to lose 23–13 to Leicester in the quarter-finals that season, and although they also claimed third place behind Wasps in the Courage League, there were tensions behind the scenes. Dick Best had lost the England coaching job to Jack Rowell at the end of 1994, despite a fine record of played 17, won 13 on his watch, and had returned to Harlequins at the end of 1995 as the club's first Director of Rugby in the professional era. This time the man who had guided Quins to cup glories in the past proved less successful and he sadly found himself at odds with his playing squad, many of whom had recently given up good jobs to turn professional. Unfortunately for all concerned, the dynamics between players and staff were very different to when Best first took charge of the team.

There had been a falling out between Best and Will Carling, but a number of other players were also deeply concerned, as Halliday, a personal friend and admirer of Best's coaching successes, discovered in his role as a Quins trustee. He recalled the 1996–97 season in his memoir, *City Centre*:

"Life was a series of confrontations, upsets and generally amateurish behaviour. I was taking an increasing number of calls from the players who were desperate for a change, threatening to leave the club if nothing happened. Eventually matters were brought to a head and at a team meeting the Chairman Roger Looker surveyed a vote of confidence. A show of hands and Dick Best's career at Harlequins was effectively over. At the time it was suggested that this was a personal issue between Dick and Will Carling and that Will was pursuing a vendetta. Certainly they had long fallen out. But this move had nothing to do with Will, it was simply fashionable and expedient for the media and Will's detractors to suggest it.

"Perhaps familiarity bred contempt but [Best's] contribution to Harlequins, England and the game of rugby in general can hardly be overstated. He was a giant in every sense and his team talks were still the best I have heard, bar none."

Andy Keast took charge for the start of the 1997–98 season – he had first re-joined the club in 1996 after a spell in South Africa and a stint as the Lions' video analyst – and Quins again fronted up reasonably well in the early stages of the Heineken Cup the following season, although some of the games were rather frenetic. A 48–40 win over Munster was one of the more remarkable matches seen at The Stoop, while a 32–31 home defeat against Cardiff was another memorable try-fest. Home and away wins over Bourgoin ensured qualification for the quarter-finals, but it all went horribly wrong as a strong Quins team were annihilated 51–10 by Toulouse at the Stade Municipal.

It was probably Toulouse's greatest ever European showing, which – given their four tournament wins – is saying something, and Harlequins captain Keith Wood certainly considered it the finest club performance he had ever seen. The sheer excellence of Toulouse's play came as a massive shock to players and fans alike, although it is likely that Quins' French duo of fly-half Thierry Lacroix and flanker Laurent Cabannes, who during their long careers playing in French club rugby had never won at Toulouse, knew better than most what was coming.

After that brief flirtation with the knockout stages, Harlequins subsequently struggled to get to grips with Europe's premier tournament. The English clubs were missing from the competition in the 1998–99 season as the RFU and ERC (now the EPCR)

indulged in a protracted stand-off about the division of monies, and the following season Quins contrived to somehow finish bottom of a pool containing Cardiff, Montferrand (now Clermont Auvergne) and Benetton Treviso. The Italian club completed a double over a Quins side that registered just a solitary win in the whole campaign – a scrappy 11–9 victory over Montferrand.

The Heineken Cup had not proven to be a happy hunting ground for the club, yet frustratingly Quins performed exceptionally well in the Challenge Cup, even rising above some indifferent domestic form to win the competition in 2000–01 – a curious season in all respects.

After finishing tenth in the 1999–2000 season and languishing in 11th place come Christmas the following year, the club parted company with coach Zinzan Brooke on New

Above: With the advent of professional rugby came the Heineken Cup which Harlequins immediately embraced, although in 1997 they were defeated 51–10 in Toulouse in one of the French giants' finest performances

Right: The pennant presented to Harlequins before the Toulouse match

Above: All Black legend Zinzan Brooke was followed as Head Coach by Chief Executive Mark Evans (below) in 2000

Year's Day. Brooke had succeeded another former All Black, John Gallagher, who had himself taken over from Keast in 1998 as Quins continued to look for the right man to unlock the potential of the club. Following Brooke's departure, Quins' new Chief Executive Mark Evans – a former coach at Saracens – stepped into the resultant breach, greatly assisted by England A coach Richard Hill.

"When I arrived in the summer of 2000 I think it's fair to say the club was struggling a bit with the realities of professional rugby," recalls Evans. "The day I took over we only had seven contracted full-time professionals for the season ahead, attendances were dropping and we were failing to tap into the rugby potential of south-west London. The owners and the board were very committed and ambitious, though, so it was possible to plan for the future but the immediate challenge was a playing one – survival. We made a couple of very good signings with players

like David Wilson and Paul Burke. Zinnie was a hugely popular guy at the club, an incredible player, but it wasn't working for him so I took over in the New Year."

With Evans in charge of the playing side there was no great revival in Premiership fortunes, with Quins finishing the season in 11th place, but the second half of the season saw a remarkable improvement in form in two cup competitions. Quins reached the final of the Tetley's Bitter Cup (the old Pilkington Cup), losing a thrilling game to Newcastle 27–30 in front of a 71,000 crowd at Twickenham Stadium, but at the end of the season took home the Challenge Cup after beating Narbonne in yet another nail-biting extra-time final.

Skippered by Wilson, a World Cup-winner with Australia in 1999, Quins seemed utterly unrecognisable from the rather plodding side that did battle in the league. In the Tetley's Cup they accounted for Manchester (38–8), Sale (11–6) and Leicester (22–18) before squaring off against a star-studded Newcastle team in a rip-roaring final. Quins led from the 14th to the 84th minute until, with the last play of the game, David Walder stole in for the winning try.

It was doubly frustrating for Harlequins in that, as TV replays showed, Walder's try had come from a Newcastle line out that should clearly have been awarded to Quins after Falcons prop Ian Peel had been ushered into touch. Wilson and Burke touched down for the London club, with centre Will Greenwood having a hand in both, while Burke also kicked 17 points in an outstanding performance from the Irish international. For Newcastle, Tom May scored a fine brace of tries and Jonny Wilkinson kicked two conversions and two penalties.

If the 2001 Tetley's Cup ended in disappointment, then the European Challenge Cup (widely known as the European Shield at the time) finally brought a smile to Harlequins faces after a tough phase in its existence. Nonetheless, despite Quins' lowly league position there was never any danger of relegation because the club was always a good 20 points ahead of Rotherham, and so the cups provided a welcome outlet.

The pool was an interesting and competitive affair, with Quins gaining home and away wins at Ebbw Vale and Perigueux and just about getting the better of Dax, winning 25–3 at home but losing 23–22 in the return leg the following week. The points difference in those games proved the crucial factor that saw Harlequins pip the French side to top spot in the pool and advance to the knockout stages, which bore witness to two of Quins' best performances in a long while.

In the quarter-finals, Harlequins journeyed to Brive and responded to the challenge with a stunning 20–13 win at a ground where away victories were, at the time, very rare. Tries from Greenwood and flanker Steve White-Cooper did the trick and meant Quins had the opportunity to redress the balance against Newcastle in the semi-final.

The resultant 17–12 triumph was probably Scotland fly-half Craig Chalmers' finest hour at Harlequins. Coming in for Burke, who was out with a broken hand, Chalmers scored all 17 points through a try, conversion, three penalties and a drop-goal. The match itself was a fierce contest – at one stage both captains, Wilson and Doddie Weir, were sent to the sin-bin – but this time Quins kept Newcastle out at the death to become the first English club to reach the European Challenge Cup Final.

Held at the Madejski Stadium in Reading, the final was a brilliant match and a real rollercoaster ride for the club's supporters, which was rather fitting given the season Quins had endured. Narbonne, with Pumas legends Ignacio Corleto and Mario Ledesma very much to the fore, were formidable opposition, and it was helter-skelter stuff with the score 26–26 after 80 minutes. Thereafter Quins drew ahead with Burke enjoying another prolific afternoon, scoring 27 points from his boot, while there were tries for Ben Gollings, Pat Sanderson and Daren O'Leary. Victory was tinged with sadness, though, when Wilson suffered a serious knee injury early in extra-time. It looked bad at the time and ultimately proved career-ending for the Quins skipper, who might have been 34 but was playing well and certainly had a couple more seasons in his legs. To lose him, just when the club was beginning to build some genuine momentum, was a huge blow.

Left: After a dramatic 22–18 semi-final victory against Leicester at The Stoop, (*from left*) Roy Winters, Keith Wood and Rory Jenkins celebrate reaching the 2001 Tetley's Bitter Cup Final

Below: The final itself was a less happy occasion for Harlequins, a dejected Ryan O'Neill summing up the day as Newcastle Falcons celebrate Dave Walder's match-winning last-minute try

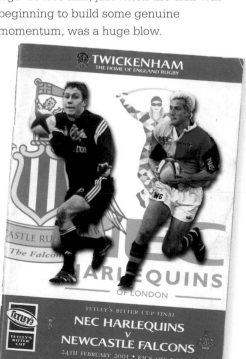

Right: David Wilson (*right*) starred in the 2001 European Shield triumph against Narbonne before tragically suffering an injury that would ultimately end his career

Below: Will Greenwood, going through his blonde phase, helps Keith Wood lift the European Shield aloft as the club celebrates winning its first European trophy

Opposite: Let the party begin!

Yet again though Quins had shown their proven talent for cup competition. In a season when they frustratingly finished second to bottom in the Premiership, they had reached the Tetley's Cup Final and won the European Shield against absolutely outstanding opposition.

"The truth is we weren't good enough or consistent enough to challenge for the Premiership then," recalls Ireland and Lions hooker Keith Wood. "But we had plenty of

EUROPEAN SHIELD FINAL 2001
Harlequins 42 Narbonne 33
(Madejski Stadium)

Harlequins: J Williams; B Gollings, W Greenwood, N Greenstock, D O'Leary; P Burke, M Powell; J Leonard, K Wood, J Dawson, G Morgan, S White-Cooper, P Sanderson, D Wilson, R Winters
Replacements: E Jennings for B Gollings (32 mins), R Jenkins for R Winters (72 mins), A Codling for G Morgan (72 mins), B Starr for J Dawson (79 mins), T Fuga for D Wilson (88 mins)
Tries: Gollings, Sanderson, O'Leary
Conversions: Burke (3) **Penalties:** Burke (6)
Drop-Goal: Burke

Narbonne: I Corleto; A Joubert, D Douy, A Stoica, S Rouch; G Quesada, G Sudre; A Martinez, M Ledesma, F Pucciarello, C Gaston, O Merle, P Furet, M Reynaud, S Reid
Replacements: F Azema for I Corleto (77mins), JP Poux for Martinez (78 mins), C Mathieu for P Furet (100 mins)
Tries: Corleto, Ledesma, Reid
Conversion: Quesada **Penalty:** Quesada
Drop-Goal: Quesada

Referee: Nigel Whitehouse (Wales)
Attendance: 11,211

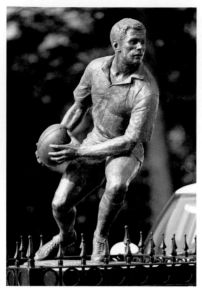

Above: The rugby world was shocked by the death of Nick Duncombe in 2003, and a statue commemorating the blossoming Harlequins and England star was unveiled at the entrance to The Stoop in 2005

Right: The morning after the night before... Will Greenwood and Jason Leonard pose with the Webb Ellis Cup in their Harlequins shirts on Manly Beach, Sydney, just hours after England's 2003 triumph

talent and when the force was with us and the stars aligned we could be very good and formidable opponents. That tended to make us a very dangerous cup team."

This solid cup form was not transferred to the Heineken Cup the following year, however, as Harlequins again found the going tough, with only a double over Bridgend to enthuse over. In particular, a 51–17 walloping by Munster at Thomond Park demonstrated the gulf in class between Quins and Europe's elite at the time. However a return to the Challenge Cup saw the club rediscover its inspiration, winning the competition for a second time during the 2003–04 campaign.

Sadly, tragedy had struck earlier in the season when scrum-half Nick Duncombe was cruelly struck down by illness in February 2003 and died suddenly, at the age of 21, while on a week's winter training break in Lanzarote. Nick was capped twice by England and Sir Clive Woodward had spoken often of him being the obvious long-term successor to Matt Dawson and Kyran Bracken when they retired. A former pupil at RGS High Wycombe – where Dawson was also once a student – Nick had been a stand-out England schoolboy international and had shown his incredible determination by overcoming a broken neck he suffered while playing for England Schools in 2000. He had also represented England at the Commonwealth Games Sevens tournament in Manchester in August 2002. As a memorial, a statue of Nick in typical pose passing the ball onto his fly-half was commissioned and is situated in the north-west corner of the Twickenham Stoop Stadium.

After qualifying easily from the pool stages, Quins thrived in the knockout matches, registering a thumping 41–8 win over old rivals Brive in the quarter-finals and a hard-fought 31–22 semi-final victory over Connacht – a club it was to become well acquainted with over the coming years.

Come the final, Quins faced Montferrand – one of the best sides in Europe at the time – but on this occasion, captained by Springbok Andre Vos, the team was inspired by the occasion, emerging 27–26 winners. Fullback Gavin Duffy and wing Simon Keogh scored the tries, while Burke slotted four penalties and his replacement, Andy Dunne, also added a penalty and a conversion to complete a fine win and add more silverware to the Harlequins trophy cabinet.

In truth, however, success in the European Shield had papered over a lot of cracks at the club, which still had not fully adapted to the day-to-day realities of professionalism. And this was brought into sharp focus in the following season when the 'unthinkable' happened and the future of Harlequins was suddenly on the line again.

EUROPEAN CHALLENGE CUP FINAL 2004
Montferrand 26 Harlequins 27
(Madejski Stadium)

Montferrand: A Floch; A Rougerie, R Chanal, T Marsh, S Kuzbik; G Merceron, P Mignoni; C Soulette, O Azam, D Attoub, H Louw, T Privat, M Reynaud, O Magne, E Vermeulen
Replacements: E Pearce for H Louw (50 mins), A Audebert for E Vermeulen (50 mins), S Viars for S Kuzbik (59 mins), L Emmanuelli for C Soulette (73 mins)
Tries: Azam, Mignoni **Conversions:** Floch (2)
Penalties: Floch (3)
Drop-Goal: Merceron

Harlequins: G Duffy; G Harder, W Greenwood, M Deane, U Monye; P Burke, S Bemand; M Worsley, T Fuga, J Dawson, S Miall, J Evans, P Sanderson, A Vos, T Diprose
Replacements: S Keogh for M Deane (55 mins), A Dunne for P Burke (60 mins), C Jones for M Worlsey (60 mins), L Sheriff for J Evans (67 mins), J Leonard for J Dawson (73 mins)
Tries: Duffy, Keogh **Conversion:** Dunne
Penalties: Burke (4), Dunne

Referee: Nigel Whitehouse (Wales)
Attendance: 13,123

Top left: Gavin Duffy goes over the line to score Harlequins' first try in the 2004 European Challenge Cup Final against Montferrand

Top right: Simon Keogh is congratulated on scoring the second

Bottom left: The ecstatic Andre Vos lifts the trophy…

Bottom right: …but retiring hero Jason Leonard steals the show

CENTRE OF EXCELLENCE

A big part of the professional rugby set-up at modern-day Harlequins is the state-of-the-art training headquarters at Surrey Sports Park in Guildford.

The £35m centre, opened in 2010 and situated in the grounds of Surrey University, houses a 50-metre Olympic-size swimming pool, three multi-sports halls, a squash centre, 700 square metres of fitness facilities, two artificial all-weather floodlit pitches, outdoor and indoor tennis courts, four real tennis courts and a climbing centre.

More importantly for Quins, however, is that there are also a number of excellently maintained full-size rugby pitches and, after initially basing themselves in an old student union complex, the club has added its own clubhouse containing medical facilities, meeting rooms and player dining areas.

The Sports Park has a strong rugby tradition, having hosted the Women's Rugby World Cup in 2010, which proved a great success, and served as a much-prized training base for a number of teams during the 2015 Rugby World Cup.

"A world-class training base is very important, in fact vital, for a club like Quins," explains Conor O'Shea, who took over as Quins' Director of Rugby in 2010 and played an integral part in the club's move to the Sports Park later that same year. "It's the heartbeat of the elite playing section of the club, where all the hard work gets done, where the squad plots and plans, where players recuperate and recover come rain or shine. You can get so much concentrated work done in a place like this. It's the kind of place you look forward to going. Training is never a chore or just routine.

"For most of the players it becomes a second home and as such needs to be a place where everybody feels comfortable. It's quite an inspiring environment to work in, with elite athletes from all sorts of disciplines. Quins has always been very pleased to be part of that overall sports community and there is a very useful swapping of expertise and ideas. It's a very buzzy place to train and operate out of.

"The club has enhanced the facilities available to it considerably since 2010 by adding a dedicated clubhouse, but the players utilise all that the wider Sports Park offers. The pitches are excellent, the top pitch in particular always seems to be in good condition no matter what the elements throw at it, and the whole complex is pretty accessible to most of the guys, a drive down the A3 from London."

Right: The facilities at the Harlequins training headquarters at Surrey Sports Park are designed to get the very best out of the squad

The sweatshop. Intensive gym sessions are a part of daily life for elite rugby players, and to that end Quins make use of the excellent gym facilities at the Sports Park.

▨ **Above:** Quins' Head Coach Mark Mapletoft leads a review session

▨ **Far left:** Assistant Kitman Tommy Fuller makes sure the players' equipment is in tip-top shape

ATTACK
IMPOSE QUINS STYLE
ROLE CLARITY
BREAKDOWN
TEMPO
PHYSICALITY   WORKRATE

Above: Director of Rugby John Kingston leads a full team meeting. Analysis is a vital part of the elite game and uses the latest video technology (right)

Far right: Quins coaches for 2016–17 (*from left to right*): Nick Easter, Graham Rowntree, John Kingston, Mark Mapletoft and Collin Osborne

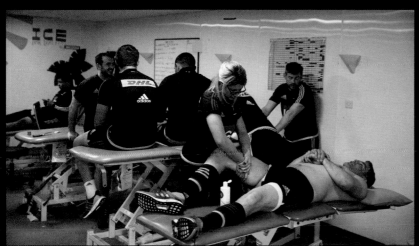

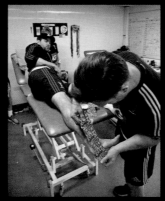

Rugby is a physically demanding sport, making expert medical support and physiotherapy essential. Players can burn thousands of calories during a training session, and their diet is carefully monitored by the club to ensure they have everything they need to be at their sharpest

Above: Changing rooms are the inner sanctum for any club. Jack Clifford chats with Adam Jones (top left) while Danny Care (above) and Mike Brown (far left) prepare for another session

Opposite: Charlie Matthews soars high during line out practice

Left: Field of Dreams: The main practice pitch at Surrey Sports Park

Above: A Quins training session is an exhausting but rewarding experience

197

Kicking back in the Players' Lounge after training is always good for morale. The bespoke team room provides the squad a place to relax and catch up, as well as offering pool shark Adam Jones the chance to take on all comers and a quiet place to sign some memorabilia

11

Down but not out

2005–2011

11

Relegation was a massive shock to Harlequins when it came at the end of the 2004–05 season. However, ultimately many consider it to be the best thing that could have happened as it forced the club to concentrate on putting in place the structures required to ensure its long-term prosperity. A rocky road lay ahead but – as can be seen throughout the history of Harlequins, especially during hard times – somehow it seemed to energise the club to reach greater heights.

Title page: Mehrtens reflects on his brief but hugely influential spell at Harlequins following his final game for the club against Sale in April 2007

Right: James Hayter (*sitting*) and captain Andre Vos (*standing*) are devastated after Quins' defeat to Sale condemns the club to relegation

Mark Evans had been confronted with myriad challenges when he arrived at Quins in 2000, with the process of re-aligning the club in the professional era as important as improving the competitiveness of the squad.

"We had to take a good look at ourselves again," he explains. "The ground was looking shabby and we had no real identity. We started looking at considerable ground improvements, but in the meantime simply painting the ground in the club colours helped brighten the place up.

"The recruitment advantages Quins used to enjoy, connections with the universities and perhaps being able to find jobs in the City, no longer really mattered. Being a professional rugby player was now a stand-alone job. Harlequins wasn't producing its own players – the club had relied too heavily on signing players – so the first thing I did was to get Tony Russ and Collin Osborne to establish an academy and that has made a massive contribution ever since.

"We were right in the middle of a rugby hotspot but gates had become very small. We had to engage with that community so the first thing we did was offer very competitive prices for season tickets. Harlequins, in the professional era, had to identify its core support and start nurturing it."

The coaching situation remained fluid as Evans appointed John Kingston – more of an out and out coach – as Director of Rugby at the end of the 2000–01 season but soon took over responsibility for the team once again. For a while there was evidence of steady if unspectacular improvement with successive Premiership finishes of ninth, seventh and sixth between 2001–04, and off the pitch the rebuilding of the club was looking promising.

For the 2005–06 season Dean Richards, so successful during his spell as Director of Rugby at Leicester, had been lined up to fulfil a similar role at Quins and All Blacks fly-half Andrew Mehrtens had put pen to paper. But then, seemingly almost from out of nowhere, came relegation.

In retrospect the 2004–05 Premiership season was probably as competitive as it has ever been. Quins' final total of 38 points would have seen the club survive most years and Leeds Tykes, sitting in eighth position, had only accumulated five points more than Quins. When it came to losing bonus points, Quins had the top total in the league with nine, which suggests that the team was very competitive but unable to convert pressure into points and narrow defeats into wins. Even on the last day, when Quins squandered a 12–0 lead to lose 23–22 to Sale, just one more Quins try would have resulted in a bonus point win and seen the club climb above Northampton Saints to safety in the league.

Yet the bottom line was that Quins probably deserved to be relegated. The team never really recovered from an appalling start which saw eight straight losses in the league, and come the day of reckoning – no matter what gloss was applied – Quins had ultimately won two fewer games than any other side.

The initial fall-out was painful and costs had to be cut immediately. There were redundancies amongst the club's staff and players had to take significant wage cuts. Mentally, the entire club had to quickly take on board the reality of relegation and, in fact, the very real need to bounce back and earn promotion at the first attempt. Relegation can make or break a club: some clubs have emerged stronger for the ordeal, but the likes of West Hartlepool and even Orrell – highly regarded rivals of Quins for so long – plummeted down through the leagues and into obscurity. Which was it to be?

With its back up against the wall, however, the situation quickly steadied for the club. Skipper Andre Vos resisted other lucrative offers and recommitted his future, while Mehrtens arrived and Will Greenwood stayed, and the sponsors, NEC, were still fully on board along with the owners, Duncan Saville and Charles Jillings. Membership inexplicably started to increase, while the ground development plans continued unabated and Evans and Tony Copsey continued to work hard to commercialise the club. From the off Harlequins rolled up their sleeves and decided to embrace National Division One rugby, as did the spectators.

The fanbase continued to build, as is often the case when a side starts winning the majority of its matches, and the average home gate that season was an impressive 8,996, which was higher than the previous

season in the Premiership. A significant number of those fans also decided to hit the road and follow Quins to new rugby venues such as Manchester, Plymouth, Doncaster, Truro and Birmingham

The team hit their stride quickly and proved pretty much unstoppable, registering 25 wins out of 26 games, but many of the matches were very competitive and Exeter did emerge victorious at the County Ground in February thanks to a fine 13–8 win. Away from the spotlight and media there was also the opportunity for promising players such as Chris Robshaw and Mike Brown to learn their trade, while the elder hands including Vos, Mehrtens and Tony Diprose had far more opportunity for one-on-one coaching and mentoring than would probably have been the case in the Premiership.

"The accepted wisdom is that relegation was the making of the new Quins, but I would only partly go along with that," recalls Evans. "The plans for regeneration were already in place, the new stand had been signed off, high-profile signings had been completed, the fanbase was growing and the general progression of the club on the pitch had been slowly but definitely upwards. We were poised for lift off but then we had one of those inexplicable seasons and suddenly found ourselves out of the Premiership. I look back and accept that, personally, I was trying to do too much at times – Chief Executive and Director of Rugby – but sport is sport; if it wasn't for a couple of close calls we would have won two or three more games and finished mid-table.

"What our time down in the National Division One did do was enable Dean to build a winning team, establish that winning mentality and blood young players like

Brown and Robshaw earlier than perhaps he might have done in the Premiership. And of course when you are building up a fanbase it helps considerably to be winning just about every week; a feel-good factor starts to kick in, even though you are playing in a lower league. The owners and sponsors were fully committed and the supporters were really buying into the club."

Above: All Blacks legend Andrew Mehrtens arrived for the 2005–06 season, despite the club's relegation to National Division One

Above: Dean Richards' modern approach to coaching galvanised the team to bounce straight back up after relegation

Right: Richards brought the best out of the likes of Nick Easter, seen here breaking through the Pertemps Bees' defence during Harlequins' first fixture in National Division One

Opposite: Harlequins celebrate promotion back to the Premiership at the first time of asking, having recorded 25 wins in 26 games

Colin Herridge also observed a change in the general approach under Richards: "Dean was very keen that everybody enjoyed the ride and insisted the team always stay for a few beers with the opposition afterwards. In fact, he even arranged a few overnighters for some old-fashioned bonding sessions. I understand one evening in Plymouth got particularly lively, ending with a breakfast dip in the freezing Atlantic the following day. There were plenty of long coach journeys home from various distant destinations and they were great for building team spirit as well. There were a lot of smiles around and the squad became very tight."

Richards was a very influential figure who instinctively knew the practical realities of the club fighting its way out of the second tier, but he was also exceptionally good at encouraging the younger brigade, as Robshaw confirms: "That promotion season was an important one personally and for the club. I'd had some pretty serious injury problems and was beginning to fret, but I had got myself very fit ahead of that season and Dean was very encouraging at training. I'd set my sights on a place in the 'A' team or on the bench at best – with the likes of Andre Vos, Nick Easter, Tony Diprose, Luke Sherriff and others around I wasn't counting any chickens – but he insisted I should be aiming to start in the first team. I shouldn't settle for anything less.

"He was as good as his word and picked me to start in a dozen or so league games until I broke my leg in a Monday morning training session. It was the week after our defeat at Exeter, which I had missed as I was away with England Under-21s, and I wandered into a pretty full-on, snarly session as the boys worked off their frustration. I wasn't quite switched on and clumsily got my leg trapped at a ruck. I was absolutely furious with myself but even then Dean was very supportive.

"Next season, when we had been promoted, I had another big injury, rupturing an ACL playing Sevens. I seemed jinxed and Quins would have been fully entitled to release me from my academy contract after six months but straight away Deano assured me that I was still part of his plans. That gave me peace of mind and allowed me to fully commit to the rehab and come back properly in my own time.

GUINNESS PREMIERSHIP

WE'RE GOING UP

NEC HARLEQUINS

COMEBACK COMPLETED!

DIVISION ONE
CHAMPIONS 2005/06

Commitment · Loyalty · BELIEVE

Right: Will Greenwood celebrates scoring a try in the 2006 Powergen National Trophy Final against Bedford at Twickenham, while skipper Andre Vos lifts the trophy (far right)

Below: Winning the trophy was the icing on the cake at the end of the promotion season and proved that Harlequins' winning mentality had well and truly been restored

to watch everything Vos did at training and in matches and learn because he was one of the best."

Harlequins' priority on returning to the top flight was simply to remain there, and in the next couple of seasons the club achieved this goal with a fair bit to spare. Quins never remotely threatened to get in on the hunt for trophies, but the team wasn't scrabbling to avoid relegation either. Performances at the time were considered 'ball-park' and there was time to learn and grow as a team.

In the 2006–07 season there was, briefly, a worrying start with five defeats on the bounce, but the club found its stride with a 34–19 win over Saints in the first week of November and thereafter recovered to such an extent that it finished seventh in the Premiership. With an average home attendance of 11,091, the support continued to grow – Harlequins had found its modern-day identity.

Outstanding young players like Robshaw, Brown and Danny Care were beginning to come to the fore, while a slightly older generation, including the likes of Ugo Monye and Easter, were flexing their muscles. The ambition was palpable, and this was underlined in May 2007 when Richards pulled off a major coup by signing All Black fly-half Nick Evans, who was to join the club after the conclusion of the 2007 World Cup. Many overseas players had joined Premiership clubs at the end of their careers, but very few of Evans' stature had made the move in their pomp and with a long career still ahead of them.

The circumstances were slightly unusual. Many observers would have conceded that Evans was one of the top three or four fly-halves in the world, but it was his

Left: Future stars! (From left to right) Chris Robshaw, Danny Care and Mike Brown all made a significant impact during Quins' promotion season and kicked on impressively when the club returned to the Premiership, with Brown winning the rather distinctive Player of the Season award for 2006–07

misfortune to be a contemporary of Dan Carter, possibly the best fly-half in the history of the game, which prevented him from ever holding down a regular starting spot for the All Blacks. With Carter looking to continue to the 2011 World Cup and well beyond, there was little realistic hope of Evans becoming a regular for New Zealand, and so he was attracted by the prospect of playing full-time in England and putting down roots in the UK.

Indeed, Evans did exactly that in 2013 when he became a British citizen, and with the fly-half in the side from Christmas onwards Harlequins continued to progress in 2007–08, finishing in sixth place after a purple patch in March where they beat both high-flying Gloucester and Bath to hint at exciting days ahead.

For the time being, though, Europe was very much on the backburner. In that first season after promotion Quins showed some promise in the Challenge Cup but failed to qualify from their pool, finishing second behind Bath – although a 37–27 win at

Montpellier provided a definite highlight. The 2007–08 European campaign saw Quins enter the Heineken Cup, but it proved a baptism of fire as, in a brute of a pool that also included Stade Francais, Cardiff and Bristol, the club failed to register a single win. Competitive against the two British teams, Richards' side came a distant second in the two matches against star-studded Stade Francais, losing 37–17 in Paris and 31–10 at home. It was both a painful experience and a huge learning curve for those willing to take the lessons on board – this was the level every player had to aspire to.

And so to the 2008–09 season which, for the most part, included some of the best rugby ever seen by Quins in the professional era, both in the Premiership and in Europe. Ultimately, however, the season would end in tears with the club in disgrace after the 'Bloodgate' scandal. But where did it all go wrong?

At the start of the season Richards, with the X-factor that Evans provided at fly-half,

felt he had a squad strong enough to fight on all fronts and set both the Premiership and the Heineken Cup as objectives. In the Premiership Harlequins appeared much more consistent – finishing in second place in the regular season and qualifying for the play-offs – and proved free-scoring throughout, logging 60 tries in 22 regular season matches and recording some mighty wins along the way, including doubles over Bath and Saracens and a spectacular 32–10 victory over Wasps. Frustratingly the team then produced its one truly sub-par performance of the season, losing 17–0 to eventual finalists London Irish. Most of the time, though, there was a buzz around the place, and this was epitomised by the 50,000 crowd the team attracted to Twickenham for the inaugural 'Big Game' against Leicester Tigers on 27th December, which resulted in an entertaining 26–26 draw.

In the Heineken Cup Harlequins finally started to put its best foot forward and topped an ultra-competitive group that included Stade Francais, Ulster and Scarlets.

Quins came of age with a magnificent 15–10 win over Stade Francais in front of over 70,000 roaring fans at the Stade de France, when some heroic defence and tries from Tom Williams and Jordan Turner-Hall saw the team home. Then, just a week later, Quins claimed arguably the most dramatic win in its history in the return game. On this occasion, after an injury time passage of play that lasted over four minutes, Evans clinched victory at the death with a drop-goal that sent Quins into the quarter-final against Leinster. Life could not have been sweeter for Harlequins and its growing army of supporters.

It was on a murky afternoon on 12th April 2009 at The Stoop when the urge to win and the desire to finally become a recognised force in the Heineken Cup overcame common sense and fair play. The quarter-final against Leinster was a scrappy, intense affair with none of the open rugby that both teams were famed for, and as the game progressed it became increasingly likely that one score – most probably a penalty or drop-goal – would decide the match either way.

Evans had been doubtful before kick-off with a thigh muscle injury and, although he started the match, he had to come off in the 47th minute to be replaced by Chris Malone with the score at 6–0 to Leinster. Thereafter Quins were in the ascendancy and a try from Brown 14 minutes from time put them right back in contention at 5–6. Easter and Will Skinner both went close and Quins also had a try disallowed when referee Nigel Owens couldn't see enough to award the points.

With 11 minutes left Malone picked up an injury and limped off to be replaced by Williams. At this crucial stage of the game, the season and – arguably – the club's

Opposite: When the going gets tough… Paul Volley in action against Bath in 2007

Left: Harlequins recorded two famous victories against Stade Francais in 2008, in front of 70,000 at the Stade de France (left and below) and at home when Nick Evans' famous last-minute drop-goal sent The Stoop into ecstasy

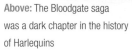

Above: The Bloodgate saga was a dark chapter in the history of Harlequins

history, Quins suddenly had no recognised goal-kicker or drop-goal exponent on the pitch. Panic ensued.

It was at this point that Richards, in his desire to win a game that Quins should probably have already wrapped up, overstepped what is permissible and fair. Even though Evans was injured, Richards needed him out on the pitch on the off chance that a kickable opportunity presented itself. The fly-half proceeded to have his injured knee heavily strapped and to warm up on an exercise bike on the touch line. Then Richards arranged with physiotherapist Steph Brennan for Williams to fake a blood injury, which was the only way Evans would be permitted to return to the field.

To these ends a theatrical blood capsule, apparently purchased from a joke shop in Clapham Junction, was sent out for Williams

to complete the subterfuge, but with the Sky TV cameras in attendance the watching rugby world was quickly alerted that something untoward had happened. In any case the Leinster players and staff protested furiously to Owens, but Evans was allowed to return to the field and did get one attempt at a drop-goal, although mercifully it sailed wide. If Quins had won the match and progressed in the tournament the consequences, dire as they turned out to be, are scarcely worth thinking about.

After the match Leinster lost no time in lodging an official complaint about the incident. Richards proclaimed Quins' innocence and insisted that all involved had acted within the laws of the game, but already TV replays revealed that something irregular had occurred and the ERC ordered an investigation, as did Harlequins itself.

Richards eventually admitted that he had orchestrated the whole affair with Brennan and Williams. Most disturbing of all, however, was that pressure had been put on the club's duty doctor, Wendy Chapman, to cut Williams' lip with a scalpel in the changing room so there was 'evidence' of a genuine injury when the player was examined after the game.

The incident eventually resulted in a £259,000 fine, a three-year ban for Richards and a two-year ban for Brennan, while Chapman was suspended temporarily by the General Medical Council before being officially warned and allowed to continue practising as a doctor. Williams received a one-year ban for his part, but this was later reduced to four months on appeal.

Club Chairman Charles Jillings also resigned, saying: "We, Harlequins, acknowledge that we failed to control Dean Richards. I trusted Dean. As a result of the board's failure to exercise control, the club cheated. This is totally unacceptable. Ultimately this happened on my watch and the failure to control must fall at my door."

Harlequins did, however, escape expulsion from the following year's competition for which they had qualified by virtue of finishing second in the Premiership. It would be hard to think of an incident more at odds with the club's history and general ethos.

"It was a sorry affair," says Club President Bob Hiller. "Harlequins cheated, got caught, and were heavily punished. There can be no complaints. It sent shockwaves around the club, our name was mud for a while and it took a couple of seasons at least to fully move on. I can't really offer any logical explanation. Having played a fair bit of top-level rugby myself, I know how that desire to win can almost become an obsession and fill your mind. It was a huge game, a Heineken Cup semi-final place was within touching distance after all the club had gone through since being relegated a few years earlier, but ultimately it's still just sport and there is always a line you must never cross."

Just four years after being relegated, the scandal was another massive test of Harlequins' resolve and club spirit. Initially there was the shame and guilt to deal with, and unsurprisingly that loss of self-esteem and confidence translated itself on to the field the following season when Quins struggled to eighth place in the Premiership, the ever-loyal John Kingston taking over as temporary coach and doing a stalwart job. There was also the sense that, going forward, Quins would be more closely scrutinised than any other club in rugby history. Everything had to be whiter than white, there could be no shortcuts. Everybody was waiting for the club to trip up.

"Bloodgate was a bombshell, there is no other way of looking at it, and a lot of very good people got caught up in it," recalls Mark Evans. "It was totally out of character. Dean had done a fantastic job for Quins over four years, but we got what we deserved and it took fully 12–18 months to recover. In playing terms we lost a season at a time when the club was making great strides. I was actually considering leaving that summer for a fresh challenge but couldn't depart under those circumstances and remained. The entire club had to earn its good reputation afresh through hard work and honesty."

In December 2009, Evans unveiled Conor O'Shea as the new Director of Rugby. Given the recent past, it was clearly a key appointment and Quins had launched a worldwide search for the right man to lead

the club, if not out of the wilderness then at least to a better place. He came with impressive credentials, both as a player and coach with London Irish and as an academy manager with the RFU, while he also had that extra dimension of having served as Director of the English Institute of Sport (EIS) for the 18 months prior to his appointment at Harlequins. He certainly knew his rugby, but he was also at the cutting edge of sports science.

"We had a good look around but actually Conor was our first choice from early in the process," says Evans. "His CV was excellent but most of all we had seen with our own eyes the great job he had done with limited resources at London Irish. He took some persuading, mind. He was heavily committed to the EIS and ideally wanted to see that through to London 2012."

One of the first appointments O'Shea made was to give Chris Robshaw the captain's armband. O'Shea recognised a quality player who even during Quins' recent bad times had been voted Premiership Rugby Player of the Season by his peers and fellow professionals. Robshaw would be a captain who led by his honest hard work and personal example, and given that Bloodgate was still so recent in everybody's minds this was no bad thing. As a player and individual, Robshaw would always stand up to the closest scrutiny.

In the Premiership that first season under O'Shea, Quins hardly set the world alight with a seventh-place finish, yet the eight losing bonus points suggested the club could be real contenders if it converted those narrow defeats into victories.

Not for the first time it was the European Challenge Cup that ignited Quins, and the

club's third title was perhaps the most significant in that it kick-started a surge of confidence and momentum that was to pay dividends the following season.

With no relegation worries in the Premiership and the realisation that it was probably a year too early to have serious title ambitions, Harlequins threw the kitchen sink at Europe in 2010–11, qualifying as pool winners over Connacht, Bayonne and I Cavalieri. This set up a compelling road to the final, which in short order saw Quins tackle European giants Wasps, Munster and old rivals Stade Francais. These high-profile games against Europe's elite were incentive enough, but they also offered a chance for England hopefuls to stake their claim for inclusion in Martin Johnson's 2011 World Cup squad.

First up was Wasps at The Stoop, where 22 points from the boot of Evans and tries from Care and Maurie Fa'asavalu heralded a deeply impressive 32–22 win. But then came the big one, an away semi-final against Munster at Thomond Park, the graveyard for so many European hopes. This was a key match for Quins in so many ways – a rite of passage for a young team – but if they could leave Ireland with a win then it would be a pure rugby story to finally banish any thoughts of Bloodgate.

Above: The appointment of Conor O'Shea as Director of Rugby in December 2009 heralded a new era for the club

Left: Get that man! Paul O'Connell of Munster is tackled by Joe Gray and George Robson (*left*) during the impressive 2011 European Challenge Cup semi-final victory away at Munster

Centre: Oh yes, that felt good! Nick Easter (*left*), Robson and Ugo Monye enjoy the moment

Right: Man of the match Maurie Fa'asavalu takes the acclaim from the crowd flanked by Chris Robshaw (*left*) and Easter

In front of a 26,000 crowd at Thomond Park in warm weather, it was quality all the way as Quins took the game to Munster with two first-half tries from Care and Fa'asavalu, and there could have been two or three other scores before the break.

Munster did hit back with a Felix Jones try and had an effort from Doug Howlett disallowed for a forward pass as the nerves started to jangle, but a brace of penalties from replacement Rory Clegg stretched Quins' lead.

A late sending off for Easter saw Harlequins play out the final 10 minutes with 14 men, but the team defended with aplomb to secure a 20–12 victory. At the time it was only the second occasion that Munster had been defeated at Thomond Park in either European tournament.

"That was a huge win for us a team," recalls Robshaw. "As Conor said in the changing room afterwards, we had that in our locker forever. Wins like that change your entire mindset. If you can beat Munster at Thomond in Europe, you are capable of beating anybody. It doesn't mean to say you will, you still have to put all the hard work in, but after winning at Munster you know big

results and titles are possible. I always look back on the win at Thomond and then taking the cup against Stade a few weeks later as the foundations of our Premiership title the following season. No question."

Man of the match against Munster was Samoan flanker Fa'asavalu, who was revered by his colleagues for his professionalism and commitment to the cause. A star for Samoa in the 2003 World Cup, Fa'asavalu enjoyed a long and successful career in rugby league with St Helens and Great Britain before becoming one of O'Shea's first signings. During his time at the club he brought a new dimension to Quins' back row play, with his power-packed ball carrying adding much to the dynamism of the pack and his tackling striking fear into opposition teams. And never was that seen to better effect than in his barnstorming performance at Thomond Park.

The victory over Stade Francais at Cardiff City Stadium in the final was a dramatic affair as the Harlequins players had to keep their cool and come from behind at the end through a late score by Gonzalo Camacho. The try put Quins 17–18 behind with a touch line conversion to follow, but Evans was born for such moments and sent the ball soaring

through the posts with a minimum of fuss. Quins had won a third European Challenge Cup, but this time it really felt like it might be the start of something even bigger.

EUROPEAN CHALLENGE CUP FINAL 2011
Harlequins 19 Stade Francais 18
(Cardiff City Stadium)

Harlequins: M Brown; G Camacho, G Lowe, J Turner-Hall, U Monye; N Evans, D Care; J Marler, J Gray, J Johnston, O Kohn, G Robson, M Fa'asavalu, C Robshaw, N Easter
Replacements: W Skinner for M Fa'asavalu (60 mins), R Chisholm for G Lowe (75 mins)
Try: Camacho **Conversion:** Evans
Penalties: Evans (4)

Stade Francais: M Rodriguez; J Arias, M Bastareaud, G Bousses, D Camara; L Beauxis, J Dupuy; R Roncero, R Bonfils, D Attoub, T Palmer, P Pape, J Haskell, A Burban, S Parisse
Replacements: JM Leguizamon for A Burban (37 mins)
Penalties: Beauxis (4)
Drop-Goals: Bastareaud, Rodriguez

Referee: George Clancy (Ireland)
Attendance: 12,236

Champions 2011

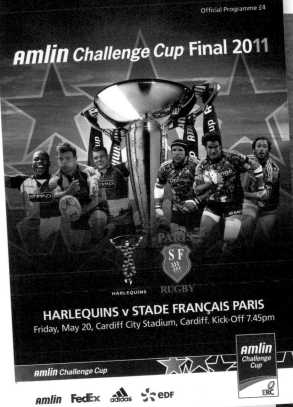

Official Programme £4

amlin Challenge Cup Final 2011

HARLEQUINS v STADE FRANÇAIS PARIS
Friday, May 20, Cardiff City Stadium, Cardiff. Kick-Off 7.45pm

amlin Challenge Cup

Amlin   FedEx   adidas   ⁕ eDF

Above: Beating Stade Francais 19–18 in the final in Cardiff, thanks in no small measure to Gonzalo Camacho's try (top, centre), was a watershed moment for the club after a difficult period

CLOSE QUARTERS

GOOD EVANS!

There have been many dramatic moments at The Stoop over the years, but none match the conclusion of Harlequins' Heineken Cup pool match against Stade Francais on the evening of 13th December 2008, where Nick Evans' last-minute drop-goal snatched a heroic victory in front of a raucous home crowd.

■ **Above:** Every Harlequins supporter's heart is in their mouth as Nick Evans, after almost five nerve-shredding minutes of extra-time, takes aim

Harlequins had notched up a famous win against the same opponents in France the previous week and a second success would all but guarantee a place in the quarter-finals. But the star-studded Parisians were in an uncompromising mood for the return game, and when Juan Martin Hernandez put Stade Francais 17–16 up with a 72nd-minute drop-goal the match seemed to be going their way. Then, with just over a minute to go, the following passage of play unfolded…

78.54: An uncharacteristic mistake by Italian legend Sergio Parisse, twice a nominee as IRB World Player of the Year, opens the door for Harlequins as the No. 8 decides to clear a 22-metre drop out from Nick Evans straight into touch. Quins have a line out 30 metres from the Stade line.

79.25: Flanker Will Skinner takes the ball cleanly and, though the Quins pack is forced to retreat under severe French pressure, the ball is recycled and kept in hand.

80.00: Full-time is up on the clock and the next stoppage, other than a penalty, will see referee Nigel Owens blow the final whistle.

A ruck forms on the 10-metre line as Quins adopt a pick and go approach, advancing towards the Stade line inch by inch.

80.20: Scrum-half Danny Care clearly thinks a drop-goal attempt is now on and wants Nick Evans to drop back into the pocket. He shapes to make a pass in Evans' direction but the former All Black fly-half signals to continue the surge forward.

80.40: Harlequins patiently recycle the ball and slowly advance forward over the chewed up turf. Stade Francais, conscious of conceding a kickable penalty, are not contesting the breakdown and simply concentrate on forming an impenetrable defensive line.

81.02: The clock ticks away as Quins enter the 11th phase of play since that first attacking line out. Evans is now definitely interested in a drop-goal and takes a good ball from Care, but instantaneously assesses that the kick is still not quite on. Instead he uses a moment of hesitancy from the Stade defence to break dangerously right to left, but then, with the ball wet and slippery, throws a poor pass to Jordan Turner-Hall out on the left wing. Turner-Hall bends low to take the ball on the half-volley and fumbles – did the ball go forward? Stade have no doubt and appeal loudly, but Owens waves play on. Quins breathe again.

81.30: Quins regroup after that heart-in-mouth moment and start methodically going through the phases again. The game remains in the balance.

81.50: The 16th phase unfolds and the fans at The Stoop are dying a thousand deaths. Evans positions himself 30 metres out and waits for Care to deliver the pass. The crowd momentarily goes silent... and Evans bails out again, not liking the odds. Instead he accelerates sharply past the charging defenders and gets to within 10 metres of the goal posts before being tackled.

The home side are now in striking distance, but their playmaker and drop-goal expert is at the bottom of a ruck.

82.00: It's the 17th phase and a try now seems a very real possibility. Quins break left from the ruck and Ugo Monye goes very close – just a few blades of grass between Harlequins and an epic victory – but it is certainly not clear and Owens has no choice but to play on as Quins continue to attack.

82.36: It's siege warfare on the Stade line and the Parisians have committed 13 players to the ruck, with just two outfield players defending the width of The Stoop pitch. If Quins look up now and swing it wide they are home and hosed, surely? The crowd is screaming to that effect but down on the pitch 30 exhausted players are in a world of their own, operating on instinct and memory as the oxygen debt accumulates and rational thought becomes difficult.

83.10: Chris Robshaw puts his head down and lunges for the line. Close but no cigar.

83.30: Quins finally look up and decide to move the ball right, but Stade have somehow reorganised their defence and the moment disappears.

83.39: The 27th phase arrives and Quins now seem intent on trying to win the game with a try. Care snipes away and Tom Williams on the right wing cuts in on the switch and sets off on a mazy run, beating a string of defenders. He makes virtually no ground going forward but crucially moves play back into the middle of the pitch and a ruck forms some 10 metres from the Stade posts. Suddenly Quins are in prime drop-goal territory again.

83.53: It's the 28th phase and Evans, standing 27 metres from the posts, calls for the ball from Care. The pivotal moment of the match has arrived.

83.56: Evans collects the pass and takes aim, but the alert Stade defence has read the play and are advancing quickly, straining every sinew in an attempt to cut off the opportunity. Evans knows that if he launches the ball high, in the textbook

fashion, there is still every chance it will be charged down, so he opts for a low, drilled kick, almost threading the ball through the onrushing defenders.

83.57: 13,000 fans hold their breath. The trajectory of the ball, as Evans said himself afterwards, resembles that of a dead duck falling to the ground, and as it heads into the murk under the posts in front of the South Stand, where the floodlights offer less than perfect illumination, it is difficult to see whether the ball has made it over the bar. Evans is sure from the off and wheels away in celebration, but the Stade players are less than convinced.

84.15: Owens isn't sure either and refers upstairs to the TMO. There is a short, agonising wait as the video referee examines the footage, but the cry of delight from those watching the monitors in the private boxes tells its own story. The replay shows the ball dropping over the crossbar – but only just – and the crowd erupts as Owens receives the official word in his earpiece and blows the final whistle to signal Harlequins' incredible 19–17 triumph.

■ **Above:** The Quins fly-half guides the ball through the onrushing Stade defence and over the bar, sealing an epic 19–17 triumph in the process

215

12

Champions at Last
2011–2012

12

In many ways the 2011–12 Premiership season was the perfect storm for Harlequins, with all sorts of factors coming together to bring about the club's greatest moment to date. A youngish side had been maturing together over the past few seasons and the European Challenge Cup success the previous year – especially those wins over Munster at Thomond Park and against Stade Francais in the final – had instilled a confidence that had previously been lacking. In particular, there was a new ruthlessness in tight games as the losing bonus points of past seasons were turned into vital wins – Quins claimed no fewer than 10 Premiership games by seven points or less during the campaign.

Title page: Chris Robshaw lifts the Aviva Premiership trophy after Harlequins' triumph over Leicester Tigers in the dazzling Twickenham sunshine on 26th May 2012

Below: The Quins players assemble for the pre-season squad photograph on the eve of the ultimately glorious 2011–12 campaign

Other more subtle factors were also at work, however, especially among key individuals who were feeling even more motivated than usual: Danny Care had initially been selected for England's 2011 World Cup squad but had to withdraw with an ankle injury; Chris Robshaw was unfortunate not to make the trip after impressing in the summer training camp; and Mike Brown unluckily missed out on selection at fullback. Meanwhile, Nick Easter was performing as well as any English forward in the Premiership, but when new

coach Stuart Lancaster came in was told that he was too old to be considered by England. As a result the club had four very fit, hungry players determined to prove a point.

After a summer training camp at Harlequins' new Surrey Sports Park base in Guildford, the rest of the squad was formidably fit as well. A busy pre-season schedule included the JP Morgan Sevens series and home matches against Esher and Nottingham, where younger players and those returning from injury were tried out,

before two tough away 'friendlies' against full-strength Ulster and Castres sides. Both these latter fixtures resulted in defeats but Quins wanted to start the Premiership campaign off the back of two serious, intensive workouts to make sure the team hit the ground running.

And that is exactly what Harlequins did, winning the first 10 Premiership matches of the season in a row – a stunning start and a real statement of intent. Such a run could never have gone on indefinitely in such a

218

competitive league, but like all good frontrunners Quins reserved sufficient gas to finish the season strongly, eventually beating Leicester Tigers in front of 81,000 fans at Twickenham Stadium. In rugby terms, wins don't come much bigger.

The road to the final started with a 29–24 victory over London Irish in the Premiership double header at Twickenham and, although the final score was much closer than Harlequins would have liked, it set the club's stall out for the season. The team was going to play high-tempo, adventurous rugby whenever possible, backing its skills and pace as all the best Quins teams have done down the years.

Brown enjoyed a memorable match at fullback to start a season that would end in his selection for England, and the only

downside was a broken arm for back row forward Tom Guest that meant he did not feature again in the Premiership until the end of December. By the time Guest returned for the narrow win at Exeter on New Year's Eve, the club was riding high at the top of the table, although the unbeaten run had come to an end on 27th December when Saracens won the Christmas 'Big Game' 19–11 in front of a full house at Twickenham, with Quins old boy David Strettle clinching victory with an interception try.

The setback against Saracens highlighted how close the Premiership was becoming. In fact, during Quins' autumn run of success the team had won five tight contests by fewer than seven points. Quins had led the table from the third round of games when a five-try 42–6 demolition of Gloucester had

propelled the club into first place ahead of second-placed Exeter, who had lost their unbeaten record to Bath, 23–19.

One of the high points of Harlequins' sparkling autumn form came in the shape of a first win at Leicester's Welford Road ground since 1997, a hugely significant result that was perhaps overlooked a little with the eyes of the world focused on the Rugby World Cup taking place in New Zealand. Leicester's coach Richard Cockerill could have justifiably pointed to his many absentee players as a factor in the defeat, but Quins won the match in style with an all-court game. There were tries for wings Sam Smith and Seb Stegmann, but the sweetest moment of all was the sight of Olly Kohn rumbling over from a rolling maul, a favourite ploy of the Tigers on their own patch.

Left: Playing a brand of fast, attacking rugby epitomised by livewire winger Ugo Monye, Harlequins won 10 matches on the trot at the start of the season, including the Premiership double header against London Irish

Above: Mike Brown excelled in the early part of the season, although Quins' unbeaten run came to an end in the Christmas Big Game against Saracens

Right: Playing them at their own game! A famous victory over Leicester was recorded at Welford Road thanks to a Tigers-style pushover try by Olly Kohn

Below: The popular away shirt from the 2011–12 season became synonymous with the team's style and success

The win at Leicester demonstrated again that the team was now capable of winning in the toughest environments, especially as it followed another notable success on the road, a 17–15 win over Worcester at Sixways on a Friday night. The home side led 15–3 at one stage, but a try from Smith and a penalty try, from more forward pressure, in the second half overturned the deficit – exactly the kind of game prospective Premiership champions needed to be winning.

Harlequins also gained a reputation for playing attractive rugby, even if the 48–41 win over Sale gave many supporters palpitations after a particularly hectic match at The Stoop. Sale scored four tries in the final 20 minutes after Quins had posted an initial lead of 38–12 at half-time, Brown scoring two tries. It was a warning shot over the bows, though, and coughing up a losing bonus point like that could have been costly indeed.

The season was full-on from start to finish and, as well as trying to conduct a successful league campaign, Quins seemed determined to produce a credible push for the Heineken Cup, having qualified by virtue of their Challenge Cup victory the previous year. It started well enough with wins over Connacht and Gloucester, but tough back-to-back games against Toulouse loomed. The French side won the battle of the breakdown to leave The Stoop with an outstanding 21–10 win, but Quins then produced yet another great away performance in the return match, winning a scintillating contest 31–24 with Brown capping another fine match by scoring two tries.

Qualification was still in the balance in a particularly even pool, and though Quins made it four wins out of five with a 20–14 victory against Gloucester in their next European game, the team still needed to win against Connacht at the Racecourse Ground in Galway to ensure a quarter-final place. However, Connacht dug deep to cling on 9–8, with a late Nick Evans penalty going just wide.

Elimination from Europe's premier cup competition was a big blow, with success on club rugby's biggest stage continuing to elude Quins. But fighting for league and European Cup honours in the same season requires huge resources beyond the reach of most, and being forced to concentrate on the league on this occasion was no bad thing.

There was a definite minor dip in form at this juncture – almost inevitable given the length of the season – and a 24–3 defeat at Northampton did not see the team at its best and allowed Saracens to move to within three points of the top of the table. Quins needed to regroup and with LV= Cup matches against Leicester and Cardiff in the offing O'Shea took the opportunity to rest the majority of his First XV squad before the next Premiership game, at home to London Irish on 11th February.

Robshaw and Brown were away on England duty at this point but, with George Robson deputising as skipper, Quins held off a late London Irish charge in an entertaining encounter to squeeze home 30–23 and complete a league double over the Exiles.

Robson had a major impact on the season, starting 22 of the 24 regular season and play-off matches for Quins at lock and putting in consistently high-quality performances at the heart of the pack. An England Under-16 and Under-18 player, Robson was – like Robshaw and Brown – a product of the Harlequins youth academy and played for the club for 11 years, including their season in National Division One, before eventually moving on to Oyonnax in the T14 after over 200 first team appearances.

Not huge for a top-level lock, Robson punched above his weight in everything he did on the pitch and won a huge amount of line out ball against much bigger opponents. Every title-winning side needs a George Robson in its ranks.

Next, a mix of grit and grunt up front and Evans' kicking proved to be crucial in helping Quins to a 16–14 win over Worcester in a scrappy match at The Stoop. A powerful rolling maul, led by Easter, earned a penalty try which cancelled out an opening effort from Worcester wing Miles Benjamin. With Saracens losing 19–20 to Leicester, the hard-fought win stretched the margin at the top to six points and Quins maintained the lead in the last round of games in February. Despite losing 29–23 at Gloucester, a try in the 80th minute from Ross Chisholm and a touch line conversion by Evans gained a

valuable losing bonus point on a weekend when Saracens lost 16–11 at Worcester.

To finish a gruelling but vital spell of games that coincided with the Six Nations, Harlequins grabbed another crucial two points when Evans' kicking gained a 9–9 draw at Newcastle, the fly-half landing his third penalty goal in the final minute to earn the points. And though Saracens beat Northampton 18–12, Quins still topped the table by four points.

Nevertheless the tired squad was in desperate need of a break and O'Shea's decision to grant the team a week's recuperation while the Six Nations finished was, in hindsight, a very sensible move. Harlequins returned refreshed for the final third of the campaign and promptly beat Bath 14–6 at The Stoop. The match featured another strong second-half display, which

was topped off by Maurie Fa'asavalu's try in the 73rd minute. The win also returned Quins to the top of the Premiership after Saracens, who had thumped Sale 45–9, had headed the table for 48 hours.

A week later the top two met at Wembley in a contest that attracted a crowd of 83,761 – a world record for a club game at the time. It was another brutal affair against a side that had developed into Quins' modern-day bogey team. However, the match will be remembered for Quins having three players sin-binned – Joe Marler, Care and Easter – but still managing to manufacture a priceless 24–19 win thanks largely to a quick start and first-half tries from Jordan Turner-Hall and George Lowe. The countdown to the play-offs was now fully underway and the onus fell on nailing down the top spot to secure a home draw for the semi-final.

Left: Harlequins recorded a famous victory against Saracens at Wembley – in front of a then world record crowd for a club game – despite having three players sin-binned

First there was the small matter of a Challenge Cup quarter-final at Toulon, but the players' minds may well have been on the Premiership campaign when they put in a disappointing performance to go down 37–8 at the Stade Mayol. However, Quins bounced straight back to form by flattening Wasps 33–17 in the next match. With two matches to go the victory over Wasps guaranteed a top four place, but Quins still needed to win one of the last two regular season games to guarantee a home draw.

The victory did not come at home to Leicester, with the Tigers winning an absolute humdinger of a game 43–33, Thomas Waldrom's late try and Toby Flood's conversion even denying Quins a losing bonus point. To get nothing out of the game was tough to take, but Quins bounced back the following week to beat Sale 24–10 and finish top of the pile. The club had led the league since the third week of the season and its reward was now a home semi-final against Northampton.

The home advantage may have proved the crucial factor in the semi-final play-off as Quins, nervous and misfiring, advanced with a narrow 25–23 win. The high drama came three minutes from time as most of the Quins team, cheered on by the home crowd, piled over the Saints line from a rolling maul before facing the agony of a prolonged TMO decision.

After leading the Aviva Premiership for 19 weeks of the regular season, Quins probably deserved the benefit of any doubt when Graham Hughes, the television match official, advised referee Andrew Small, whose vision had been blocked by a mass of bodies, that he could award the try with Marler getting the vital touchdown. Marler's try levelled the scores at 23–23 before Evans added the conversion to inflict Northampton's third successive Premiership semi-final defeat.

For Harlequins, the victory was another significant milestone and came a few days after Marler, then just 21, had been one of nine players from the club named in England's squad for the tour of South Africa that summer. Quins' players were finally beginning to get noticed in high places.

For the opening hour of a typically tense semi-final, goal-kickers Ryan Lamb and Evans had traded blows and the Saints led 18–15 before registering the first try of the match through scrum-half Lee Dickson, brother of Quins' Karl, who took advantage of a slick breakout put together by George Pisi, Vasily Artemyev and James Downey.

That 64th-minute score put Northampton 23–15 ahead, but the momentum of the game then swung in Harlequins' favour. A spell of ferocious pressure started when Lamb was

Opposite: George Robson celebrates as Joe Marler (not pictured) touches down to level the scores at 23–23 in the final minutes of the semi-final against Northampton, although there was an agonising wait until the try was awarded

Above: The Harlequins players celebrate reaching the club's first ever Premiership final while Saints skipper Lee Dickson (far right) sinks to his knees in despair

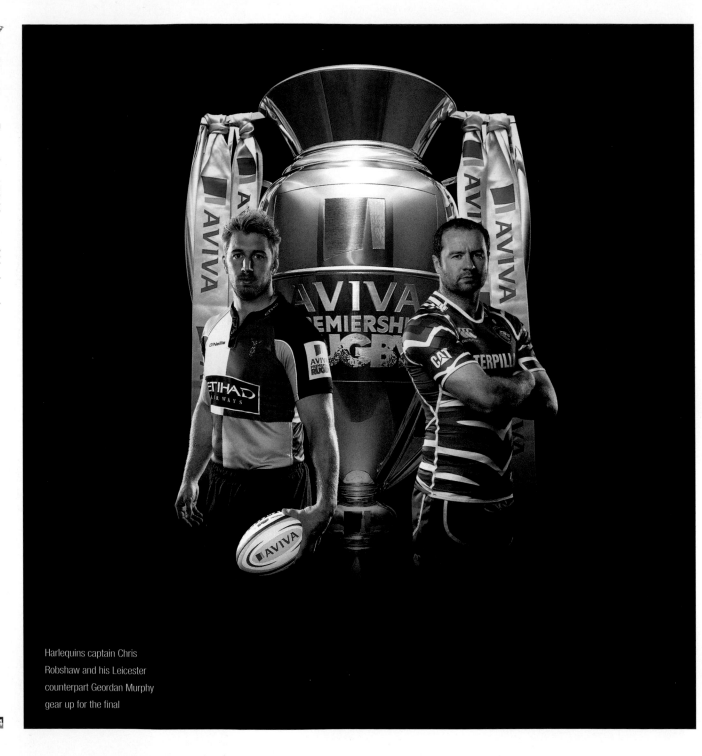

Harlequins captain Chris
Robshaw and his Leicester
counterpart Geordan Murphy
gear up for the final

caught in possession on his own try line and
Northampton were eventually penalised for
holding on. Evans landed his sixth penalty to
bring Harlequins to within a score at 18–23 in
the 71st minute and, from then on, Quins
dominated the contest until, after forcing
Northampton back, Marler's try levelled the
contest and Evans completed the comeback.

It was far from the most stylish or
convincing of performances, but O'Shea
remained unperturbed. "My dad won a lot of
All-Ireland Gaelic football finals for Kerry and
he always told me 'good semi-finalists never
make good finalists,'" he said. "We weren't
good today so hopefully we will make good
finalists. We have done nothing yet. We have
one game to go and we have a performance
in us, we know that."

And so it proved. Everything went right on
the day and Harlequins became the sixth club
to win the Premiership title. It had been an
emotional day from the off, not least a couple
of hours before the kick-off when thousands
of supporters lined the route from The Stoop
to Twickenham Stadium as the squad walked
from the club's HQ to the famous
international arena via the A316 footbridge. It
proved to be an inspirational journey.

Going into the match some observers felt
Quins had taken something of a risk, O'Shea
deciding to take advantage of the opportunity
to fly the squad to Abu Dhabi for four or five
days to recover from what had been a brutal
season. Quins had looked a little lacklustre in
the play-off semi-final and O'Shea believed
that, with a little TLC, he could conjure a
performance from his team. His players were
never going to beat Leicester Tigers in a
Twickenham final by being average – the
team would have to rediscover its zest and
put in the performance of a lifetime.

Above: Steely determination is etched on the faces of the players as they embark on the now traditional walk from The Stoop to Twickenham Stadium for the final, flanked all along the way by hordes of colourful and expectant Quins supporters

Right: Harlequins owners (*from left to right*) Charles Jillings, Duncan Saville and former Chairman Malcolm Wall soak up the pre-match build-up in the company of club legend and Sky Sports commentator Will Greenwood

Below: Chairman David Morgan (*right*) and club stalwart Colin Herridge soak up the pre-match atmosphere

Opposite: The two teams emerge to one of the great sights in rugby – a packed Twickenham Stadium on Aviva Premiership Final day with cheering supporters from both teams mingling and enjoying the moment

AVIVA PREMIERSHIP RUGBY FINAL 2012

HARLEQUINS v LEICESTER TIGERS
SATURDAY 26TH MAY, TWICKENHAM STADIUM, KICK OFF 15.00

After the enthralling 43–33 encounter at The Stoop only a month earlier, and given the Tigers' incredible track record of success at Premiership finals, the bookmakers made Leicester slight favourites. Harlequins, however, looked dangerous from the first whistle, shifting the point of attack often in a first half played at a fierce pace considering the hot conditions. Tapped penalties and 22 drop-outs were used as a ploy to keep things moving and Care's incessant sniping summed up the attitude, as did the work-rate of Robshaw and his pack who were quick to look for deft offloads.

Quins' reward was not long in coming, a fine Tom Williams try conjured after excellent hands from Robson and Easter opening up an 8–0 lead within 10 minutes, Evans having kicked an earlier penalty. George Ford replied for Leicester but a further penalty from Evans stretched the lead to 11–3 as Quins remained on the attack.

Such an attacking policy was not without its dangers, however, and Leicester always looked capable of counter-attacking. Ford quickly landed his second penalty to cut the margin to 11–6 and Leicester's most decisive intervention came on the half-hour mark when a loose Quins line out enabled Tigers prop Dan Cole to put flanker Steve Mafi in the clear on a 60-metre gallop to the line. Ford's conversion gave the Tigers a 13–11 lead, but a penalty from Evans just before the break, for which Waldrom also received a yellow card, re-established Quins' ascendency at 14–13.

The Harlequins players will have wondered how they had contrived to be only a single point ahead at half-time. The team had dominated territory, had the bulk of possession and were posing questions that Leicester were struggling to answer. Undeterred, Quins continued in the same vein after the interval and surged ahead during the next 16 minutes. Evans kicked his third penalty, and another three-pointer came after a promising attack almost brought a second try, Care's grubber kick to the corner after some inventive offloading just evading Brown and Ugo Monye.

Waldrom returned for Leicester having seen his side concede nine points while sin-binned and Quins soon struck again when Robshaw crashed over after good work by Joe Gray and Turner-Hall. Evans converted and, after Marler and James Johnston had forced a scrum penalty, he landed the kick for a lead of 30–13 and a personal contribution of 20 points.

The match looked done and dusted at this point, but Leicester's Ben Youngs led two attacks and from a quick tap penalty he worked a try for centre Anthony Allen. Ford converted and added a final penalty, and Leicester really went for broke in the final 10 minutes. However, despite some horrifically nerve-jangling moments, Quins held firm to claim the club's first Premiership title.

"It was a great feeling going up the steps to receive the trophy, but for me the best part of the day was when we reversed the pre-match walk from The Stoop and took the trophy back home," recalls Robshaw. "The supporters came with us and poured onto the ground while somebody produced a microphone in the grandstand and various players said a few words. Nick Easter took over as MC and introduced us all one by one and started a sing-song with one of his Chas & Dave numbers.

"It was a brilliant, happy evening. We wandered around in the sun drinking beers

Opposite: Tom Williams scores the first try of a pulsating match as Harlequins open up an 8–0 lead (top); Ugo Monye evades the tackle of Leicester's Alesana Tuilagi as Harlequins continue to attack, but the Tigers clawed their way back into the game and only trailed by a single point at half-time (middle); with Nick Evans kicking 20 points, Harlequins dominated the second half and, despite a late rally by Leicester, were worthy of their 30–23 victory (bottom)

Left: 'We've done it!' Jubilation greets the final whistle as Harlequins are Aviva Premiership champions for the first time in the club's history

Below: Winners! One of the medals issued to players and staff

and signing shirts and stuff, and then somebody said the coach was leaving for Kensington Roof Gardens, which had been quietly booked for a bash if we won the cup. A very good evening was had. That season had brought me the very great honour of captaining my country, but there is something very special about winning a major trophy with the club, colleagues and mates you have been playing and training with for years, in a number of cases since my early days with the academy. We had won the Premiership and we had won it the Harlequins Way."

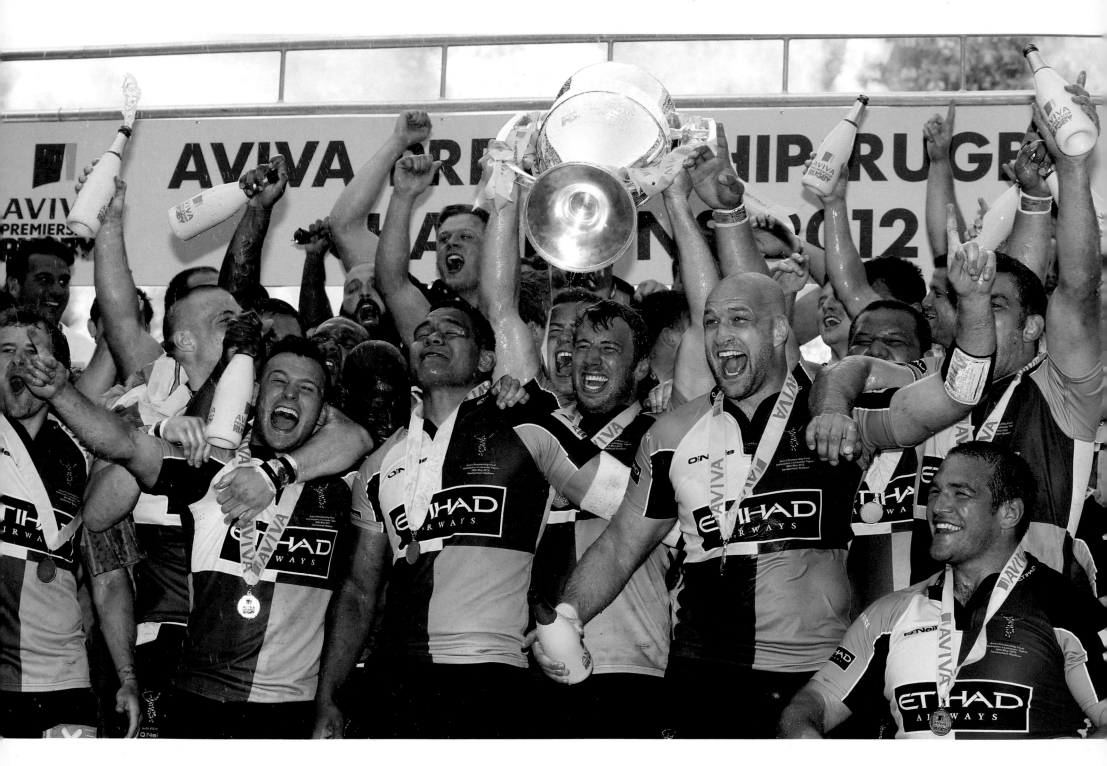

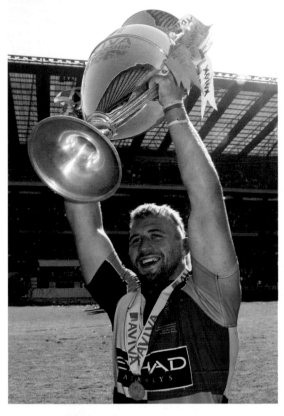

Champions all! With the Aviva Premiership trophy safely within Chris Robshaw's grasp (opposite), it was promptly passed around the team as the party went into full swing. Assisted by Mike Brown and Ugo Monye, Jordan Turner-Hall used it as an impromptu hat (top left), Joe Marler lifted it to the fans one last time (top right), captain Robshaw and delighted Director of Rugby Conor O'Shea posed for a photo (bottom left) together before it entered the Harlequins dressing room

Above: The celebrations continued long into the night back at The Stoop where thousands of Harlequins supporters gathered on the pitch to acclaim the players and to see the trophy one more time as skipper Chris Robshaw addressed the fans

Far left: George Robson and Danny Care share the moment

Left: Master of ceremonies Nick Easter poses for one final shot

AVIVA PREMIERSHIP 2011–2012

Match 1: 3rd Sept: v London Irish (A) **Won** 29–24
Tries: Johnston, Monye **Conversions:** Evans (2) **Penalties:** Evans (5)

Match 2: 9th Sept: v Northampton (H) **Won** 26–13
Tries: Gray, Monye **Conversions:** Evans (2) **Penalties:** Evans (4)

Match 3: 17th Sept: v Gloucester (H) **Won** 42–6
Tries: Smith, Wallace (2), Monye, Brooker **Conversions:** Evans (3), Clegg **Penalties:** Evans (2), Clegg

Match 4: 24th Sept: v Worcester (A) **Won** 17–15
Tries: Smith, Penalty Try **Conversions:** Evans (2) **Penalty:** Evans

Match 5: 1st Oct: v Sale (H) **Won** 48–41
Tries: Brown (2), Lowe, Kohn, Lambert, Evans **Conversions:** Evans (6) **Penalties:** Evans, Clegg

Match 6: 8th Oct: v Leicester (A) **Won** 27–18
Tries: Smith, Stegmann, Kohn **Conversions:** Evans (3) **Penalties:** Evans (2)

Match 7: 29th Oct: v Exeter (H) **Won** 19–13
Try: Brown **Conversion:** Evans **Penalties:** Evans (4)

Match 8: 5th Nov: v Bath (A) **Won** 26–13
Tries: Robshaw, Brown **Conversions:** Evans (2) **Penalties:** Evans (6)

Match 9: 27th Nov: v Newcastle (H) **Won** 39–8
Tries: Stegmann (2), Care, Wallace, Brown, Johnston **Conversions:** Evans (2), Clegg **Penalty:** Evans

Match 10: 4th Dec: v Wasps (A) **Won** 22–16
Tries: Hopper, Brown, Wallace **Conversions:** Evans (2) **Penalties:** Evans (3)

Match 11: 27th Dec: v Saracens (H at Twickenham) **Lost** 11–19
Try: Marler **Penalties:** Evans (2)

Match 12: 31st Dec: v Exeter (A) **Won** 11–9
Try: Care **Penalties:** Clegg (2)

Match 13: 3rd Jan: v Northampton (A) **Lost** 3–24
Penalty: Clegg

Match 14: 11th Feb: v London Irish (H) **Won** 30–23
Tries: Casson, Williams, Chisholm **Conversions:** Evans (3) **Penalties:** Evans (2) **Drop-Goal:** Care

Match 15: 18th Feb: v Worcester (H) **Won** 16–14
Try: Penalty Try **Conversion:** Evans **Penalties:** Evans (3)

Match 16: 25th Feb: v Gloucester (A) **Lost** 23–29
Tries: Chisholm (2) **Conversions:** Evans (2) **Penalties:** Evans (3)

Match 17: 2nd March: v Newcastle (A) **Draw** 9–9
Penalties: Evans (3)

Match 18: 24th March: v Bath (H) **Won** 14–6
Try: Fa'asavalu **Penalties:** Evans (3)

Match 19: 31st March: v Saracens (A) **Won** 24–19
Tries: Turner-Hall, Lowe, Care **Conversions:** Evans (2), Clegg **Penalty:** Clegg

Match 20: April 14: v Wasps (H) **Won** 33–17
Tries: Monye, Robson, Robshaw, Turner-Hall **Conversions:** Clegg (2) **Penalties:** Clegg (3)

Match 21: 21st April: v Leicester (H) **Lost** 33–47
Tries: Monye, Easter, Lowe **Conversions:** Evans (3) **Penalties:** Evans (4)

Match 22: 5th May: v Sale (A) **Won** 24–10
Tries: Care, Brown **Conversion:** Evans **Penalties:** Evans (4)

Match 23: Semi-final: 12th May: v Northampton (H) **Won** 25–23
Try: Marler **Conversion:** Evans **Penalties:** Evans (6)

AVIVA PREMIERSHIP FINAL 2011–12
Harlequins 30 Leicester 23
(Twickenham)

Harlequins: M Brown; T Williams, G Lowe, J Turner-Hall, U Monye; N Evans, D Care; J Marler, J Gray, J Johnston, O Kohn, G Robson, M Fa'asavalu, C Robshaw, N Easter
Replacements: R Clegg for N Evans (77 mins), T Guest for M Fa'asavalu (73 mins)
Tries: Williams, Robshaw
Conversion: Evans **Penalties:** Evans (6)

Leicester: G Murphy; H Agulla, M Tuilagi, A Allen, A Tuilagi; G Ford, B Youngs; M Ayerza, G Chuter, D Cole, G Skivington, G Parling, S Mafi, J Salvi, T Waldrom
Replacements: S Hamilton for H Agulla (74 mins), B Twelvetrees for G Ford (74 mins), L Mulipola for M Ayerza (72 mins), T Youngs for G Chuter (72 mins), M Castrogiovanni for D Cole (56 mins), G Kitchener for G Skivington (74 mins)
Tries: Mafi, Allen **Conversions:** Ford (2)
Penalties: Ford (3)

Referee: W Barnes (England)
Attendance: 81,779

Left: The press were full of praise for Quins' spectacular performance and the club produced a commemorative book to mark the occasion (above)

CLOSE QUARTERS

BIG IS BEST

The Big Game was the concept of former Harlequins Chief Executive Mark Evans, although he admits himself he borrowed heavily from the annual match between Stade Francais and Racing Paris at the Stade de France.

The idea was to make use of Twickenham Stadium to showcase the club, get a big crowd in through very reasonably priced tickets and generous concessions, and create an annual Christmas occasion that all sorts of rugby fans – not necessarily Harlequins supporters – would like to attend. It started as a loss leader and something of a gamble, with Quins needing to attract a 60,000 crowd in order to cover costs, but in no time the idea was thoroughly vindicated and the Big Game has been one of Quins' undoubted and ongoing success stories ever since. In the first eight games of the series there was a cumulative attendance of 592,473, giving an average attendance of 74,059. There is no other annual club game that currently comes anywhere near that figure.

Opposite: The Big Game just gets bigger and better, as Big Game 8 against Gloucester proved in 2015

Below: The start of a new tradition – Harlequins' first ever bespoke Big Game shirt

BIG GAME 1

Harlequins 26–26 Leicester Tigers
27th December 2008
Attendance: 50,000

Nobody knew quite what to expect from Evans' brainchild, but on a raw day a 50,000-strong crowd turned up in suitably festive mood and dress and were treated to a cracker, with Nick Evans landing a difficult touch line conversion in the final minute to secure the draw for Quins. The home side claimed a share of the honours the hard way, coming back from 23–9 down following Tigers' tries from Johne Murphy and Tom Croft. Mike Brown scored the first try for Quins and then Ugo Monye squeezed over at the death to set up Evans' dramatic late conversion.

BIG GAME 2

Harlequins 20–21 Wasps
27th December 2009
Attendance: 76,716

After a bizarre start, when the bird of prey delivering the ball headed for the crowd rather than the halfway line, Quins gifted Wasps an early try through Joe Simpson. Danny Cipriani threatened in attack but endured an off day with his goal-kicking, which could have been costly had Simon Shaw not kept the Wasps pack driving forward, and when David Walder eventually came on for Cipriani, Wasps went for the kill. Quins rallied with a try by Danny Care, but Wasps flanker John Hart scored a crucial try to secure victory and David Strettle's last-minute score offered little consolation for a Quins side that only truly hit their straps in the final quarter.

The eagle has not landed! The bird of prey tasked with delivering the match ball for Big Game 2 went slightly off course

Above: Joe Marler used Big Game 3 to show his support for the Great British banger – and fellow Quins forward Olly Kohn's company – in his own unique style

Right: The Harlequins players emerge for Big Game 4 wearing one of the most imaginative Big Game shirt designs so far (below)

BIG GAME 3
Harlequins 28–18 London Irish
27th December 2010
Attendance: 74,212

Goal-kickers Nick Evans and Chris Malone hogged the limelight during the first half – notching six and four penalties respectively – in an unsurprisingly cagey match given that Irish were low on confidence following seven straight Premiership defeats. George Lowe scored a nice try from a Jordan Turner-Hall kick after the break, but Irish rallied and went in search of a losing bonus point and might have felt a little aggrieved not to be awarded a penalty try when Quins coughed up three penalties inches from the try line without conceding a yellow card.

BIG GAME 4
Harlequins 11–19 Saracens
27th December 2011
Attendance: 82,000

The sell-out 82,000 crowd was officially a world record for a club game, but Saracens proved party poopers as Quins slipped to a first league defeat of the season. Sarries went 19–3 up in no time with four penalties from Owen Farrell, who also converted David Strettle's breakaway try. Quins hammered away for the rest of the game but, apart from a Joe Marler try and a second Nick Evans penalty, got little joy. "It wasn't the cup final out there today, this was just one match in 22," insisted Quins Director of Rugby Conor O'Shea after the game. "The cup final is in May and we will be there and we will be ready for it." And indeed they were…

Nick Evans is tackled by London Irish's Sailosi Tagicakibau during Big Game 5

BIG GAME 5
Harlequins 26–15 London Irish
29th December 2012
Attendance: 82,000

Irish were in the middle of a depressing run without a league win since September and never really got on terms with a Quins side not firing on all cylinders either. A poor first half in difficult wet conditions finished 6–6, with a brace of penalties apiece from Nick Evans and Ian Humphreys, and soon after the break it was 9–9. But Quins then finally started to exert some authority before Danny Care dived under three would-be tacklers to score. Evans and Humphreys continued their kicking duel but the matter was finally decided when referee Greg Garner awarded Quins a decisive penalty try.

BIG GAME 6
Harlequins 22–6 Exeter Chiefs
28th December 2013
Attendance: 74,827

Harlequins consolidated the club's hold on fourth place in the Premiership in a match that packed virtually all the relevant action into the first half. Quins scored two early tries through Nick Evans

and Charlie Walker, the latter from a nicely timed pass from Matt Hopper, with Exeter claiming just a Gareth Steenson penalty in reply. Quins sealed the victory when a trademark break from Danny Care sent Mike Brown flying in under the posts. A big win seemed likely but Exeter managed to batten down the hatches after the break in an anti-climactic second half.

Below: Mike Brown (*right*) celebrates his try against Exeter Chiefs during Big Game 6 with Sam Smith (*left*) and Danny Care

Harlequins mascot Charley gets the crowd going during Big Game 8

Care hit back to leave the home side trailing 17–15 at half-time. Gloucester nudged further ahead with a Harry Trinder try before Quins came storming back through Nick Easter and Ross Chisholm. A second try for Trinder and another from fullback Rob Cook seemed to have clinched the issue, but Quins earned a draw with a second try by Chisholm, converted by Nick Evans, who was then just wide with a drop-goal attempt that would have won the game. Frenetic but fun.

Left: The first adidas Big Game shirt, a stylish black number produced for Big Game 8, proved extremely popular with the fans

BIG GAME 7
Harlequins 25–30 Northampton Saints
27th December 2014
Attendance: 82,000

Not a vintage season for Quins as injuries and Test call-ups took their toll – Chris Robshaw and Nick Evans missed the match – but this was a cracker against the reigning champions. Quins took an early lead through a George Lowe try before going down the tunnel 13–8 down, Samu Manoa hitting back with a try and Stephen Myler kicking two penalties. After the break George North and Jack Clifford swapped tries before Saints took a decisive lead through Kahn Fotuali'i. Young lock Sam Twomey scored a late try for Quins, but it wasn't quite enough for the home side.

BIG GAME 8
Harlequins 39–39 Gloucester
27th December 2015
Attendance: 70,718

A riotous game of rugby with five tries apiece and the honours rightly shared. Gloucester were first out of the traps with tries for Jeremy Thrush and James Hook, but Marland Yarde and Danny

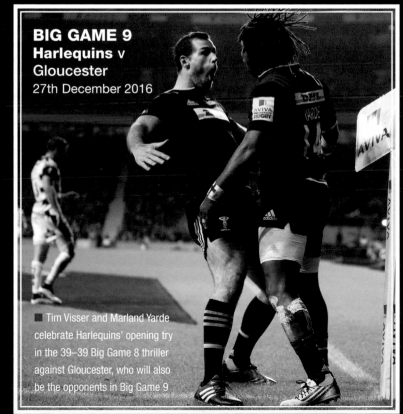

BIG GAME 9
Harlequins v Gloucester
27th December 2016

Tim Visser and Marland Yarde celebrate Harlequins' opening try in the 39–39 Big Game 8 thriller against Gloucester, who will also be the opponents in Big Game 9

13

Past, Present and Future

2013–2016

13

Taking home the Premiership title in 2012 was undoubtedly the high-water mark in Harlequins' history to date, but the club has been there or thereabouts in subsequent years, twice reaching the Premiership play-offs and winning more silverware in 2013 when a predominantly young team triumphed in the LV= Cup. It is often said that the only thing harder than reaching the top is staying there, but Quins performed strongly across the board in the 2012–13 season with little evidence of a hangover following their title-winning campaign.

Danny Care passes the ball during the 2012–13 Heineken Cup quarter-final against Munster at The Stoop, which Quins narrowly lost 18–12

In the 2012–13 Premiership season Harlequins finished third in the league table to reach the play-offs before losing 33–16 in their semi-final against Leicester, while in the Heineken Cup Quins reeled off six wins on the bounce in the pool stage to qualify as the top seed for the quarter-finals. Resisting the temptation to take the match over the road to Twickenham Stadium, almost 15,000 fans squeezed into The Stoop – the minimum capacity allowed for a quarter-final – for the game against Munster. But although Quins went in at the break leading 9–6, the powerful Irish side boxed very clever in the second half with Ronan O'Gara kicking all the points in a 18–12 victory.

Yet again it wasn't to be in Europe, but everybody in the squad was firing on all cylinders and some of the less high-profile players showed up extremely well in the successful LV= Cup campaign. Impressive pool wins over Northampton, Bath, London Welsh and Ospreys preceded a 31–23 semi-final win over Bath to set up a showdown with Sale Sharks at the Sixways Stadium, Worcester. Harlequins dominated the final from the start and emerged 32–14 victors after tries from Tom Williams, Tom Guest, skipper Luke Wallace and Tom Casson, with Ben Botica kicking the other 12 points.

The following season was a largely successful one as Quins again reached the Premiership semi-final play-offs – making it

LV= CUP FINAL 2013
Sale Sharks 14 Harlequins 32
(Sixways)

Sale: N MacLeod; T Brady, J Leota, S Tuitupou, C Ingall; D Cipriani, N Fowles; A Dickinson, T Taylor, T Buckley, F McKenzie, T Holmes, J Gaskell, D Seymour, A Powell
Replacements: A Croall for T Taylor (75 mins), R Harrison for A Dickinson (55 mins), H Thomas for T Buckley (50 mins), A Ostrikov for F McKenzie (50 mins), D Braid for D Seymour (50 mins), D Peel for N Fowles (50 mins), C Amesbury for C Ingall (67 mins), M Cueto for T Brady (50 mins)
Try: Leota **Penalties:** Cipriani (3)

Harlequins: R Chisholm; T Williams, G Lowe, T Casson, S Smith; B Botica, K Dickson; M Lambert, R Buchanan, W Collier, S Twomey, C Matthews, M Fa'asavalu, L Wallace, T Guest
Replacements: D Ward for R Buchanan (55 mins), D Marfo for M Lambert (71 mins), J Johnston for W Collier (50 mins), P Brown for S Twomey (68 mins), J Trayfoot for M Fa'asavalu (53 mins), J Burns for K Dickson (76 mins), R Clegg for T Casson (64 mins), C Walker for T Williams (59 mins)
Tries: Williams, Guest, Casson, Wallace
Conversions: Botica (3) **Penalties:** Botica (2)

Referee: Greg Garner (England)
Attendance: 8,100

three years in a row – before losing to Saracens at Allianz Park. However, the 2014–15 campaign saw Quins drop to eighth position, while the club's tilt at the European Champions Cup (formerly the Heineken Cup) was a curate's egg affair, winning four of the six games in a tough pool but failing to progress after a curiously off-key 23–3 home defeat against Wasps, a game Quins dominated territorially despite the scoreline.

Title page: Centre Matt Hooper spectacularly touches down against Exeter Chiefs at The Stoop during the 2014–15 season

Left: Luke Wallace keeps a strong grip on the LV= Cup as the fireworks and the champagne go off around him following the 2013 victory over Sale at Sixways

Below: It's thirsty work winning these trophies you know! Rob Buchanan gets a well-earned drink during the post-match celebrations

243

Right: The Harlequin Amateurs First XV line-up, ably led by captain David Love (*front row, third from the right*)

Below: Stars in the making! The Under-10s side enjoy making new friends and learning to play rugby the 'Harlequins Way'

Harlequin Amateurs

Harlequin FC had to adapt or perish in the mid-1990s when the game turned professional, but once the elite team had been established the amateur ethos was maintained by the formation of Harlequin Amateurs, which looked to continue the old traditions of the club and provide an opportunity for all ages and abilities to wear the famous colours.

The club runs mini rugby sides for children from the age of five and youth sides all the way up to Under-17, while there are a selection of senior teams ranging from the First XV, who play in the Herts/Middlesex 2 league, to the Veterans. The latter enthusiastically maintain the Quins tradition of being rugby tourists, with Dubai being their most recent destination, and adopt the mantra: 'You don't stop playing rugby because you are too old; you get old because you stop playing rugby.'

The Quins Amateurs enjoy great support from St Mary's University, Twickenham, where the tennis hall and their Broom Road playing fields are made available for some of the younger teams to train and play, while a number of St Mary's students also provide invaluable coaching. The older youth teams, along with the senior XVs and Vets, play at St Mary's Waldegrave Road campus. As part of the 150th anniversary celebrations there are plans to bring the Harlequin Amateurs under the administrative umbrella of the professional club.

Top left: Playing rugby for Harlequins at all levels is about enjoying your rugby as much as Vets XV player Gareth Igo

Top right: The Vets XV prepare for battle!

Bottom left: The First XV pack down

Bottom right: Former First XV captain Jon Lowe gets fixed up by the physio

The Harlequins players pause for a minute's silence before the 2016 European Challenge Cup Final v Montpellier to remember 20-year-old Seb Adeniran-Olule, a young Quin with huge potential who tragically died in a road collision in the week preceding the match

The Conor O'Shea era ultimately came to a close at the end of the 2015–16 season, the disappointment of a 26–19 defeat against Montpellier in the European Challenge Cup Final in Lyon concluding a horrendous week which had begun with the tragic death of academy player and England Under-20 international Seb Adeniran-Olule in a road collision. "Seb was an incredible talent and had already represented England at under age level as well as making his senior debut for Quins at just 20," O'Shea said when the news broke. "He will be sorely missed."

Quins gave it everything against Montpellier and finished the match strongly, with Marland Yarde's 72nd–minute try briefly raising hopes that O'Shea – who, after six years with the club, had agreed to take charge of Italy at the end of the season – would receive a fitting send-off. But it wasn't to be as the French side, impressively physical throughout, held on to secure a deserved victory.

"Everyone was devastated but I'm proud of what we as a club achieved over the years," explains O'Shea. "We lost one of our own before the game and everyone at Quins will be upset about that for a long, long time to come, but it showed the character of the team that even at 26–9 they never folded, they played to the bitter end.

"Obviously I was disappointed – you don't want the last emotions you feel at a club to be sad ones – but I'm also proud. I'm leaving behind a special group of guys, fellas who have contributed so much to Harlequins and to England, who made me proud every time they pulled on a Quins jersey. This club has given me more than I could ever give to it. The supporters have been amazing, the players have been incredible – they will be back.

Rugby doesn't build character, it reveals your character and guys like Nick Easter, Chris Robshaw and Danny Care have it in spades. Quins are going places, of that I have no doubt."

The club conducted a worldwide search for O'Shea's successor but ultimately elected to promote from within, John Kingston taking over as the new Director of Rugby with Mark Mapletoft moving up to Head Coach and former England Assistant Coach Graham Rowntree coming in as Forwards Coach. And with such expertise at the helm, as well as international stars like Jamie Roberts, James Horwill, Tim Visser and Adam Jones bolstering the homegrown talents of Robshaw, Mike Brown and Joe Marler, O'Shea's conviction that the club is going places looks well-founded indeed.

Of course, Harlequins will be hoping for a particularly strong showing in the 150th anniversary season but as well as being a cause for celebration the sesquicentennial is also an opportunity to reflect and plan for the future, exploring not only where the club has been but where it is going. What will Harlequins rugby look and feel like in 20 years' time, or indeed in another 150 years' time? The difference between those pick-up games at Hampstead Cricket Club 150 years ago and the club's current status seems almost infinite – from that band of brothers roaming the Metropolitan Line in search of a game, a home ground and a friendly pub to change in, to the high profile players of the professional game. Vastly different eras, challenges and, in the early days, a different game, but still the same club.

So what can Harlequins members and supporters expect in the future? How can Quins continue to expand and improve?

Which avenues will open up? What next? And how will the precious link with the past and that distinctive Harlequins ethos be maintained? Two individuals who can contribute most pertinently to this debate are Chief Executive David Ellis and owner Charles Jillings, the latter the club's joint owner alongside Duncan Saville – all of whom are at the heart of the club's major decisions going forward.

Firstly, to set everything in context, Ellis explains the two-pronged importance of the 150th anniversary celebrations:

"Reading through this book, I am struck massively by the larger-than-life qualities of those Harlequins who went before us, their sense of fun and their pursuit of excellence, both in their sporting and professional lives. We need to take this opportunity to look back with pride on these remarkable individuals and the imprint they left on this club.

Above: Seb Adeniran-Olule

Top: Conor O'Shea is applauded off the pitch by the players following the final home match of his Harlequins' career at the end of the 2015–16 season

Above: Sharnie Van Lyth crosses the line for her first ever try away at Millwall

Above right: Leah Carey goes in for a big hit away at Guernsey, supported by Kate Goater and Danie Martin

Right: Bryony Skinner, Jess Dawson and Roisin Hyde celebrate after a muddy victory

Harlequin Ladies

Harlequin Ladies was established in September 1995 when a couple of Quins supporters moved into the area and wanted to set up a ladies team. With support from the main club, the idea soon grew into a squad of players that went on to win their first league campaign, ending the season unbeaten.

During the early years, Harlequin Ladies went from strength to strength, establishing a highly successful youth side and forming stronger links with the main club and the local community, all the while developing an enviable social calendar which included quizzes in The Albany pub, an annual boat race in Marble Hill Park and regular tours. The Quins Ladies also support a number of charities, including the Injured Players Foundation and Restart, regularly volunteering to bucket shake at The Stoop to help raise funds and awareness.

During the past five seasons, the club has successfully worked hard to rebuild after a number of players retired or relocated. Since 2014 alone, over 20 brand new players have been introduced to the great game of rugby, and have been training and playing regularly in our famous shirt. The ethos of the club is now more about introducing new players to the game, and acting as a link for those Under-18 players wishing to continue into adult rugby. However, with an ambitious 10-year development plan well under way, the future is certainly looking bright for Harlequin Ladies!

Top left: Meet the forwards — club captain Kate Goater, First XV captain Laura Stephenson and Lauren Bosley

Top centre: Motivational words at half-time

Top right: Lauren Bosley offloading the ball to scrum-half Jo Plinston away at Guernsey

Left: Shauna Kiernan and Rhiannon Needham secure a turnover in a National Cup match against Teddington

Above: The commemorative badge and 'retro' shirt, designed by adidas for the 150th anniversary in 2016–17

"There has always been a pioneer spirit at Harlequins. Without puffing out our chests too much, we have always been at the cutting edge of whatever has been happening in the rugby world. From the moment Hampstead FC decided to reform as a club, voted for the name Harlequins and opted for our bright, extrovert club colours we were marked out to the rest of the rugby world as being a little unorthodox and mischievous – and it seems to be an internal ethos that has never changed.

"When we came together a few years ago to decide what the next five years would look like, we tried to encapsulate what the club was about, and a few of the words that cropped up were remarkable, innovative, adventurous, passionate, courageous, committed and iconic. And the inspiration for all of that were those who went before us. They gave us the club's DNA. They created something quite unique and we need to remember and celebrate that wholeheartedly.

"We need to tell their stories and keep drawing from them. As part of that process of reconnecting with our past, we intend to bring the amateur club back under the umbrella of the professional operations.

"They are incredibly closely connected, we have seen that, and they shouldn't be separated. We are the custodians of the past and we need to do that in style. We can safely assume, at the very least, that our

founding Quins and those who built the club up and kept it going despite two World Wars would expect us to throw a decent party. I occasionally bump into 'survivors' of the Centenary celebrations of 1966 and let's just say that the bar has been set very high!"

The 150th anniversary celebrations include the production of a new retro-style playing shirt by adidas – inspired by a classic Harlequins jersey from 1902 – as well as a documentary produced in association with BT Sport. The events taking place include a special pre-season day at The Stoop that features a friendly match with Glasgow Warriors and a veterans' match between a Bob Hiller President's XV and a Jason Leonard RFU President's XV. A challenge match with the Maori All Blacks (a reprise of the famous encounter in 1926), Big Game 9 and a special 150th Anniversary Celebration Dinner in the Dorchester Hotel are among the other highlights. In addition, there will be a host of supporters, past players, women's and girls' rugby and community events throughout the course of the season, while plans are in hand to include each of the eight affiliated overseas clubs in the festivities.

"The celebrations are one part of the sesquicentennial," explains Ellis. "The second part is to drive forward and realise our vision – in the short, medium and long term. It is incumbent on us because of our heritage to take a leadership role in the development of the game and set sail on the next 150 years."

In the short term that future includes the continued chasing of success in the Premiership and Europe, but Jillings has strong ideas of how the future of Harlequin Football Club might look:

"At the start of professionalism there were some very real question marks as to whether

professional club rugby in England was a viable business proposition. But today it is much more than viable – it is vibrant. As with any sport, the challenge is to make sure we continually invest, and that the benefits are shared for the longer term rather than just the short term. In 20 years' time my expectation is that the landscape will be very different from today, but there will be absolute features remaining. The Stoop will be The Stoop. It will always remain The Stoop and we will always play there. I can't imagine us ever moving.

"Harlequins is not an island, and we benefit from the group around us and their investment in Premiership rugby. But within the Premiership we must also be proactive innovators and not be frightened to take the lead. Historically, that has often been our role within the game.

"We need to deepen and expand our involvement with rugby generally. It will take time but it must happen. The one thing we cannot do is stand still. The minute we think we are good enough, we will be found out. In the nearly 20 years since I became involved, we haven't stood still for a day and that is how it must remain. The club motto 'I never sleep' is so apt. We don't know exactly who came up with that phrase 150 years ago, but it truly became the club's mantra.

"Outside of The Stoop I would like to see the footprint expanded, particularly in North America and Asia. We have barely scratched the surface in terms of the potential international element of the club and we need to engage new groups of people. Harlequins will definitely become more international, but the club here at The Stoop will always be at the centre.

"And always we need to be aware of our role within the community in which we live.

Left: Always looking to broaden its horizons, in 2015 the club visited the USA. As well as a friendly match against the USA Eagles at PPL Park in Pennsylvania (below), which Quins won 24–19, a series of coaching sessions run by Harlequins coaches Mark Mapletoft (left) and Tony Diprose (right) proved immensely popular

Quins Supporters' Association

The Quins Supporters' Association (Quinssa) was formed in 2003 with the simple aims of supporting Harlequin Football Club, representing the interests of Quins fans and providing opportunities for supporters to meet and enjoy each other's company. Nothing has changed since then, including the £5 membership fee!

Two of Quinssa's key roles are organising coaches to away matches – with discounted prices for all members – and block booking tickets for European fixtures to help ensure the team receives plenty of support when they play abroad. Quinssa also arranges regular social events, often attended by Quins players, coaches, club officials, referees and high-profile pundits who each provide fascinating insights into the latest developments at the club and across the wider game – for example, during Conor O'Shea's time as Director of Rugby he hosted an annual supporters' debrief where fans were invited to pick over the bones of the season and learn more about the club's future goals.

The supporters' association also holds an annual dinner – a social highlight attended by the squad – where they present the player and club awards voted for by the supporters, run fundraisers for the Quins academy and local charities, and organise collections on behalf of the Shooting Star CHASE children's hospice charity every Christmas, providing an array of gifts to help this amazing cause.

Quinssa
Quins Supporters' Association
www.quinssa.org.uk
Proudly supporting Quins since 2003
PLAYERS MAKE A TEAM
SUPPORTERS MAKE A CLUB!

Quinssa
Membership No: Expiry Date: July 20
First Name:
Last Name:
Contact Details: members@quinssa.org.uk
Harlequins

Above left: The Under-18 Sevens team from Future Hope – the Harlequins affiliate club in Kolkata, India – with 2016 India Under-19 Sevens trophy in hand

Above centre: During a visit to Kolkata in June 2015, Harlequins players took part in an inspirational training session with local players

Above right: Olly Kohn made a whole bunch of new friends during the Kolkata trip!

Right: Harlequins Chief Executive David Ellis is already planning for the club's next 150 years

The minute we become 'just' a rugby club we will lose the magic of Harlequins and we will lose momentum. We badly want to win at rugby but we also want to become a positive influence in the environment. At Abu Dhabi Quins, for example, it's important that we help with a flourishing rugby club, but possibly the most important achievement would be to offer a sporting outlet for young women in that region. At Future Hope Harlequins there is a huge potential for Harlequins Rugby to be a force for the good in a city with considerable challenges. At all our affiliate clubs there is the opportunity to do more than simply play rugby.

"When I got involved back in 1997 I had no idea it would dominate such a large part of my life, but I suspect there are owners and investors all over the Premiership who will share the same experience. It permeates most things. I am emotionally involved 24/7 and I can't remember a day since then when I haven't enjoyed some kind of Quins conversation. However, as owners it's important that we are not 'hands on' and trying to micromanage and run the club from day to day. That's not our role. We have excellent staff running the club."

Ellis heads up the team tasked with the day-to-day management of the club, but he is also putting flesh on upcoming projects and is excited by the future:

"Our priority will always be the rugby. We have the stated ambition of becoming the best rugby club in the world and that is what we will continue to aim for. We will always spend up to the salary cap trying to attract the best players and coaches, and we will continue to invest in our academy and the very best training and medical facilities. We will strain every sinew to play successful winning rugby the Harlequins Way.

"During one of my first weeks as Chief Executive, I went to Surrey Sports Park with Conor O'Shea to watch training for a day, sit in on all the meetings and try and understand what makes our players tick. Chris Robshaw got up at one stage and made a short but very powerful speech. I quote it here to the best of my memory: 'Let's never be ordinary. Let's never be content with a safe sixth or seventh in the table and occasional great wins over the very top teams. Let's not play routine, predictable rugby. Let's not play safe, let's push it all the time.' New to the job

these words made a big impression on me, and I have tried to incorporate this as our theme behind the scenes as well.

"We want to increase our involvement at all levels. Women's rugby is at last beginning to get the recognition it deserves and our long-term aim is to run a professional Harlequins team because in the future we have no doubt that there will be a professional women's league run along the lines of the Premiership. In the future we also envisage

running a Sevens team to take up the increasing opportunities to compete around the world as Sevens grows year on year.

"As Charles says, our affiliate clubs give us a fantastic global dimension – clubs who share our name, club colours and core values. This is a very real relationship. We keep in touch, representatives of those clubs will be at our festivities during the sesquicentennial celebrations, and as the mother club we try to help and advise. But I believe we are only scratching the surface in what this relationship could really mean. The potential for scouting and developing players around the world with the seven senior clubs among those affiliated is enormous, while it also gives us a foothold in the market place. Meanwhile, with the very special case of Future Hope Harlequins in Kolkata, the school and team for orphans and street children, there are opportunities to do great things, both socially and in terms of nurturing a small but fanatical rugby community.

"Even as Chief Executive I'm sometimes taken aback at the 'reach' of the Harlequins name and colours. Our friends in adidas recently told me of anecdotal evidence that the Quins jersey is the third most recognised rugby shirt in the world behind the All Blacks and the British and Irish Lions, which is remarkable. Our website and social media channels are among the most popular in sport in this country. There is a resonance about the Harlequins name and ethos, and the challenge now is to maximise everything we have, in the right order, so we grow as a club and reinforce our values in all sorts of different directions. There has never been a more exciting time in the club's history."

As part of Quins' forward-looking strategy the club launched a bond issue in April 2016

Left: The emergence of exciting prop Kyle Sinckler epitomises the ethos of a club that is always looking to push on to the next level – Never Sleeping!

which provided an opportunity for partners and supporters to invest in the club's future.

"We want to raise £7.5 million from the bond and that will help us to accelerate all our exciting plans for the club as we continue to stay ahead of the game as it grows," Ellis explains. "The focus for the club is to continue to invest in the areas that make us great, including our players, supporters and partners, with the aim of underpinning our sporting achievements with commercial success to lay the foundation for the next 150 years."

And perhaps the final word should go to Jillings:

"Quins is bigger than all of us; the club will exist long after we have all gone. Our job for a period of time is to steer the ship and put

wind in her sails whenever we can. Recently, for example, it was of course a wrench to lose Conor O'Shea as our Director of Rugby, but such moves are absolutely the norm within the business. What is important is that Conor totally bought into the Harlequins Way, worked around the clock to contribute and mastermind the winning of trophies, and built a squad capable of taking us forward. On the eve of the 150th anniversary he left the club having contributed massively and leaving it in a better place than when he arrived. And that is what we are all trying to do in our various ways."

It is tough to think of a better description of the ethos behind the Harlequins Way than that…

Harlequin FC Season by Season Record: 1971–2016

| Season | LEAGUE/PREMIERSHIP | | | | | | | EUROPE | | DOMESTIC CUP | |
	Division	Pos	P	W	D	L	PLAY-OFFS	TOURNAMENT	ROUND	TOURNAMENT	ROUND
1971–72										Knockout Cup	QF
1972–73										Knockout Cup	1st round
1973–74										Knockout Cup	2nd round
1974–75											
1975–76											
1976–77										Knockout Cup	1st round
1977–78										Knockout Cup	SF
1978–79										Knockout Cup	2nd round
1979–80										Knockout Cup	SF
1980–81										Knockout Cup	3rd round
1981–82										Knockout Cup	QF
1982–83										Knockout Cup	QF
1983–84										Knockout Cup	SF
1984–85	National Merit Table	7th	5	2	0	3				Knockout Cup	QF
1985–86	National Merit Table	6th	4	2	0	2				Knockout Cup	QF
1986–87	National Merit Table	10th	6	2	0	4				Knockout Cup	4th round
1987–88	**League 1**	**3rd**	**11**	**6**	**1**	**4**				**Knockout Cup**	**Winners**
1988–89	League 1	8th	11	5	0	6				Knockout Cup	SF
1989–90	League 1	7th	11	6	0	5				Knockout Cup	3rd round
1990–91	**League 1**	**3rd**	**12**	**8**	**0**	**4**				**Knockout Cup**	**Winners**
1991–92	League 1	8th	12	5	1	6				Knockout Cup	Finalist
1992–93	League 1	8th	12	5	1	6				Knockout Cup	Finalist
1993–94	League 1	6th	18	8	0	10				Knockout Cup	SF
1994–95	League 1	8th	18	6	1	11				Knockout Cup	SF
1995–96	League 1	3rd	18	13	0	5				Knockout Cup	QF
1996–97	League 1	3rd	22	15	0	7		Champions Cup	QF	Knockout Cup	SF
1997–98	Premiership	10th	22	8	0	14		Champions Cup	QF	Knockout Cup	4th round
1998–99	Premiership	4th	26	16	1	9				Knockout Cup	QF
1999–00	Premiership	10th	22	7	0	15		Champions Cup	Pools	Knockout Cup	QF
2000–01	**Premiership**	**11th**	**22**	**7**	**0**	**15**		**Challenge Cup**	**Winners**	**Knockout Cup**	**Finalist**
2001–02	Premiership	9th	22	5	3	14		Champions Cup	Pools	Knockout Cup	SF
2002–03	Premiership	7th	22	9	0	13		Challenge Cup	2nd round	Knockout Cup	QF
2003–04	**Premiership**	**6th**	**22**	**10**	**2**	**10**		**Challenge Cup**	**Winners**	**Knockout Cup**	**6th round**
2004–05	Premiership	12th (R)	22	6	1	15		Champions Cup	Pools	Knockout Cup	6th round
2005–06	**National 1**	**1st (P)**	**26**	**25**	**0**	**1**		**Challenge Cup**	**Pools**	**National Trophy**	**Winners**
2006–07	Premiership	7th	22	10	0	12				Anglo–Welsh Cup	Pools
2007–08	Premiership	6th	22	12	0	10		Champions Cup	Pools	Anglo–Welsh Cup	Pools
2008–09	Premiership	2nd	22	14	1	7	SF	Champions Cup	QF	Anglo–Welsh Cup	Pools
2009–10	Premiership	8th	22	9	2	11		Champions Cup	Pools	Anglo–Welsh Cup	Pools
2010–11	**Premiership**	**7th**	**22**	**9**	**2**	**11**		**Challenge Cup**	**Winners**	**Anglo–Welsh Cup**	**SF**
2011–12	**Premiership**	**1st**	**22**	**17**	**1**	**4**	**Winners**	**Challenge Cup**	**QF***	**Anglo–Welsh Cup**	**Pools**
2012–13	**Premiership**	**3rd**	**22**	**15**	**0**	**7**	**SF**	**Champions Cup**	**QF**	**Anglo–Welsh Cup**	**Winners**
2013–14	Premiership	4th	22	15	0	7	SF	Challenge Cup	SF*	Anglo–Welsh Cup	Pools
2014–15	Premiership	8th	22	10	0	12		Champions Cup	Pools	Anglo–Welsh Cup	Pools
2015–16	Premiership	7th	22	10	1	11		Challenge Cup	Finalist		

*dropped down from Champions Cup

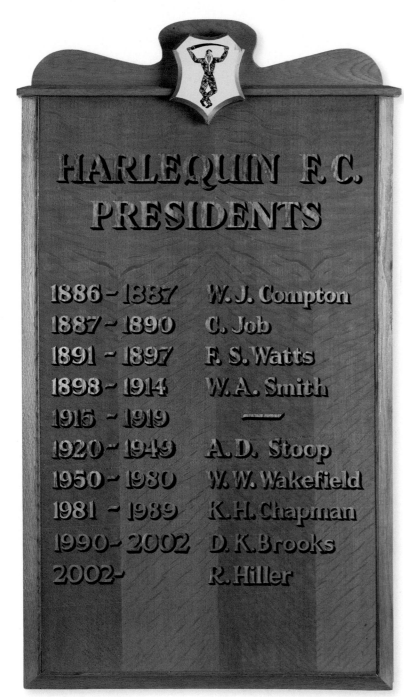

HARLEQUIN F.C. PRESIDENTS

1886 – 1887	W. J. Compton
1887 – 1890	C. Job
1891 – 1897	F. S. Watts
1898 – 1914	W. A. Smith
1915 – 1919	—
1920 – 1949	A. D. Stoop
1950 – 1980	W. W. Wakefield
1981 – 1989	K. H. Chapman
1990 – 2002	D. K. Brooks
2002 –	R. Hiller

Harlequin FC Presidents, Captains and RFU Presidents

Captains of Harlequins

1867–1868: No appointment
1868–1869: E E Clarke
1869–1870: W E Titchener
1870–1871: P Wilkinson
1871–1874: E Walker
1874–1875: W Watson
1875–1876: G W Perham
1877–1878: C E Graseman
1878–1879: A Tillyer
1879–1880: H Watts
1880–1885: F W Burnand
1885–1886: A A Surtees
1886–1887: G B James
1887–1888: A B Cipriani
1888–1892: A A Surtees
1892–1894: A B Cipriani
1894–1896: S B Pcech
1896–1897: C M Wells
1897–1898: J D Wittaker
1898–1900: R F Cumperledge
1900–1901: H O Mills
1901–1902: W L Furrell
1902–1905: C E L Hammond
1906–1914: A D Stoop
1919–1920: N B Hudson
1920–1921: W W Wakefield
1921–1922: H B T Wakelam
1922–1923: V G Davies
1924–1925: W W Wakefield
1925–1926: V G Davies
1926–1927: H P Marshall
1927–1929: W W Wakefield
1930–1931: P W Adams
1932–1933: J C Gibbs

1933–1936: P E Dunkley
1936–1938: K H Chapman
1945–1946: K H Chapman
1946–1947: B D Napper
1947–1948: J R C Matthews
1948–1949: W W Jackson
1949–1952: J C R Matthews
1952–1953: D K Brooks
1954–1959: R M Bartlett
1959–1961: R W D Marques
1961–1962: J S Abbott
1962–1965: C M Payne
1965–1966: G C Murray
1967–1968: D F B Wrench
1968–1970: R B Hiller
1970–1972: R H Lloyd
1972–1973: E Kirton
1973–1974: M J Mason
1974–1977: N O Martin
1977–1979: D A Cooke
1979–1980: A C Alexander
1980–1981: T Claxton
1981–1983: R F Best
1983 1987: D H Cooke
1987–1990: J Olver
1990–1993: P J Winterbottom
1993–1994: A R Mullins
1994–1995: B C Moore
1995–1997: J Leonard
1997–1998: K G M Wood
1998–1999: M Z V Brooke
1999–2000: W D C Carling
2000–2001: D J Wilson
2001–2002: G J Morgan
2002–2006: A N Vos

2006–2008: P C Volley
2008–2010: W J Skinner
2010–2014: C D Robshaw
2014–2015: J W G Marler
2015– : D S Care

Harlequins members who have become President of the RFU

1928–1929: V H Cartwright
1932–1933: A D Stoop
1934–1935: J E Greenwood
1947–1948: B C Hartley
1950–1951: W W Wakefield
1963–1964: A G Butler
1973–1974: M R Steele-Bodger
1974–1975: K H Chapman
1981–1982: D K Brooks
1984–1985: A E Agar
1986-1987: A A Grimsdall
1989–1990: D L Saunders
1993–1994: I D S Beer
2015–2016: J Leonard

Nunquam Dormio: 150 Years of Harlequins
List of Subscribers

Charles Abram
Douglas N Adamson
John Aitken
Oliver Jack Aldridge
Calum Alexander
David Alexander
Cullen R Allain
Ryan A Allain
Roger & Linda Allard
Laurence Allcorn
David Allen
John Allen
Simon H Allen
Harry David Allingham
Terrance Allsopp
Gary Anderson
Graham Anderson
Paul R Anderson OBE
James S Andrew
Ben Annis
Charles Ansley
Edith Armfield-Shepherd
John Arnold
Paul Arnup
Peter Ashdown
Kim Ashton
Tim, Tessa, Edward &
   William Atkin
David Augustus
Nick & Sally Avis
Raymond Aylward

John Bailey &
   Philip Gordon Young
Billy & Jackie Baker
Jack James Baker
Paul Baker
Geoff Ball
Alex Balm
Andrew Barker
Chris Barker
Tim Barker
John Barletta
Michael J Barnes
Tim Barnes
Jackie, Graham, Edward &
   Freya Barnetson
Gordon Barnett
Darren, Kelly, Eva &
   Henry Bartlett
Guy Barton
Stewart & Noelle Baseley
Robert Bass
Charlotte, Simon, Tom &
   Alex Bates
Paul R J Beard
Tom Beardon
Paul & Debbie Beaumont
John Benson
James Bentham-Wood
Rodney Bentham-Wood
Liz Oliver & Russ Bequette
Guy Billington

Graham Birkett
Sue Birnage
Laurence & Tina Bishop
David Blackburn
Joe Blakeney-Edwards
Paul Bloom
Paul Otway &
   Mima Boardman
Fiona Bond
Nigel Bond
Toby Bonney
Chris Bonsey
Robert Bourne
Fletcher James George
   Bowley
Richard Bowley
Dominic J Boyle
Richard J Bradwell
Richard Braithwaite
Paul & Vivienne Bramall
Andy & Ted Brampton
Alan & Elaine Bridle
John & Vicki Bromwich
The Brooker Family
Shirley & Simon Broomfield
A K Brown
Andrew & Sara Brown
Chris Brown
Norman Brunskill
Paul Burgess
Paul C V Burgess

Robin Burn
Robin Burnett
Dan Burns
Carole Bushell
Paul Butcher
James Butler
Tony Byrne
Matt Caffyn
Tim Caffyn
Nicki Callan
Nigel Callow
Philip Cambray
Noel Cameron
Jean L Carlaw
John T Carlaw
John W D Carlaw
Jim Chalmers
Stephen A Champion
The Champion Family
Beena Chanda
Andrew E Charman
Tim Charman
Brian Cheney
Arun Cheta
Sandra Christian
Giles Clark
Ian & Robyn Clark
Adam Clarke
Alan Clarke
Mike & Nicola Clarke
Tony Clarke

James Clarkin

Andrew Clayton

Roger Clement

Jilly Clifton

Michael Coady

Simon Coleman

Ben Coles

Dom Coles

Ian Collie

Ian Collier

Brad "Biglad" Collins

Paul & Mandy Collins

Adam Cook

Alan D Cooke

Claire & Scott Cooke

David Cooke

Simon Cooke

Chris Corfield

Chas Cowie

Lee A Cox

Max Christopher Craigie

Christopher Crosby

John Crouch

Neil Crowe

Richard Crowe

Andrew Crowley

Chris Cullen

Anthony David Curtis

Giles Curtis

Paul Curtis

Dallas Harlequins Rugby
  Football Club

John Dallimore

David Dance

Peter & Lynne Daniels

Craig Darby

Alison Davie

Christopher Davies

Dai Davies

Gavin Davies

Hannah Davies

Janette Davies

Mike Davies

Peter Davies

Rhys Davies

Jill Davies & Charles Smith

Gaynor Davies &
  Chris Twiss

Graham Davis

Stephen Davis

Ian & Andy Davison

Michael & Susan Day

Rebecca de Garston-Webb

Jan de Walden

Marilyn Swales &
  David Dean

Paul & Juliet Deane-Williams

Ian Mark Defty

Andre "KATO" Dent

Ian Dilks

Simon Dilloway

James Dinnage

Mike Dobie

Tim Dobie

Julian Donnelly

Mustafa, Durmus &
  Ibrahim Dourmoush

Mark & Jodie Douse

Scarlett Lea Olivia Dowling

John & Elisabeth Dugdale

Martin Durham

Jack Durrans

John Durrans

Mark & Sue Dyer

Alex Dyke

Jonathan, Elizabeth &
  Emily Ede

Stephen Edlmann

James Edmonds

Neil Edwards

Paul Edwards

C J M Ellerington

Barry Elliott

Gareth Elliott

Ian Elliott

Martin Elliott

Russell Elliott

Harry Ellis

India Ellis

Jon Ellis

Simon Elmer

David Elphinstone

The Elvin Family

Mark Evans

Toby & Di Everett

Hugo Eyre

Jim Eyre

Nick Fardey

Martin Farrelly

David Felton

Aaron Fereday

Stefano Filopei

Gareth & Christina Fitzgerald

Craig Fletcher

Peter C Forbes

Les Ford

Wayne Ford

Finlay Fowler

Lesley Frazer

Alan Frei a.k.a.
  Frenchy/Blondie

Ben Fretwell

Bryony Fucile

Paul Fuller

Michael Furnell

Nick Gadsby

Chris & Joan Galpin

Tim Gardiner

Lily Gardner

Alister Garratt

Imogen Gaunt

Richard Gee

Lucas George

John Gibbs

William Gibbs

Jane Gibson

Karen Gibson

Christine Gidlow

Michael Gilbert

Michael Gillin

Lyn Glaves

Mark Gledhill

Robert Glenister

Kate & Paul Goater

Michael Goddard

Debbie Godfrey

Roger Golding

Abigail Sophia Gomez

Donna Goverd

Jack Graham

Martin Graham

Etta Elizabeth Gray

Jon Gray

Pete Greed

Del Green

Gary & Lorraine Green

Mark Raymond Green

Rob Green

Stuart Green –
   The Cabbage Patch
Peter A D Griffiths
Martyn & Sue Guess
Nigel Gunn
The Colonel &
   Oscar Gunter-Hays
Iris Avaline Guyett
Violet Lucy Guyett
Julian Hall
J P G Hamilton
Robin Hammond
Bruce Hampton
Steve Hancock
Lyndon Harper
Paul Harrington
James Harris
Mark Harris
Chris Harrison
Sam Harrison
John A Hartley
Jeff Harvey
Simon, Lisa, Joshua &
   Lucy Harvey
Ian Harvey-Piper
Samuel Robert Hase
John Hatton
Chris & Julie Hawkins
Paul Hawkins
Karen Ruth Hay
Richard Graham Hay
Brian Haynes
David Ian Haynes
Alan & Peter Hayward
Joshua & Oliver Hayward
George James Hearne
John Heigham

Garreth Hemmings
Gary Hemmings
Colin Herridge
Alistair Hill
Peter Geoffrey Hill
Bob Hiller
Gill Hiller
Bob Hobley
Benjamin Hodges
Daniel Hogg
David Hogg
Nigel Holden
David Holland
Trevor A Holland
Brian Hollingsworth
W T & G R Hollins
Malcolm & Pat Hollins
   (in memoriam)
Simon & Raphael Hollister
Ian Holloway
Ken Holloway
Rodger Homer
John Honeysett
Chris Hook
Diane & Clive Hook
Lewis Hook
Bob Hope
Alan R Horten
Chris Horton
Sean Horwood
Ian Howard
Faye Howell
Graham Howell
Neil Hudson
Paul Hudson
Dan Huish
Ellis Isaac Hunt

Kevin Hunt &
   Dawn Hopson
Robin Hunter
Simon Hunter
John Paul Hutchings
Nick Hyams
Shawn Imeson
Graham Indge
Peter Ingham
Andrew Thomas Inwood
David Ireland
Robert Ireland
Garry, Mary, Sadie &
   William Irwin
Benjamin James Jackson
Matthew Jackson
Paul D Jackson
Peter Jackson
Aaron Jacobs
Mike James
Paul Terence James
The James Family
Michael Jameson
David Janes
Carl Jansen
Michael Jelley
David G Jenkins
Simon David Jenkins
Pam & Keith Jenner
Charles Jillings
Karl Jochem
Dan Johnston
Jay Jolliffe
Keith Graham Jones
Mark & Adam Jones
Megan Jones
Nicholas C Jones

Paul Jones
Rebecca Jones
Valerie Jones
David Joyce
David Judd
Brendon &
   Frances Kavanagh
Chris Kelly
Michael A J Kelly
Peter Kelly
Stuart Kelly
David & Sheila Kennedy
Donald Kerr
John Kerr
Pamela & John Kerr
Andrew Kerslake
Benjamin King
Philip King
Tom Kingsbury
John & Dylan Kingston
Matt & William Knight
Jeremy Kohler
Alan Kurtz
Emm-Jane Kurtz
Steve & Rebecca Laffey
Richard Lambert
Francis Land
Daryl Lankshear
Andrew Lawrence
Phil Lawrence
Andrew Lawton
Charles Le Bosquet
Peter Le Bosquet
Adrian Lear
Mervyn Ledbury
Gareth Ledger
Jonathan Lennard

The Lennon Family
Colin Levins
Neal Lewtas
Bob Lloyd
Philip Lofthouse
Richard Lofthouse
Paul Lovelock
Sam Luckin
John Luffingham
Josh Lyddon
The Lynch Family
David Macfarlane
Jonathan Macfarlane
Laura Macfarlane
Nick Macintyre
Aurora MacKenzie
Finlay MacKie
Miles MacKinnon
Mark Maley
Rhys Mallet
Jules & Julia Mancell Smith
Fi & Nick Marley
Barry & Sarah Marshall
Ashley Marston
Tom Marston
Alexander Joseph Martin
Geoffrey J Martin
Steve Martin
Helen E L Mason
M J Mason
Jon & Hazel Masters
Anne McCarthy
Maximilian McGill
Robert McHardy
James McKane
Audrey McKenna
Michael McKenna

Alain McKinnon
Sharon McKinnon
Paul McLean
Dominic McNeice &
  Ann Fletton
Charles Mead
Paul, Sue & Bethany Mead
Richard Meehan
The Meek Family
Carl Mellings
Steve Mellors
Toby Mersh
Lauren Michael
Paul R Michael
Mike Millard
Antonia & Miranda Miller
Jeremy & Emma Miller
Graeme P Mills
Henry Mitchell
Sue Mitchell
Mike Molyneux
Barbara & Tony Moore
Duncan & Patsy Moore
Stephen Moore
Guy Moorfoot
Laurence Morley
Maggie Morrell
Andy Morris
Kevin Morris
Alasdair Morrison
Tom Moses – 4th Official
Jim Munns
Chris Munton (Mr Harlequin)
Alan Murphy
James Jonathan Murphy
Michael James Murphy
John Neilson

Nev's Left Boot
Paul Nicholson
Simon Nicholson
Bartlomiej Niedzinski
Anne Noakes
Robin Noakes
Justin Roy Norman
Barney North
Chris North
John Norton
Robin Norton
Nigel O'Brien
Richard &
  Carole O'Callaghan
Paul O'Hanlon
Alex, Isabella &
  Olivia O'Shea
Mickey O'Sullivan
Nigel Oatway
Mike Oehlers
F Op den Kamp
Stephen Owens
Andy Page
Brian Page
David Page
Tim Page
Stephen Pam
Paul Parker
Zak Parker
Paul S Parkin
Rick Parry
Roger Parsons
Subhash Patel
Derek Patey
Bryan Roy Patrick
Lee Patterson
Shaun Patterson

Angela &
  Michael Pawley
Anthony Payne
Diana Payne
Edward G Payne
Noah Payne-Frank
Stephen Pays
Simon Peacock
Steve Peacock
Sharon Peaker
Darren Pearce
Malcolm Pearce
Mark Green &
  Lynn Pearcy
Dave Pendleton
Michael Perkin
Chris Perks
Jonathan Perrée
Mike (Perkins) Peskin
William Petch
Mike Pettit
Andrew Victor Pheasant
Jonathan Phillips
Nigel Pickup
Allan Pidding
Richard & Trudy Piggot
Mike Pilcher
Mark Pinney
Nick Piper
Alan Plom
Wendy Plumb
Barry Pool
Sandra Pope
David Poulter
Jo Powell
Neil D Powell
Catherine Power

Stephen H Powis
Howard Preece
Michael Preece
Chris Price
Colin & Donna Pridham
N & C Priestley-Wall
Chris Procter
Darren Pullinger
Brian Pullman
Katie Purcell
Tom Rameaux
Linda Randall
Sally Stripp & Lynda Randall
Linda Read
Thomas Frederick Reavie
Ashleigh Reed
David Reed
Mark Reed
Stuart Reed
David & Frances Regan
John Rendall
Barry Reynolds
Jeremy Jon Reynolds
Gary Rhoades-Brown
John Richards
Alex Richardson
James Richardson
Philip Richardson
Mark Richings
Daniel Ridge
Michael Ridge
David Ridgway
Christopher Roberts
Graeme Roberts
Richard Roberts
Ian Robertson
Ali & Stuart Robertson-Fox

Martin Robins
Tony Roche
David Rooke
John & Helen Root
Bill Ross
Mark Rowe
Anthony Royle
Michael Russell
Matthew Ryder
John Sackett
Maggy Sadler
Jamie Salmon
Sanna Sand
Chris Savage
Duncan Saville
Peter Robert Saving
Trevor Saving
Veronica Joyce Sayer
 (nee Gamble)
Telfer Saywell
Tom Saywell
Paul Scarborough
Chris Scoggins
Janet Scott
Simon Scott
Steve & Pat Scott
Stuart Scott
Chris Scovell
André Scruton
Andrew Scrutton
Richard Seaborne
Nick Seaward
Martin, Caroline, Stephen,
 Kathryn & Jessica Self
Janette Semmens
Alasdair Shand
Andrew Sharp

Craig Sharp
Ross Sharp
Nick Shaw
Quinlan J Shea, III
Terry & Jane Short
Sam Shufflebotham
David J R Sibree
James P Sibree
William P Sibree
Andy Silk
Paul Simmonds
Mark, Lai-Gain &
 Toby Simmons
Peter Simmons
Angela Simpson
Tom Sims
John & Jane Sinfield
William Sinfield
Pat & Tony Slonecki
Oliver Slot
Peter Slot
Adam Small
Katy Small
Alex & Holly Smith
Charles Daine Smith
James, Kelly, Niamh &
 Caitlin Smith
Martin C Smith
Michael R Smith
Robert Smith
Terry Smith
Emma Louise Smythe
David M Snare
Keith & Harry Springall
Alex & Jenny Stables
Keith Stait
Matt Stait

Jonathan Stephens
Paul Colin Stevens
S Ann Stevens
Emma & Molly Stewart
John Stockdill
Jonathan Wainscott Stocker
William Wainscott Stocker
Kevin A Stockwell
Alexander J Stokes
Jonathan & Andrea Stokes
Michael & Vivien Stoney
Ian "Stoppers" Stoppani
Robert Storey
Simon Stormer
G F Stormont
Bob Stoyle
Tim Strong
James Stuart
Simon Styles & Mo Reeve
Richard Sunderland
Glenn Sutcliffe
Simon J Sutton
Shirley Swann
Oliver Syers
Geoff & Maggie Sykes
John B Sylvester
Noel Tappenden
John Taverner
Chris & Gill Taylor
David Taylor
Stephen Taylor
Thelma Taylor-Morgan
Andy Tharp
Pamela L Thom
Carl Anthony Thomas
Iestyn Thomas
Nigel Thomas

David Thompson
Gavin Thompson
Pam Thompson
Simon Thomson
Edward Thornton
The Thornton Family
Andrew Tillbrook
John Titcombe
James E F Tommey
Peter Townsend
Christopher Tredway
Nigel Tribe
Anthony Fiennes Trotman
Ian Trussler
Charlie Tuff
Chris Turner
Ian & Jennifer Turner
Karen & Charlie Turner
Matthew, Sarah, Luke & Natalia Turner
Paul, Sarah, Isabel, Eliza & Alice Turner
Richard Turner
Henry Turrell
Pauline Tweedale
Chris Upton
Brandon Pierre van der Westhuizen
Ashley Varley
Phil Vaughan
Martyn Verlander
David Vincent
J Vink
Hugh Vosper
Steve Wade
Patrick Wadsted
Dominic Waggett

Oli Wainwright
Jez Walder
Andrew Walker
George Walker
Malcolm Wall
David Waltham-Hier
Derek Walton
Peter Waring
Alexander J Warman
James O Warman
Richard M Warman
William A Warman
Gareth Watkins
Matthew Watkins
Mike Watson
David & Edna Watts
Ian Watts
Ben & Alec Webley
Jeremy Webster
Christopher J S Welch
John Welch
Alan West
Stephen Paul Westerman
Paul David Westhead
Alan Whalley
David Wheatley
Alan Wheeler
Mark Whitby
Rob White-Cooper
Steve White-Cooper
Mike Whiteside
Jon & Claudine Whitmore
Barry Whittle
Nick & Gill Wickers
Richard Wiggs
Nicholas E G Wilby
Alan Wilkinson

Mark Wilkinson
Alexandra & Richard Williams
Andy Williams
Bill Williams
Maurice Williams
Peter Williams
Rhys Williams
Robert Williams
Ron Williams
Sebastian Williams
Tudor Williams
Zoe Williams
David Williamson
Ilsa Williamson
Neil Willingham
Andrew Willis
Vince Willows
Bev Wills
Nico & Aileen Wilson
Woody & Penelope Wilson
Lyndon John Wingrove
David Withers
Stephen Wooding
Tony Woodward
Will Woodward
Jade Wooldridge
Alan Woolford
Percy & Janet Wraight
David Wright
Steven & Laura Wright
Andy & Cathy Wythe
Debbie Lynn & Graham Yeomans
Robert Yonge
Bennett Leon Young
Leon Young

Descendants of Robert Corry (Great Grandfather of Adrian Stoop)

Sandy Brown (nee Trembath)
Sir James Corry 5th Bt
Lt-Col Timothy Corry
Nicholas Corry
Cdr Simon Corry RN
Trish Hassall (nee Corry)
Oliver Hassall
Rebecca Hassall
George Hassall
Amanda Jones (nee Corry)
Jane Redman (nee Corry)
Anthony Trembath
Timothy Trembath

Acknowledgements

The publication of a special book like this would not have been possible without the support and encouragement of many individuals who gave generously of their time and their knowledge of Harlequins. They include:

David Ellis, Mark Evans, Brendan Gallagher, Mike and Gill Hagger, Colin Herridge and Bob Hiller.

Graham Howell, Charles Jillings, Anne McCarthy, David Morgan and Callum Shepherd.

Conor O'Shea and the players and staff of the rugby department.

Kate Goater, Andy Brampton and Scott Cooke of Harlequins Ladies, Amateurs and QUINSSA respectively.

Graeme Roberts and the club's heritage team.

Michael Rowe and Deborah Mason of the World Rugby Museum at Twickenham.

Jim Drewett and Toby Trotman of Vision Sports Publishing.

The club is most grateful to them all.

**Paddy Lennon,
150th Anniversary Co-ordinator for
Harlequins,
May 2016**

Author acknowledgements

Huge thanks must go to Paddy Lennon for his ringmaster's role in masterminding this project and to Graeme Roberts for his very considerable assistance and in particular his painstaking and on-going research to compile the definitive Roll of Honour for those Quins who gave their lives in the First and Second World Wars. Others, and in no particular order, who gave their time willingly – sometimes over an agreeable lunch – include Paul Ackford, Peter Winterbottom, Mike Davis, Mark Evans, John Olver, Conor O'Shea, Chris Robshaw, Colin Herridge, Bob Hiller, Charles Gillings, David Ellis, Donald Kerr, Rhys Williams, Keith Wood, Paul Parkin, Tim Grandage at Future Hope and Alex Hinde at adidas.

A massive debt is owed also to those two who have trod this path before and chronicled Quins' history over the years. H B T Wakelam's *Harlequin Story*, published in 1954, was manifestly a work of love by a devoted Harlequin and speaks eloquently of the early years and is particularly poignant when modestly chronicling the huge contribution various Quins made to the national cause in time of war. Philip Warner, meanwhile, brought the story up to date in 1991 with his celebratory *The Harlequins – 125 years of Rugby Football*.

The little known but invaluable *The Complete Who's Who of England Rugby Union Internationals* is a tome that no self-respecting rugby journalist can function without and the *Centenary History of Oxford University Rugby Club* by Ross McWhirter and Sir Andrew Nobel in 1969 often filled in any biographical details of pioneer players. *The Story of Adrian Stoop* by Ian Cooper, published in 2004, is an exceptional and insightful sporting biography as is *For Poulton and England: The Life and Times of an Edwardian Rugby Hero* by James Corsan. Both are highly recommended. *The Life of Ronald Poulton*, written by his grieving father Professor Edward Bagnall Poulton, is also an emotive read.

Finally Jim Drewett, Ed Davis, Paul Baillie-Lane and designer Neal Cobourne at Vision Sports Publishing have enhanced the project massively with their inspired designs and use of pictures which so accurately capture the essence and style of Harlequins through the decades.

Brendan Gallagher, May 2016

Photography

A key element in this book is the high quality of the photography it contains; many of the images are appearing in print for the first time. Harlequins and Vision Sports Publishing are most grateful to the past and present generations of talented photographers who have contributed to the images published. They include the work of Getty Images, Pinnacle Photography and 3 Objectives Photography who have so superbly photographed all the historic memorabilia.

Every effort has been made to contact the copyright holders of the photographs used in this book. If there are any errors or omissions the publishers will be pleased to receive information and will endeavour to rectify any outstanding permissions after publication.

Picture credits

Harlequin FC: p8, 9, 11, 13, 20, 25, 26, 27, 28, 29, 30, 34, 36, 37, 38, 40, 50, 52, 53, 56, 57, 59, 60, 62, 63, 66, 67, 70, 72, 76, 77, 78, 79, 80, 81, 82, 83, 84, 87, 88, 90, 91, 92, 93, 94, 95, 97, 100, 103, 104, 106, 108, 109, 112, 113, 124, 127, 131, 133, 134, 135, 136, 137, 140, 141, 143, 146, 147, 148, 150, 151, 152, 153, 156, 158, 162, 164, 165, 166, 167, 168, 169, 170, 171, 173, 178, 180, 181, 183, 207, 213, 220, 225, 226, 229, 232, 233, 234, 236, 239, 244, 245, 248, 249, 250, 254

Getty Images: 4, 5, 7, 8, 9, 10, 16, 17, 18, 19, 22, 23, 29, 51, 56, 68, 69, 74, 89, 102, 114, 115, 116, 117, 118, 119, 120, 121, 122, 123, 126, 128, 130, 138, 142, 144, 145, 148, 149, 150, 151, 152, 153, 154, 156, 157, 162, 163, 166, 174, 177, 178, 179, 180, 181, 182, 183, 184, 185, 186, 187, 188, 189, 190, 191, 192, 193, 194, 195, 196, 197, 198, 199, 200, 202, 203, 204, 205, 206, 207, 208, 209, 210, 211, 212, 213, 214, 215, 216, 218, 219, 220, 221, 222, 223, 224, 225, 227, 228, 229, 230, 231, 234, 235, 236, 237, 238, 239, 240, 242, 243, 246, 247, 251, 252, 253, 254, 255

World Rugby Museum: 5, 6, 12, 31, 37, 39, 40, 41, 42, 43, 44, 45, 46, 47, 48, 49, 52, 53, 54, 58, 60, 61, 62, 63, 64, 65, 73, 75, 86, 89, 96, 105, 106, 107, 110, 111, 129, 132, 141, 147, 159, 170

Colorsport: 8, 15, 112, 126, 128, 160, 161, 176

PA Photos: 14, 131, 151, 152, 153

Foto Graffic: 225, 226, 232

adidas: 172

Ian Hewitt & Sampson Lloyd (from the book *Immortals of British Sport*): 186

Karen Davis: 80

nunquam dormio

1866   2016

150 years Harlequin FC